NIETZSCHE, GOD, AND THE JEWS

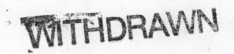

NIETZSCHE, GOD, AND THE JEWS

His Critique of Judeo-Christianity
in Relation to the Nazi Myth

by
Weaver Santaniello

foreword by David Tracy

Published by
State University of New York Press, Albany

© 1994 State University of New York

All rights reserved

Printed in the United States of America

For information, address the State University of New York Press,
State University Plaza, Albany, NY 12246

Production by Christine Lynch
Marketing by Fran Keneston

Library of Congress Cataloging-in-Publication Data

Santaniello, Weaver, 1958-
    Nietzsche, God, and the Jews : his critique of Judeo-Christianity
in relation to the Nazi myth / by Weaver Santaniello ; foreword by
David Tracy.
        p.   cm.
    Includes bibliographical references and index.
    ISBN 0-7914-2135-X (alk. paper). — ISBN 0-7914-2136-8 (pbk. :
alk. paper)
    1. Nietzsche, Friedrich Wilhelm, 1844-1900—Religion.
2. Christianity and antisemitism. I. Title.
B3318.C35S26 1994
261.2′6′092—dc20   93-46690
                                                        CIP

10 9 8 7 6 5 4 3 2 1

The author and SUNY Press sincerely thank the following publishers for permission to use excerpts from copyrighted works:

RANDOM HOUSE: *The Gay Science* by Friedrich Nietzsche. Copyright © 1974 by Random House, Inc. Reprinted by permission of Random House, Inc. *On the Genealogy of Morals* by Friedrich Nietzsche. Copyright © 1967 by Random House, Inc. Reprinted by permission of Random House, Inc. *Ecce Homo* by Friedrich Nietzsche. Copyright © 1967 by Random House, Inc. Reprinted by permission of Random House, Inc. *Beyond Good and Evil* by Friedrich Nietzsche. Copyright © 1966 by Random House, Inc. Reprinted by permission of Random House, Inc. *The Will to Power* by Friedrich Nietzsche. Copyright © 1967 by Walter Kaufmann, Reprinted by permission of Random House, Inc.

VIKING PRESS: "The Antichrist" by Friedrich Nietzsche, edited by Walter Kaufmann, "Nietzsche Contra Wagner" by Friedrich Nietzsche, edited by Walter Kaufmann, "Thus Spoke Zarathustra" by Friedrich Nietzsche, edited by Walter Kaufmann, "Twilight of the Idols" by Friedrich Nietzsche, edited by Walter Kaufmann, from *The Portable Nietzsche* by Walter Kaufmann, editor, translated by Walter Kaufmann. Translation copyright 1954 by the Viking Press, renewed © 1982 by Viking Penguin Inc. Used by permission of Viking Penguin, a division of Penguin Books USA Inc.

CAMBRIDGE UNIVERSITY PRESS: *Daybreak: Thoughts on the Prejudices of Morality* by Friedrich Nietzsche, translated by R. J. Hollingdale. © Cambridge University Press 1982. Reprinted with the permission of Cambridge University Press and R. J. Hollingdale.

THE UNIVERSITY OF CHICAGO PRESS: *Selected Letters of Friedrich Nietzsche*, edited and translated by Christopher Middleton. Copyright © 1969 by The University of Chicago. Reprinted by permission of The University of Chicago Press.

HARVARD UNIVERSITY PRESS: *Nietzsche: A Self-portrait from his Letters*, edited and translated by Peter Fuss and Henry Shapiro. Copyright © 1971 by Harvard University Press. Reprinted by permission of Harvard University Press.

Dedicated with thanks and respect
in memory of Erich Heller

*. . . the heights where you find him link him in friendship to
. . . the unrecognized of all times.*

—Nietzsche (1882-85)

CONTENTS

FOREWORD

Of the three great 'hermeneutes of suspicion'—Marx, Freud, Nietzsche—of contemporary thought, Nietzsche continues to prove the most radical and most unsettling. The central insights of both Freud and Marx have become—as W. H. Auden foresaw—part of the whole climate of educated opinion. Other aspects of their thought, that part of Marx (and it is there) which leads to Leninism, Stalinism, and Maoism; the part of Freud which led to a therapeutic culture of individualist self-proclaimed victims, are so disturbing as to demand the kind of attacks (indeed often Nietzschean attacks) that they now endure.

With Nietzsche the reality is quite clear. Many earlier receptions of his thought beginning with the notorious editings and interpretations of his sister, Elisabeth Förster-Nietzsche and her circle were so disastrous and dishonest that it took decades to recover from them. Some, it seems, have still not recovered. And yet through it all Nietzsche's impact survived. It has never been possible to read Nietzsche honestly and not be at once shaken and strengthened. It is not only Nietzsche's ideas (although surely it is that) but his power of mind and energy of spirit that demands the attention of any serious person.

Nietzsche forces an active, not reactive response. His dazzling array of styles neither decorates nor obfuscates. The style drives home, from every side, barring every desired escape, a relentless barrage of insights which, once grasped, free one not so much to new answers as to new questions and, above all, a new style of questioning. Then all one's former hopes, desires, fears, drives, resentments and strengths undergo a strange sea-change; some never to return. Only an active response—never finished, always probing—is worthy of Nietzsche.

In this clear and systematic study of Nietzsche Donna "Weaver" Santaniello has found her own active voice to hear and to respond to Nietzsche, especially in his fierce but complex critique of Christianity and his even more complex and often ambivalent responses to Judaism united to his consistent attack on the growing antisemitism of his period. This is a book with singular clarity of purpose, style, and design on these difficult questions of interpretation. With the possible exception of Nietzsche's readings of the Greeks, there is nothing more central to Nietzsche nor more difficult to understand and assess than Nietzsche's interpretation of Christianity and Christendom, of classical Judaism and modern antisemitism.

Santaniello knows all this with singular purpose and clarity. She develops her persuasive reading of Nietzsche on these issues by a complex union of historical-contextual study, a careful speculative psychology and, above all, attention to the appropriate details of Nietzsche's own texts. Nietzsche himself would surely endorse a 'strong reader' on these issues, especially the 'ressentiment' underside of so much of what passes for 'Christian' love and humility.

This deliberate clarity of purpose and interpretation differs from both the earlier purely existentialist readings of Nietzsche and the more recent radically rhetorized and pluralized 'new Nietzsche' by its fascinating union of historical-psychological context and clear, singular, active, but never arrogant reading of texts which can bear, as Santaniello insists, many readings. This union of historical context and existential-vital reading, of psychology portrait and detailed exegesis yields a reading of Nietzsche which all—even the 'new Nietzscheans'—can learn from even where they do not agree. Santaniello is the opposite of a reductionist on these issues of interpretation. She sees how Nietzsche's life and thought, his theory and practice, unlike most modern philosophers but like the ancient philosophers cannot be separated. Nietzsche has returned; for like Wittgenstein or Weil or Foucault, his thought resists the modern obsession with splitting theory-praxis and one like Nietzsche. Unlike both Marx and Freud, he survives not as an increasingly ambiguous part of a wider climate of opinion; Nietzsche survives as he foresaw he would, as a hammer against all opinions—including those of all Nietzscheans, old and new. He always feared disciples and longed for honest, courageous readers, for active respondents. In this work he receives exactly that.

David Tracy

ABBREVIATIONS
OF NIETZSCHE'S
WORKS AND LETTERS

BT	*The Birth of Tragedy* (1872)
UM	*Untimely Meditations* (1873-76)
HU	*Human, all-too-Human: A Book for Free Spirits* (1878)
MO	*Mixed Opinions and Maxims* (1879)
WS	*The Wanderer and his Shadow* (1880)
D	*Daybreak: Thoughts on the Prejudices of Morality* (1880)
GS	*The Gay Science* (1882)
Z	*Thus Spoke Zarathustra: A Book for All and None* (1883-85)
BGE	*Beyond Good and Evil: Prelude to a Philosophy of the Future* (1886)
GM	*Toward the Genealogy of Morals: A Polemic* (1887)
TW	*Twilight of the Idols: Or, How One Philosophizes with a Hammer* (1888)
AC	*The Antichrist* (1888)
EH	*Ecce Homo: How One Becomes What One Is* (1888)
CW	*The Case of Wagner: A Musician's Problem* (1888)
NW	*Nietzsche Contra Wagner* (1888)
WP	*The Will to Power* (also referred to as the *Nachlass*)
SL	*The Selected Letters of Friedrich Nietzsche* (trans. Ludovici)
L	*The Selected Letters of Friedrich Nietzsche* (trans. Middleton)
SP	*Nietzsche: A Self-Portrait from His Letters*
NWC	*The Nietzsche-Wagner Correspondence*

ACKNOWLEDGMENTS

Numerous individuals have inspired this book.

I thank my family, Janet, Bernie, Garry, Joanne and Loomis, for their unfailing support and encouragement throughout this voyage called life. I also thank the Riddles for sharing their home and friendship at a decisive turning point. Alice Cooper, who artistically looks "beneath surfaces," first sparked my interest in theology many years ago. I remain grateful to him for that and for the carte blanche treatment he and Brian "Renfield" Nelson have furnished.

It is infeasible to name all those scholars who have provided academic assistance generating this work; yet the following professors are singled out for their vital contributions—although the views presented throughout are not necessarily theirs: Peter Hayes, Susan Herbst, Lallene J. Rector, and Rosemary Radford Ruether, who tirelessly advised my dissertation out of which this book has arisen. I especially thank David Tracy, at the University of Chicago Divinity School, for longevity as a "kindred soul" and for writing the Foreword, and Jacob Golomb, at the Hebrew University of Jerusalem, for his powers of discernment. I also thank the staff at SUNY Press, especially Cari Janice and my editor, Carola Sautter, for their earnest support and for orchestrating this entire project.

The treasured friends who have listened to me ramble on about Nietzsche over the years are much appreciated for their admirable endurance. These include Ellie Stebner, who also helped with the acknowledgment page, Jan ("G. D.") Wojtowicz, Jeanne Matthews, Barbara Baumgartner, and Helen Kaufholz, all of whom provided a great deal of support both intellectually and emotionally. I also thank Mi-Mi, Gram, Koby Lee-Forman and Marty Forman, Joy Beth Lawrence-Clark, Regina Sullivan, Nancy Erikson, Joan Sulser, James P. Cadello, Jack Loughney, Reginald Setts, Alex and Mary Remolador, the Hampden Association of the United Church of Christ, and the inimitable department of philosophy at Westfield State College (starring Jack, Gerry, Brad, and Larry) for lending their time, energy, ears, and/or professional skills and finances.

Finally, I thank P. R. (The Reverend James Douglass Riddle) and David Kelsey, Professor of Theology at Yale University, for their invaluable mentoring.

This book is dedicated to the late Avalon Professor of German Language and Literature at Northwestern University, Erich Heller, many of whose relatives were sent to death or concentration camps when the Nazis swept across Central Europe.

INTRODUCTION

To be sure, faith alone gives blessing, not the objective
which stands behind the faith.[1]

Friedrich Nietzsche's views of Christianity, as presented throughout his fourteen major works, are multifaceted and virtually inexhaustible. He critiques
Christianity from ethical, psychological, political, historical, sociological, philological, and even scientific perspectives, and many of his key ideas are scattered
in the form of aphorisms throughout his published works, as well as in his private letters and notebooks. Nietzsche does not evaluate Christianity as an objective observer, but as one who was reared within the tradition and obsessed
with the "truth" and value of Christian claims long after he had rejected them.
Because Nietzsche's analysis of the Judeo-Christian tradition occurs on various
levels, the goal of this project is to interpret and incorporate the main ideas
prevalent throughout his writings without oversimplifying his views, and also
to animate the character of Nietzsche himself within the cultural and historical
context from which he wrote. I will analyze Nietzsche's critique of the Christian religion by exploring his personal and intellectual history in relation to
Judaism, antisemitism, and the political climate of nineteenth-century Germany.

   The depth of Nietzsche's thought and his writing style(s), coupled with the
sensationalism surrounding his name and the ideological concerns readers
themselves bring to his texts, pose hermeneutical difficulties. Nietzsche, who
has uniquely stood as a highly esteemed or despised figure, has been heralded
as the forerunner of many diverse movements including Nazism, existentialism,
death of God theologies, and deconstruction. It is not my intention to survey the
literature of these various schools; however, when appropriate, I will point out
how my interpretation of Nietzsche is both similar to and different from these
schools, especially Nazism.

   Nietzsche's philosophical views are difficult to untangle not only because
he has the power to challenge, enlighten, and enrage, but also because the politics of his day are, according to historians, disjointed and confused. The chaotic

reception of Nietzsche in Germany after his insanity, including the Nazi's use of his philosophy decades after his death, adds further complications causing division between political and apolitical commentators within Nietzsche studies today. The latter are generally regarded as those who address Nietzsche's epistemology, ontology, metaphysics, and ethics. The former focus on Nietzsche's political visions, including past renditions of those visions and their future implications. Generally, in the English-speaking world, political commentators stand in the tradition of Crane Brinton, a Harvard historian who presented his theory in the 1940s that Nietzsche was half a Nazi and half an anti-Nazi.[2] Apolitical commentators stand in the tradition of philosopher Walter Kaufmann, an emigree from Nazi Germany who, in reaction to Brinton and the Nazis, argued that "the leitmotif of Nietzsche's life and thought" was "the theme of the antipolitical individual who seeks self-perfection far from the modern world."[3] In the English-speaking world, Nietzsche has only been taken seriously as a political thinker in his own right during the past two decades, marked by the appearance of Tracy Strong's *Nietzsche and the Politics of Transfiguration*, in 1975.

Currently, the overall tendency of Nietzsche studies is ahistorical and apolitical, as represented by literary theory. This school focuses on the question of interpretation and the unusual style of Nietzsche's texts, which, as David Allison writes in *The New Nietzsche*, demands a "dangerous explosion" on the part of the reader even to follow such texts: "The Nietzschean text becomes something to be ingested, digested, transformed, and transfigured, and, together with it, the reader."[4]

Because I am concerned with Nietzsche's ethical critique of Christianity, and view Nietzsche as one who wrote to encourage critical thinking and individual transformation, my stance can formally be labeled existential-apolitical. However, because I argue that Nietzsche's life and thought was profoundly shaped by his encounter with the rampant antisemitism of his time, political dimensions are indispensable to this project which seeks to fuse both political and religious components in discerning Nietzsche's analysis of Judeo-Christianity. The historically contextualized aspect of this work, therefore, seeks to challenge Strong's claim almost twenty years ago that "there is simply for Nietzsche no coherent way to talk about politics of his day because—in genealogical perspective—the politics tend to be incoherent."[5]

Considering that scholars readily acknowledge the Judeo-Christian tradition as the nucleus from which Nietzsche's philosophy emerges, relatively minor attention has been given to Nietzsche's overall treatment of both Christianity and Judaism. In regards to Christianity, although various works and scores of essays address particular aspects of Nietzsche's analysis, efforts seeking to integrate the religious, political, and personal aspects of Nietzsche's views are rare.⁶ Perhaps the most well-known work is Karl Jasper's *Nietzsche and Christianity*, which was based on a lecture delivered in Germany in 1938, translated into English in 1961, and amounts to the length of an essay. Jaspers connects Nietzsche's thought to his personal life; he also relates Nietzsche's views on Christianity to world history and to the decline of Western culture. However, Jaspers virtually ignores Nietzsche's evaluation of ancient Judaism and modern Jewry; and he fails to mention antisemitism in nineteenth-century Germany which was of major concern to Nietzsche and central to his critique of Christianity and cultural decline.⁷

Several scholars have explored the issue of Nietzsche's treatment of Judaism and the Jews.⁸ Although the Nazis falsely claimed—and convinced much of the world—that Nietzsche was a vicious antisemite, Nietzsche's opposition to antisemitism and his high regard for his Jewish contemporaries is rarely in question by Nietzsche scholars. However, these scholars have grappled with Nietzsche's complex views toward ancient Judaism, which are both positive and negative. Nietzsche's stance has led most commentators to interpret Nietzsche's negative evaluation of Judaism in light of the fact that Judaism gave birth to Christianity, which is his major enemy; others to simply dismiss his views as contradictory; and yet others to gross distortions of Nietzsche's texts.⁹

Howard Duffy and Willard Mittelman's "Nietzsche's Attitudes Toward the Jews," published in 1988 is pivotal. The article sketches the development of Nietzsche's views concerning ancient Judaism and modern Jewry over the course of his personal life and literary career, and also makes a threefold distinction regarding Nietzsche's overall perspective. The authors distinguish Nietzsche's attitude toward ancient Hebrews, the prophetic and priestly Judaism out of which Christianity arose, and modern Jewry.¹⁰

The authors demonstrate that Nietzsche favors the ancient Hebrews and modern Jews; he is ambivalent toward prophetic-priestly Judaism which he believes gave rise to Christianity. The authors state that Nietzsche is strongly and consistently opposed to antisemitism. They conclude their essay by asserting that "contemporary Christianity and contemporary anti-Semitism represent the vengeful ones who would prevent the *new* revaluation by holding down the Jews."¹¹

Assuming these threefold distinctions, which fully emerge in Nietzsche's later writings, this book further explores the personal and religiopolitical aspects of Nietzsche's stance toward Judaism, Christianity, and antisemitism. By situating Nietzsche in an argument against nineteenth-century Christianity and culture, I argue that Nietzsche's views toward Judeo-Christianity, while complex, are coherent, and are best interpreted in the context of the theological and political categories that existed in Germany. I argue that his family's Christianity initially fueled his contempt for the Christian tradition, that his disdain for antisemitism strengthened this contempt, and, in light of Nietzsche's personal history, offer explanations as to why Nietzsche identified strongly with the Jewish minority in his culture. Therefore, Jewish-Christian relations in nineteenth-century Germany are central to an understanding of Nietzsche's thought, and will be the focus of this study.

My approach to Nietzsche is rooted in two primary assumptions. First, I assume that his writings are deeply personal and thus cannot be severed from history and his life experiences. Second, I assume that Nietzsche had motivations for critiquing the Judeo-Christian tradition and that these were twofold, psychological and ethical. On the one hand, his preoccupation with Christianity was largely driven by his own reaction against his family's religion, including his rebellion against several generations of ministers and his father, who died before Nietzsche's fifth birthday. On the other hand, he was immensely driven by ethical and political concerns in regard to what he viewed as a deteriorating state of German culture, typified by antisemitism as well as by egalitarian movements. Part 1 of the book predominately will concern itself with psychological considerations and biographical elements. Part 2 will focus on the ethical and political aspects as presented in Nietzsche's mature writings: *Thus Spoke Zarathustra, Toward the Genealogy of Morals*, and the *Antichrist*. By explicating these texts, and placing them in dialogue with Nietzsche's major religious and political opponents, I demonstrate the extent to which Nietzsche's contempt for antisemitism shaped his religious and political viewpoints, especially in his last productive years, which is a topic that has been neglected in Nietzsche studies.

Part 1 will provide an overview of Nietzsche's life and ideas, situating Nietzsche within his biographical and cultural context. Psychological components which prompted and drove Nietzsche's critique of Christianity will be suggested. Among other things, Nietzsche's turbulent relationship with his mother, his sister Elisabeth, his misogyny, and his "break" with Wagner and Elisabeth, will be discussed. Providing an account of Nietzsche's early influences and interests is necessary for approaching his mature philosophy, for it reveals that Nietzsche was preoccupied with the same issues throughout much of his life.

The first chapter will sketch Nietzsche's early intellectual history, focusing on how his life and religious ideas were shaped by Darwinism, Strauss, Schopenhauer, Wagner, and Christianity. His painful break with Wagner, which was prompted by his mentor's antisemitism and German nationalism, will be highlighted. The second chapter will present a detailed but concise biographical sketch of Nietzsche's turbulent life in the months immediately surrounding his writing the first part of *Zarathustra*. This will reveal that Nietzsche's contempt for Christianity was intermingled with his infamous misogyny. I will also discuss his disdain for his sister Elisabeth's Christianity and the breach between them which occurred during her courtship and marriage to Bernhard Förster, a prominent leader in the antisemitic movement. The chapter will conclude with a summary of Nietzsche's life until his mental collapse in 1889, Elisabeth's role in creating Nietzsche's image in Germany after his death, and her later relationship to Hitler and National Socialism. The third chapter will draw upon the corpus of Nietzsche's writings, presenting a holistic but concise picture of how Nietzsche viewed cultural Christianity in nineteenth-century Germany. Nietzsche's overall picture of Christianity, including that of the Lutheran state-church, the theological elements he despised, and the image of God that prevailed in German culture, will be portrayed. This chapter will provide a foundation for part 2. Before a focused view of Nietzsche's ethical critique can be undertaken, one must be clear about what Nietzsche is critiquing.

Part 2 of the book will address the three texts wherein Nietzsche's assessment of Christianity is presented in detail: *Thus Spoke Zarathustra* (1883-85), *Toward the Genealogy of Morals* (1887), and the *Antichrist* (1888). I will approach these texts with a specific focus on the religiopolitical aspects of Nietzsche's cultural critique, demonstrating how the concepts of suffering and revenge, in relation to Christianity and antisemitism, inform that critique. Chapter 4 will present *Zarathustra* as Nietzsche's theological polemic against traditional Christian themes. The central concepts of the *Übermensch*, the will-to-power, and the eternal return, will be presented as alternative concepts serving as replacements for the Messiah, creation, and redemption as traditionally understood within the Christian religion. Throughout, Nietzsche's conviction that heaven and hell are human projections and products of revenge will surface, as will his role of a solitary eccentric who withdrew from public and political life.

Chapter 5, which is marked by Nietzsche's literary shift to an essay style and his development as a political thinker, will offer explanations for this change. Situating the *Genealogy* in its historical context will illuminate Nietzsche's views toward Judaism in relation to Christianity and in lieu of other Aryan myths which prevailed during his time. I show that the *Genealogy* was in part a polemic against both Christian and secular antisemitism which were becoming a more potent social force in Germany and which Nietzsche became increasingly preoccupied with in the mid-1880s.

The sixth chapter will briefly compare the first essay of the *Genealogy* with the *Antichrist*, showing how the two texts relate to Nietzsche's ideal master race, designed to differ with the Aryan mythology of the Germans, based on the exclusion of Semites. I will then discuss the *Antichrist* in its nineteenth-century theological context, showing that the work, in many aspects, was in striking contrast to Christian theological trends which tended to demean contemporary Jews. The conclusion will summarize Nietzsche's life in relation to his writings, offering suggestions as to why his Jewish contemporaries were central to his existence and why the Nazis heralded Nietzsche as a political ally decades after his death.

Overall, my interpretive position integrates both the apolitical and political traditions within contemporary Nietzsche studies in the English-speaking world. I also wish to claim two neglected but imperative traditions as central: German-Jewry which, from the turn of the century onward, assimilated Nietzsche into many aspects of its communal, cultural, and institutional life. I also claim the feminist movement in Germany which utilized Nietzsche's thought to further its political emancipation.[12] While not ignoring Nietzsche's many negative remarks toward women, these feminists saw in Nietzsche a great liberator of the human spirit who was nonetheless fettered by his own prejudices.

Altering Nietzsche's translated works in English to provide inclusive language would be an enormous task. Coupled with Nietzsche's sexism, I have chosen to leave his writings in their gender-specific form; doing otherwise would conceal his sexual politics. Due to the complex and controversial nature of Nietzsche's writings, I have provided many direct quotes not only to support my interpretation, but to encourage readers to formulate their own. Because of the uncertain status of the *Nachlass*, a vast collection of notes Nietzsche accumulated over a long period of time, I will generally use them only to support or to clarify his published works.[13]

Part I

Nietzsche's Life and Cultural Christianity, 1844-1900

Nietzsche was, with regard to a *certain* moral tradition, the Christian, his own, eminently perceptive in registering its decadence and thus its waning authenticity, its lagging vitality and thus its spiritual obstructiveness, its lack of genuine conviction and thus its culturally enfeebling effect; and goaded on by his spiritual discontent, he was inexhaustibly ingenious in analyzing the psychology of the Christian "camel-spirit": the pleasure it takes in carrying the burden of its cross . . . the sensation of power it enjoys in extolling the virtues of powerlessness and humility and thus afflicting the naively strong with a sense of guilt.

—Erich Heller "Zarathustra's Three Metamorphoses"

1

Nietzsche's Early Years
and the Break with Wagner

As far as Christianity is concerned, I hope you'll believe
this much: in my heart I've never held it in contempt and,
ever since childhood, have often struggled with myself on
behalf of its ideals. . . . I no longer have the slightest idea
which of my views do good, which harm.[1]

Who knows how many generations it will take to produce a few who can fully appreciate what I've done? But
this is the torment of every great teacher of humankind: he
knows that he has as much chance of becoming its curse as
its blessing. But this loneliness, ever since childhood![2]

Friedrich Wilhelm Nietzsche (1844-1900) was born in Röcken on the fifteenth
of October at 10 a.m. "to the sound of the peals of bells rung by the parish in
honour of the birthday of our reigning monarch King Friedrich Wilhelm IV"—
according to his sister Elisabeth, who is known to have a flair for the sensa-
tional.[3]

Nietzsche was the son of Karl Ludwig Nietzsche, a Lutheran pastor, and
Franziska Oehler, a Lutheran minister's daughter. When Nietzsche was two
years old, his sister Elisabeth was born. Shortly before and after his fifth birthday, he experienced the first great tragedy of his life: his father, after suffering
for almost a year from loss of appetite and migraines, died from what was
later diagnosed as softening of the brain.[4] Eight months later, Nietzsche's
younger brother Joseph died suddenly from teething convulsions a few days
after his second birthday.

Nietzsche grew up in a pious Christian home consisting of his mother, his
sister, his father's mother, and two maiden aunts. When he was nine he began
experiencing headaches which caused him to miss a great deal of school;
when he was twelve he began having serious trouble with his eyes as a result
of inheriting myopia from his father. Fellow classmates often teased

Nietzsche calling him the "little pastor" or the "little Jesus" because of his fragile physical health, his precocious mind, and his pious and peculiar disposition. He was typically melancholy, shy, and reflective beyond his years, spending most of his time in solitude playing the piano, reading the Bible, and writing poetry. His classmates' teasing further contributed to his reclusive tendencies and to his unusually close relationship with his sister. Elisabeth worshipped her brother, saved virtually everything he wrote, and regarded him as a saint.[5]

At age fourteen Nietzsche went away to Pforta, a classical Lutheran boarding school which he attended for six years. In an autobiographical essay which helped grant him a full tuition scholarship he wrote: "In all things God has led me safely as his father leads his weak little child. . . . I have firmly resolved to dedicate myself forever to his service. . . . All he gives I will accept joyfully—even death, which will one day unite us all in eternal joy and bliss."[6]

His time at Pforta was generally unhappy; the school was a blend of militarism and classicism, it resembled a prison more than a school, and its educational philosophy was geared toward keeping young minds in the classical past—and out of the contemporary world. Pforta produced some remarkable people whose minds flourished, and Nietzsche's admiration for the ancient Greeks, particularly the pre-Socratic philosophers, was cultivated there. His primary interest was still poetry, particularly Hölderlin (who was hardly known then) and Byron, both of whom Nietzsche admired for their rebellious tendencies and their roles as cultural critics.

Nietzsche was duly confirmed at the age of sixteen, and he took his profession of faith seriously. He began expressing doubts concerning the literalness of Christian doctrine, saying that the authority of the Bible and related issues were endlessly problematic. Darwinism particularly began to trouble Nietzsche during his teens, and continued to haunt him until his mental breakdown at age forty-four. An essay called "Fate and History" illustrates the struggle of the seventeen-year-old Christian who desired to adhere to traditional notions of creation that humans were made in the image of God:

[T]he doubt that power of habit, the drive towards the higher, the rejection of everything in existence . . . the doubt that humanity may have been led astray for two thousand years by a phantasm . . . —all these fight an indecisive battle until finally the pain of the experience, the sadness of the event drives our heart back into the old beliefs of childhood. But we scarcely even know whether humanity itself is only a step, a period in the universal, in evolution—whether it is not an arbitrary manifestation of God. . . . Is humanity only a means, or an end?[7]

This echoes Zarathustra's cry twenty-one years later: "If humanity still lacks a goal—is humanity not still lacking too?"[8]

Nietzsche wrote his thesis on Theognis of Megara and graduated from Pforta in September 1864 at the age of nineteen. When he, along with a group of others, was required to make a speech, he read a poem he had written for the occasion, "To the Unknown God": "Once more, before I wander on and turn my glance forward, I lift up my hands to you— . . . I have solemnly consecrated altars so that your voice might summon me again. . . . I want to know you, Unknown One . . . even serve you."[9] The pious tone of this poem however, substantially differs from one he had written the previous year, "Vor dem Kruzifix," which depicted a drunk throwing a bottle of Schnapps at a figure of Christ on the Cross.[10]

One month later Nietzsche was enrolled at the University of Bonn intending to focus on the philology of Gospel criticism and New Testament sources. Although his mother and sister expected Nietzsche to enter the ministry, by his twentieth year he refused to attend Easter services while home for the holidays. His mother wept and quarrelled with her son; his aunt intervened and explained to her that all great theologians go through periods of doubt. Because Elisabeth too was affected by her brother's questioning, Nietzsche's mother forbid them to discuss or to exchange letters concerning their Christian faith—to no avail. A few months later, Nietzsche wrote to his sister:[11]

> Is it then a matter of acquiring the view of God, world, and atonement in which one can feel most comfortable? . . . Do we in our investigations, search for tranquility, peace, happiness? No—only truth, even if it were to be frightening and ugly.
>
> One last remaining question. If we had believed since youth that salvation came not from Jesus, but from another—say Mohammed— would we not have enjoyed the same blessings? Here the ways of spirits divide. If you want to find peace of mind and happiness, then believe. If you want to be a disciple of truth, then search.
>
> Between there are many halfway positions. But it all depends on the principal aim.[12]

This letter prompted Elisabeth to consult with two uncles who were pastors. It also anticipates Zarathustra's philosophy well over a decade later: "These young hearts have all become old already— . . . only weary, ordinary, and comfortable. They put it, 'We have become pious again.' . . . Were their ability different, their will would be different too. Those who are half-and-half spoil all that is whole."[13]

Darwinism, coupled with David Strauss' *The Life of Jesus*, in which Strauss argued that the gospels were myths and the historical Jesus was a fictitious "superman" with divine attributes, were the primary reasons Nietzsche lost his Christian faith while studying theology and philology at the University of Bonn. After reading *The Life of Jesus*, Nietzsche, in a state of deep depression, dropped theology after only two semesters to concentrate solely on philology: "I craved something that would counterbalance my changing and restless proclivities, I craved an academic discipline that required aloof circumspection, logical coldness, the results of which would not instantly touch the heart."[14] Nietzsche could no longer profess a belief in the existence of God. His aimlessness led him to the philosophy of Schopenhauer, which he came to out of "need," "distress," and "desire."

A year later, when his teacher Friedrich Ritschl transferred to the University of Leipzig, Nietzsche was among the students who followed him. Nietzsche gained prominence among his contemporaries and was one of the founders of a University Classical Society in 1865. Two years later his student years were interrupted by a brief period of military service which resulted in a serious chest injury. After recuperating in Naumburg, he was back at the university in the fall of 1868 to continue his studies.

Nietzsche was recognized to be a brilliant student. After graduating at age twenty-four, upon Ritschl's recommendation, he was appointed as an associate professor of philology at the University of Basle in Switzerland without writing the usually mandatory dissertation. A year later he was appointed as a full professor. This was the only regular employment that Nietzsche ever had.

The most significant events of Nietzsche's life during this time period were twofold: he discovered the philosophy of Schopenhauer, and then several years later, the friendship of Richard Wagner. While a student at Leipzig, Nietzsche found Schopenhauer one day while browsing in a bookstore: "I trusted him at once and . . . though this is a foolish and immodest way of putting it, I understand him as though it were for me he had written."[15]

Among other things, Nietzsche was attracted to Schopenhauer's empathy toward the pain and suffering one experiences in this world, the struggle for existence, and the Buddhist notion that the satisfaction of desires was merely an escape from pain; pain quickly replenished by an endless cycle of unfilled desires and boredom. Schopenhauer held that all things were driven by the Cosmic Will, a blind nonrational force wreaking havoc on the Universe. Freedom for the individual essentially meant liberation from the Will by denying one's desires. When one became aware of the illusory character of the phenomenal world, one could become more aware of one's universal affinity with all things.[16]

Nietzsche later rejected Schopenhauer's cosmological Will and the related anthropological category of the will to existence as the primary life-force, substituting his own notion of the will to power. He adhered to Schopenhauer's conviction of the will as the primary life-force; however, he did not regard the Cosmic Will as a metaphysical principle beyond the universe, but as wholly within it.

In 1870 Nietzsche's professional career at Basle was interrupted by the Franco-Prussian War. He served as a medical orderly for three months; his service was curtailed when he contracted severe dysentery and diphtheria. Nietzsche's experience of war and suffering deeply distressed him. It strongly affected his outlook on Greek tragedy in relation to modern German culture and art, and also led to a growing restlessness with Wagner's optimism regarding the rise of the new *Reich* as an expression of Germanic health and strength.[17]

During his first month as an orderly, Nietzsche sent his mother "a souvenir of the terribly devastated battlefield, strewn with countless sad remains and smelling strongly of corpses";[18] a few months later while recovering he disclosed to his family that he was losing all sympathy for Germany's present war of conquest: "The future of German culture seems to me now more in danger than it ever was."[19]

Nietzsche returned to Basle in October. His first book, *The Birth of Tragedy* (1872) promoted a philology of the future and included a preface dedicated to Wagner. The work, in which Nietzsche celebrates Greek tragedy and compares the Apollonian and Dionysian with modern-day Schopenhauerism and Wagnerism is, as Nietzsche himself remarked, "badly written, embarrassing, and image confused," though its treatment of the relationship between art and science, Greek civilization and modernity, is often perceptive.[20] On the whole, it was unscholarly and contained no footnotes. Although the book moved Wagner to tears ("Dear friend! I have read nothing more beautiful!" . . .); Ritschl first responded with silence and then "megalomania."[21] The work earned the young professor disrepute in academic circles who had eagerly anticipated the first publication from a philologist who had secured an academic chair without writing a dissertation.

Nietzsche's early *Untimely Meditations* (a collection of four essays published between the ages of twenty-nine and thirty-one), display his continued preoccupation with Darwinism, Christianity, Schopenhauer, and Wagner. The first essay, "David Strauss: The Confessor and the Writer," was a polemic against Strauss' new work, *The Old Faith and the New*. Nietzsche not only wrote the review because Wagner was publicly criticized by Strauss and he asked Nietzsche to retaliate on his behalf, but also because Nietzsche had a concern for the now deteriorating state of German culture and saw Strauss as contributing to it. Overall, Nietzsche had personal reasons for wanting to debunk Strauss; namely, Strauss' critique of Christ in *The Life of Jesus* had, years earlier, shattered Nietzsche's Christian faith to the point of no return.

According to Strauss, Jesus could no longer be an "object of worship"—even as a mere human being—because the gospels had been discolored to such an extent that the natural Jesus could never be restored. The only thing that could be known about Jesus was that he "expected to reappear . . . in order to inaugurate the kingdom of the Messiah as foretold by him." Since this did not occur, Strauss concludes that Jesus was not the Son of God or divine. Moreover, a mere human being with such high expectations of himself must have been an "enthusiast."[23]

Nietzsche attacked Strauss for making "a bitter mockery of the nameless sufferings of mankind" and for describing Jesus as "a visionary who would . . . hardly escape the madhouse." He also blasted him for esteeming Darwin "as one of the greatest benefactors of mankind."[24] Nietzsche argued that Darwinism, without an adequate ethical basis, was detrimental to the creation of culture. Moreover, whereas Strauss assumed that no creatures were exactly alike and that evolution depended upon the law of difference between individuals, he nonetheless admonished that individuals should behave as if no differences between them existed. Strauss' philosophy of individuals, Nietzsche claimed, constituted nothing less than cultural nihilism: "Where has the moral teaching of Strauss-Darwin now gone, where has any courage whatever gone!"[25]

Nietzsche conceded that the Old Faith indeed was dying. But the New Faith, which demeaned Jesus Christ and consisted of little more than a fundamental piety toward the cosmos, was blasphemous: "Strauss . . . is not ashamed. We, however, turn aside for a moment to overcome our disgust."[26] Strauss' influence on Nietzsche remained intact throughout his life, as did Nietzsche's contempt for him. In his last productive year, Nietzsche refers to Strauss in the *Antichrist* when touching upon the "psychology of the redeemer": "The time is long past when I too, like every young scholar, slowly drew out the savor of the work of the incomparable Strauss. I was twenty years old then: now I am too serious for that. What do I care about the contradictions in the 'tradition'?"[27] Nietzsche's words are ironic; for the *Antichrist* is precisely concerned with severing Jesus from the tradition that he grew to abhor even more vehemently with time.

The point is that the young Nietzsche was torn between cultural Christianity and the historical Jesus; between Christianity's view of creation and Darwinian evolution. On the one hand, he rejected creationism but regarded Jesus as an exemplary human being. On the other hand, he adopted the empirical truth of evolutionary theory, with the understanding that a new ethic and image of humanity *had* to be constructed in order to preserve the dignity and worth of individuals. In his second meditation, "On The Uses and Disadvantages of History for Life," Nietzsche writes:

If the doctrines of sovereign becoming, of the lack of any cardinal distinction between man and animal—doctrines which I consider true but deadly—are thrust upon the people for another generation . . . no one should be surprised if the people perishes of petty egoism, ossification and greed, falls apart and ceases to be a people; in its place systems of individualist egoism, brotherhoods for the rapacious exploitation of the non-brothers, and similar creations of utilitarian vulgarity may perhaps appear in the arena of the future. To prepare the way for these creations all one has to do is to go on writing history from the standpoint of the masses.[28]

According to Nietzsche, Christianity had hitherto been the power of history and the driving force moving the masses; however, to confuse power with greatness was to confuse quantity with quality. The "truest adherents of Christianity," Nietzsche claims, "have always called into question its worldly success and power in history rather than promoted them: for they were accustomed to place themselves outside the 'world'":[29]

The noblest and most exalted things make no effect whatever on the masses; the historical success of Christianity, its power in history, its tenacity and durability, happily proves nothing with respect to the greatness of its founder, for if it did it would be evidence against him: between him and that historical success there lies a very dark and earthy stratum of passion, error, thirst for power and honour. . . . Greatness ought not to depend on success.[30]

Nietzsche affirmed Darwin's evolutionary theory but defied it by claiming that humans *could* rise above the beasts—precisely because they had the potential to overcome their natures. Though the instincts of humans were essentially no different from those of animals, the true representatives of humanity and culture were its "artists, saints and philosophers" who were "no longer animal" and whom nature created.[31] Rejecting Christian notions of eschatology which sought as the goal of humanity to be with God after death, Nietzsche, by age thirty, had formed a new theology which found the sacred in this life and an eschatology which located the sacred within history: "The goal of humanity cannot lie in its end, but only in its highest exemplars."[32]

These exemplars were referred to as "free spirits" throughout Nietzsche's earlier and later writings. In *Zarathustra* they were called Overmen (*Übermenschen*), a term Nietzsche derived from several sources, including Goethe's *Faust, The Civilization of the Renaissance in Italy* by his colleague and mentor

Jacob Burckhardt, and the essay of his favorite American author, Emerson's "The Oversoul."[33]

Free spirits were regarded as exemplary ones that had "a courage without any desire for honors" and "a self-sufficiency that overflows and gives to men and things."[34] They sought knowledge without craving certainty; they possessed intellectual integrity; they were skeptics, but they also cheerfully welcomed criticism and contradiction from others—or from themselves—"in order to receive some hint about their own injustices" of which they were unaware.[35] They had a "new conscience for truths, new eyes for what is most distant," and "new ears for new music."[36] They were relentless questioners and non-conformists, unafraid of throwing out their old convictions in order to usher in the new and improved.

Free spirits have a passion that involves using a rare and singular standard "and almost a madness." They felt heat in things that felt cold to everyone else, they discovered values for which no scales had yet been invented, and they offered "sacrifices on altars . . . dedicated to an unknown god."[37] They were faithful to themselves, followed themselves, had reverence for self, and "unconditional freedom before oneself."[38] "He too," says Nietzsche, "knows the weekdays of bondage, dependence, and service. But from time to time he must get a Sunday of freedom."[39]

Free spirits were self-creators who molded their strengths and weaknesses "to give style to one's character."[40] They were honest with themselves "on matters of the spirit to the point of hardness";[41] they were "the new, the unique, the incomparable"[42]—the artists, saints, and philosophers. They were spirits Nietzsche made in his own ideal self-image:

> Compared with the man who has tradition on his side . . . the free spirit is always weak, especially in his actions. . . . How does a strong spirit come into being? In one particular case this is how the genius is engendered. Where does the energy come from, the unbending strength, the endurance, with which one person, against all tradition, endeavors to acquire a quite individual understanding of the world?[43]

Appropriately, Zarathustra came crying in the wilderness—preparing the way for the *Übermensch*: the free spirit par excellence:

> Once one said "God" when one gazed upon distant seas; but now I have taught you to say "Overman. . . ."
>   Could you *create* a god?—So be silent about all gods! But you could surely create the overman. . . .

And you yourselves should create what you have hitherto called the world: the world will be formed in your image by your reason, your will, and your love! And truly, it will be to your happiness, you enlightened men![44]

Zarathustra is also where Nietzsche articulated his concept of the eternal recurrence and initially announced that life itself was not, in contrast to Darwin, a struggle for existence. Nor was life, in contrast to Schopenhauer, driven by a will to existence: "For, what does not exist cannot will; but what is in existence, how could that still want existence?" Nietzsche concludes: "Only where there is life is there also will: not will to life but . . . will to power."[45]

By far the most profound influence on Nietzsche's early personal, religious, and intellectual development was Wagner, to whom he paid homage in his fourth meditation, "Richard Wagner in Bayreuth." In the work, Nietzsche contrasts the two enigmatic forces within Wagner, his "tyrannical will" and his "gentle spirit," esteeming Wagner as one in whom "the desire for supreme power is translated into artistic creativity."[46]

Nietzsche, who was a fan of *Tristan und Isolde* since the age of sixteen, met Wagner three years after his conversion to Schopenhauer, at the age of twenty-four. He greatly admired the score of *Die Meistersinger* for its unconventionality, and his enthusiasm for the composer's latest work was well-known throughout the University of Leipzig when Nietzsche was in his final year as a student. By happenstance, Wagner's sister lived in Leipzig and was friendly with Professor Ritschl and his wife; through this connection, Nietzsche was awarded a meeting with his cultural hero. The meeting changed Nietzsche's life. Not only was he impressed with the composer's charm and wit, he was also surprised and ecstatic to discover that Wagner was also a Schopenhauer enthusiast. Wagner, who was notoriously egotistical and who sought disciples, enjoyed the philologist's admiration and invited Nietzsche to visit him again to talk philosophy and music. A few months later, when Nietzsche took his professorial position at the University of Basle, which was only a short distance from Wagner's Swiss villa in Tribschen, Nietzsche sought out Wagner's companionship.

Nietzsche quickly became an intimate of Wagner and his mistress Cosima (who married Wagner in 1870, but at this time was not yet divorced from composer Hans von Bülow), and became their regular house guest on weekends. The Tribschen years were by far the happiest of Nietzsche's life and he usually spent Christmas and other holidays with this family to which he felt he belonged. Wagner, who was thirty-one years Nietzsche's senior, became a mentor and a father figure to him. In turn, throughout the course of their friendship, which lasted almost a decade, Nietzsche was assigned such tasks as doing the family's Christmas shopping, editing Wagner's autobiography, buying Wagner's underclothes, and reporting to Wagner the intellectual currents within the academic community. Academicians were generally hostile towards the composer and his attempts to redeem German culture through his art.

Nietzsche's visits to the Wagner household were thoroughly enjoyed by both Richard and Cosima ("Certainly few people have so much feeling for our suffering and joys as he") and they regarded Nietzsche as Wagner's most loyal supporter.[47] This relationship was sparked by their common love for music (Nietzsche was an amateur composer and pianist) and intellectual conversations. Nietzsche often read his own essays to the Wagners, who in turn responded to and critiqued them. Moreover—at least on one occasion—Wagner read Nietzsche's essays to guests in his absence "somewhat to their dismay."[48]

It is clear that the Wagners recognized Nietzsche's exceptional intellect and had an interest in the young professor's work, but only to the degree that it was directly related to promoting their own ideas concerning the redemption of German culture. As Ernest Newman, Wagner's foremost biographer in the 1940s observes: "He [Nietzsche] was to be theirs and theirs alone, body and soul: a tight hand would have to be kept on the jesses lest the young hawk should take a flight on his own."[49] No one of Nietzsche's calibre, says Newman, "had ever come into such close relation with Wagner's intellectual life; yet towards no one else did he behave so imperiously."[50]

Wagner, who was excessively distrustful, became irate when Nietzsche did not accept invitations to visit. Wagner often interpreted Nietzsche's occasional absence as signs of defection, when, in fact, his overwhelming university obligations usually prevented him from fulfilling their frequent requests for his presence. Much of the first few years of their relationship consisted of Wagner presiding over Nietzsche and testing his disciple's loyalty ("My dear friend: Your silence surprises me. . . . I am beginning to have my suspicions about you"),[51] and Nietzsche's proving time and again his supreme allegiance to Wagner ("Most revered master! In the first onrush of the opening semester . . . nothing more stimulating could have happened to me than to receive a copy of your 'Beethoven'").[52] The young Nietzsche was enamored with the composer who possessed an artistic brilliance, a magnetic personality, and—to a large degree—Nietzsche himself. Nietzsche believed that Wagner and Schopenhauer were the greatest creative geniuses to surface in Europe after the life of Goethe.

The fourth meditation, "Richard Wagner in Bayreuth," was published in the spring of 1876 in honor of the Bayreuth opera house and festivals which were taking place there. The essay—although it has hostile undertones—was a piece of promotional propaganda paying homage to Wagner and his art. Even so, private observations recorded in Nietzsche's notebooks from 1874 onward reveal Nietzsche's growing discontent with Wagnerian principles, and thus anticipate the infamous breakup with him that became evident publicly at the Bayreuth festival during the summer of '76 (when Nietzsche fled the festival). This split was finalized at the beginning of 1878. In particular, Nietzsche was concerned with Wagner's anti-French and anti-Jewish sentiments. He refers to Wagner in his notebooks as "the tyrant who suppresses all individuality other than his own and his followers'," and then adds: "This is Wagner's great danger, to refuse to accept Brahms, etc., or the Jews."[53] Elsewhere, Nietzsche writes that Wagner offended the Jews in Germany, who owned most of the money and the press: "To start with, it was done without cause or reason, later by way of revenge."[54] In an interesting note which is of further concern here, Nietzsche observes:

> Wagner is a modern man, incapable of deriving encouragement or strength from a belief in God. He does not believe that he is in the safekeeping of a benevolent being but he believes in himself. Nobody who believes only in himself can be entirely honest. Wagner gets rid of his weaknesses by loading them on to his time and his enemies.[55]

Historically, much controversy has surrounded the breakup between Wagner and Nietzsche, particularly the reasons for it. Some insist that Nietzsche rejected Wagner because his mentor converted to Christianity (in 1876); others speculate that Nietzsche was secretly in love with Cosima, and that this caused the severance. Although these explanations may contain elements of truth, they are nonetheless superficial and are not adequate to explain Nietzsche's decision to end the friendship.

Elisabeth Förster-Nietzsche, who remained an enthusiastic admirer of Wagner throughout her life, states (1895; 1912) that Nietzsche anticipated leaving Wagner long before the festival and that he was reluctant to publish his fourth meditation because "he had lost his faith in Wagner's Art."[56] She claims that her brother fled Bayreuth because he was disappointed with the operas (and that Wagner's conversion to Christianity several months later was the main cause of the break). Newman (1946) resists Elisabeth's rendition. He demonstrates that Nietzsche had heard none of the first performances, but only a few "imperfect rehearsals," and concludes that she typically tells the story in a misleading way for the purpose of concealing that her brother was a "pitifully distempered man" who behaved like a "sick spoiled child" during his short stay in Bayreuth.[57]

Newman argues that the breakup was precipitated not by Nietzsche's discontent with Wagner's art, but by his own scientific freethinking, his "seemingly irresponsible changefulness" and the milieu of the Bayreuth festival itself—not the performances.[58] He argues that Nietzsche's increasing ill-health, his disappointment over the types of people attending the festival (well-fed, bourgeois, beer drinking pseudo-intellectuals), and the strong egos of the two men made a severance inevitable. These were the primary reasons Nietzsche became what the Wagners' later referred to as an "apostate."[59]

Kaufmann (1950), who takes issue with Newman, stresses that Bayreuth was not the *cause of* the breach, but rather the *occasion for* it. Kaufmann (like Elisabeth) stresses that the break was gradual and that the key to understanding the termination lies in how Wagner appeared to Nietzsche at the time he broke from him. Newman, Kaufmann observes, is correct to describe Wagner as an "undisputed dictator" who "worked himself into a paroxysm over Bismarck's tolerance towards the Jews."[60] And he is also correct to perceive factual errors in Elisabeth's rendering of the account concerning the events taking place that summer.

However, in the midst of his minute attention to detail in refuting Elisabeth, and in his admiration for Wagner and his music, Newman (like Elisabeth) attaches no importance to the composer's prejudices. Newman fails to see that Nietzsche, while working on his pro-Wagner essay, realized how dangerous Wagner was. Nietzsche could tolerate Wagner's personal idiosyncrasies within the confines of the household, but his public campaign and the widespread adoration and support he sought was another matter entirely. Moreover, as Kaufmann argues, Nietzsche was now heavily influenced by Enlightenment ideals and propagated the vision of the Good European (and the mixture of races), in opposition to Wagner's antisemitic German nationalism; hence, he could not reconcile his ideals with those of the Master.

While Elisabeth appeals to art (and then to Wagner's conversion), and Newman to Nietzsche's physical and temperamental disorders, Kaufmann approaches the matter from a different angle: "Bayreuth had become the Holy City of anti-Semitic Christian chauvinism."[61] The breach between Wagner and Nietzsche developed gradually, as Nietzsche became more aware that it was impossible to serve both Wagner and his own call. Instead of coming out in the open, Nietzsche's physical ailments, typified by chronic migraines and waves of nausea—although they were very real—were perhaps to a certain degree psychogenic. They were made more acute by his mental anguish and they served as an excuse to stay away from Wagner after he had moved to Bayreuth (in 1872).[62]

Kaufmann's interpretation is quite credible, agreeing both with the facts surrounding the breakup and with Nietzsche's own rendition of why he left Wagner. The best years of the Wagner-Nietzsche friendship were the first four years from 1868 to 1872, when Wagner moved from Tribschen to Bayreuth to prepare for the festivals. After that time, although Wagner often invited

Nietzsche to visit, he began to decline. Although the two men corresponded, they did not see each other from August 1874 to July 1876—much to Wagner's growing agitation ("O Friend: Why do you not come to us? . . . If you persist in doing this I can do nothing for you. Your room is ready").[63] In the summer of '76 Nietzsche attended the festival for a few days, fled to the mountains for ten days to work on *Human, all-too-Human*, and then returned again to the festival at his sister's request before going back to Basle with his Jewish friend and colleague, Dr. Paul Rée, and travelling companion, Edouard Schuré. Schuré writes: "When we left together, not a criticism escaped him, not a word of censure, but he showed the resigned sadness of a beaten man."[64]

The final meeting between Wagner and Nietzsche occurred a few months later. Nietzsche, Rée, and Malwida von Meysenbug (an active women's rights supporter who also played a mother role to younger intellectuals and artists) were staying in Sorrento wherein the three of them visited the Wagners at the end of October. On November first, Cosima wrote in her diary that Rée visited that same evening, and that his "cold and precise character does not appeal to us." She adds that "on closer inspection" she and Richard came "to the conclusion that he must be an Israelite."[65]

During that week Nietzsche visited the Wagners, which was the last time he ever saw them again. Wagner and Nietzsche took an evening walk during which Wagner allegedly raved about his new religious conversion, and also about *Parsifal*, a Christian opera he was currently working on.[66] Although a verbal dispute between the two apparently did not occur, a clash of ideals certainly did: it is clear that Nietzsche's friendship with Rée, and the Wagners' response to it, caused a further rift between them. Conversely, Wagner's sudden conversion to Christianity did not fare well with Nietzsche.[67]

Although Nietzsche continued sparse correspondence with the Wagners throughout that and the following year (the day before Christmas '76 they received a note from Nietzsche that he now rejected Schopenhauer's teachings), he nonetheless avoided personal contact with them.[68] The break was formally sealed in the winter and spring of 1878. Wagner sent Nietzsche his *Parsifal*, signing it "The Member of the High Consistory." A few months later, Nietzsche sent Wagner his new book, *Human, all-too-Human*, which was dedicated to Voltaire and included a whimsical salutation inscribed on the first page:

> To the Master and the Mistress, a cheerful greeting from Friedrich Freemind in Basle, blessed with a new child. He desires that they with moved hearts examine the child to see whether it takes after the father. . . . Whatever its fate in its earthly wandering, it wants to be liked; not by many; fifteen at most; for others it will be mockery and

torment. But before we send it out in the world, may the Master's faithful eye gaze on it and bless it, and may the wise grace of the Mistress follow it for evermore.[69]

This was interpreted by the Wagners as a betrayal. The two would never meet, speak, or correspond again after this exchange.[70]

Many have accepted Elisabeth's tale that the break ultimately occurred because Wagner converted to Christianity, expressed in his *Parsifal*, and pagan Nietzsche could not bear to see Wagner become Christian. However, Nietzsche viewed Wagner's conversion as a travesty: "If Wagner was a Christian, then Liszt was perhaps a church father!"[71] Kaufmann correctly notes that Nietzsche took Christianity quite seriously, that Nietzsche saw Wagner's *Parsifal* as simply another occasion of religious hypocrisy, and that the break occurred long before Nietzsche received the Christian opera in 1878 with a note from Wagner. Kaufmann's observations, as well as mine, stand in accord with Nietzsche's own candid remarks on the matter (to which neither Newman or Förster-Nietzsche appeal):

> By the summer of 1876, during the time of the first *Festspiele*, I had said goodbye in my heart to Wagner . . . he had condescended to everything I despise—even to anti-Semitism. It was indeed high time to say farewell: soon after, I received the proof. Richard Wagner, apparently most triumphant, but in truth a decaying and despairing decadent, suddenly sank down, helpless and broken, before the Christian cross. . . . As I proceeded alone I trembled. . . . I was henceforth sentenced to mistrust more profoundly . . . to be more profoundly *alone* than ever before. For I had had nobody except Richard Wagner.[72]

This passage reverberates in *Zarathustra*, in a section appropriately entitled "On Apostates":

> Verily, many among them once lifted their legs like dancers. . . . Then they thought better of it. Just now I saw one groveling—crawling back to the cross. . . . Did their hearts perhaps grow faint because solitude swallowed me like a whale? . . . Alas, there are always a few who retain their courageous bearing. . . . The rest, however, are cowards.[73]

Historically, one should carefully note the political games surrounding interpretations of the break, which initially stem from Elisabeth's skewed biography (and have continued to manifest themselves in countless forms to this very day). Elisabeth and Newman, although they disagree on minor specifics (art vs. Nietzsche's ill temperament), hide (or protect) Wagner's antisemitism and tend to implicate Nietzsche as somewhat "immoral" (or mentally imbalanced) for his anti-Christianity. Kaufmann exposes Wagner's antisemitism, stressing that one can be ethical without being Christian. In retrospect, from a religiopolitical standpoint, the stakes are high (especially now that Wagnerism is regarded by historians as the root of National Socialism): If the truth be known that a very sane Nietzsche indeed opposed Wagner because of his *antisemitic Christianity*, not only Wagner, but Christianity itself, suffers an embarrassment at the hands of a "pagan philosopher" who opposed Christianity on ethical grounds. Thus, politically speaking, three main counterstrategies could solve the dilemma. First, Nietzsche could be dismissed as deranged or immoral for attacking Christianity, and his opposition to antisemitism could be ignored, suppressed, and even derided (enter Elisabeth and Newman). Second, which is most interesting, Nietzsche himself could be mythologized as an antisemite which would discredit him ethically, and would also serve to intimidate Jews (the Nazis, who were Wagnerites, used this tactic). And finally, negatively portraying Nietzsche as both a vicious anti-Christian *and* an antisemite would conceivably be the perfect solution (which, in fact, is the notorious image of Nietzsche that has lingered on in the popular consciousness for nearly a century—and even more so since the time of the Second World War!).

Regardless, it is clear that Nietzsche's break with Wagner was extremely painful and was caused by (1) Nietzsche's discontent with his friend's anti-Jewish prejudices and his conviction that Wagner's pro-nationalism, which was vigorously seeking public approval, was dangerous, (2) his realization that Wagnerian art was not fated nor suited to be the salvation of European culture, and that Wagner himself was not the redeemer, (3) the fact that Nietzsche, like Wagner, was egotistical, longed to be a free spirit and cultural savior, and thus believed he needed complete independence from his Master, and (4) Wagner's conversion to Christianity repulsed Nietzsche and sealed the breakup once and for all.

In the spring of '78 when Nietzsche sent out over twenty copies of *Human* to the Wagners and various friends, it caused great shock and upheaval within the Bayreuth circle. The book's derogatory remarks against "The Artist" and Christianity, coupled with a lengthy aphorism denouncing antisemitism and German nationalism (no. 475), resulted in Nietzsche's "grand excommunication" from the clique. Nietzsche, addressing Wagnerites, writes:

Every nation, every man has . . . dangerous characteristics, it is cruel to demand that the Jew should be an exception. Those characteristics may even be . . . dangerous and frightful in him, and *perhaps* [emphasis mine] the youthful Jew of the stock exchange is the most repugnant invention of the whole human race. Nevertheless, I would like to know how much one must excuse in the overall accounting of a people which, not without guilt on all our parts, has had the most sorrowful history of all peoples, and to whom we owe the noblest human being (Christ), the purest philosopher (Spinoza), the mightiest book, and the most effective moral code in the world. Furthermore, in the darkest medieval times . . . it was the Jewish freethinkers, scholars, and doctors, who, under the harshest personal pressure, held fast to the banner of enlightenment and intellectual independence.[74]

Whereas Peter Gast, Rée, and Burckhardt applauded Nietzsche's book; Wagner, fuming in Bayreuth, blamed Rée for exerting a Semitic influence on his disciple. Richard and Cosima sensed the "guiding hand" of Rée to be the true cause of Nietzsche's apostasy. Cosima wrote to a friend: "In the end, Israel took over in the shape of a Dr. Rée, very slick, very cool, . . . representing the relationship of Judea to Germania. . . . It is the victory of evil over good."[75]

Elisabeth was unduly distressed by her brother's latest antics, for fear that her relationship with the Wagners would be ruined, which it was not. Cosima assured Elisabeth a place in their lives, while adamantly condemning Nietzsche's book as the product of a sick mind—or as Richard put it—"mental spasms."[76] Nietzsche, however, was quite clever in offending Wagner, as illustrated in aphorism 113: "When we hear the old bells ringing out on a Sunday morning, we ask ourselves: can it be possible? This is for a Jew, crucified two thousand years ago, who said he was the son of God. The proof for such a claim is wanting."[77] Wagner, who shunned institutional religion, nonetheless worshipped Jesus and fiercely insisted on his non-Judaic origins.[78]

During the fall of 1878, Wagner sniped at Nietzsche in the *Bayreuther Blätter* (without mentioning him by name); years later Nietzsche wrote two polemical works specifically directed against the composer ("Why did I never forgive Wagner? That he condescended to the Germans—that he became *reichsdeutsch*").[79] Even so, publicly and privately he continued to credit much of his early intellectual development to Wagner and spoke fondly of his memories at Tribschen: "Certainly the time I spent with him in Tribschen and enjoyed through him at Bayreuth (in 1872, not in 1876) is the happiest I have had in my whole life. . . . But the omnipotent violence of our tasks drove us asunder. . . . In any case I have had to pay dearly for my craze for Wagner."[80]

It is clear that Wagner, who served as a father figure to Nietzsche, was an object of worship who fulfilled Nietzsche's highly emotional need for a male mentor. Although Nietzsche's break with Wagner was due to ethical considerations, it was also a break that was psychologically driven: Nietzsche believed that liberation and emotional detachment from others was essential for human growth.[81]

Nietzsche's tendency to liberate himself from "externals," including family, friends, mentors, society, religion, and God(s) was formulated during his early years and became even more excessive as time went on. Nietzsche's discomfort, as well as his intense desire, to create substantial intimate relationships perhaps arose from an overwhelming fear that significant persons would ultimately forsake him, as did his father. Interestingly, although Nietzsche facilitated the break with Wagner, in a personal letter to von Meysenbug years later he wrote: "Any news from the Wagners? It's three years now since I've heard from them. *They* abandoned me too." Here, Nietzsche's reversal of events perhaps displays his need for a self-fulfilling prophecy; the hallowed prediction that those he felt closest to and trusted would eventually leave and betray him: "I knew long ago that Wagner, as soon as he realized that our aims had diverged, would do just that."[82]

By the time of *Zarathustra*, Nietzsche basically equates the notion of love with rejection, and thus regards the former as something to be resisted by "creators who must become hard": "What does he know of love who did not have to despise precisely what he loved!"[83] These sentiments are echoed when Zarathustra speaks of friendship ("You should be closest to him with your heart when you resist him"),[84] and of God ("I love him who chastens his god because he loves his god; for he must perish of the wrath of his god").[85] Nietzsche writes to Overbeck:

> I think you know what Zarathustra's warning, "Be hard!" means in my own case. My idea that justice should be done to every particular person, and that I should in the last analysis treat precisely what is most hostile to me with the greatest gentleness . . . involves danger upon danger, not only for me but also for my task: it is here that the hardening is necessary and, with a view to educating others, an occasional cruelty. . . .
>
> For my part, I mean to break off relations with everyone who sides with my sister; from now on, there can be no half-measures for me.[86]

According to Sigmund Freud (whose first great work, *The Interpretation of Dreams*, was published the year Nietzsche died), the key to understanding Nietzsche was that he lost his father at an early age and grew up in a family of women who were pious Christians. Because Nietzsche fantasized about being Christ during puberty, and labeled himself an Antichrist at the end of his life,

Freud reasons that in his denial of God, Nietzsche was merely killing his father once again.

Nietzsche's personality traits fascinated Freud and his colleagues, who included Otto Rank and Alfred Adler. In 1908, Nietzsche's autobiographical work *Ecce Homo*, written only months before his mental collapse, was discussed at length at the meeting of the Vienna Psychoanalytic Society. Among other things, the participants discussed Nietzsche's nature against the struggle of his own illness, his homosexual and narcissistic tendencies, and his paternal heritage. Many participants opined that Nietzsche displayed symptoms of severe neurosis. However, Freud and Rank dissented that neurosis was the correct diagnosis. Rank claimed that Nietzsche had a "sadistic disposition" which was accompanied by tremendous repression. And Freud diagnosed Nietzsche as a paretic. Although Freud agreed that there were indeed "disturbing elements" in Nietzsche's personality, these did not constitute a neurotic illness: "The degree of introspection achieved by Nietzsche had never been achieved by anyone. . . ." Even so, says Freud, Nietzsche forever remained the moralist: a major impediment to his personal growth was that he could not "free himself of the theologian."[87]

The influence of Wagner, Darwinism, Schopenhauer, the historical Jesus, and nineteenth-century German Christianity weighed heavily upon Nietzsche's philosophy. These forces shaped Nietzsche's psychology, theology, and philosophy. After his university retirement at age thirty-four, due to his deteriorating health, this philosophy began to flourish. As will be shown further, the echoes and responses to these influences resound in *Zarathustra*.

Nietzsche's early years were marked by a constant disillusionment with, and subsequent rejection of, personal, cultural, and spiritual gods. This is evidenced by his journey from Christianity to Schopenhauer to Wagner and beyond. As a fourteen-year-old, he believed that heaven would unite him with his father and his brother; at seventeen he wrote that the incarnation showed "that man is not to seek his bliss in eternity, but to found his heaven on earth."[88] At twenty-four Nietzsche professed that in Wagner's company he felt himself to be in the presence of "immaculate greatness";[89] then, a decade later he could find the sacred nowhere: not in Wagner, in Schopenhauer, or in the Christian religion. Even so, instead of grieving the death of God, humanity could now become its own creators, sustainers, and redeemers—there was no other hope: "Since man no longer believes that a God is guiding the destinies of the world as a whole . . . men must set themselves ecumenical goals, embracing the whole earth." "This," Nietzsche said, "is the enormous task of the great minds of the next century."[90]

Nietzsche's philosophy was consumed by efforts to establish human worth on the basis of self-affirmation and justification. It was diametrically opposed to traditional Lutheran notions of justification by faith, and to notions that morality was grounded on principles of unegoistic or selfless actions, which he regarded as dangerous psychological illusions. His break from Wagner largely informed his view that humans must first affirm themselves as opposed to sacrificing themselves to or for another, a tenet Nietzsche saw as central to Christianity.[91] From Nietzsche's perspective, the concept of God as bestowing worth upon human life and directing humanity's destiny toward a metaphysical end, was over. Human worth was abolished with the advent of Darwinism; the predestined metaphysical end had to be abolished with Christianity and replaced with a new ethic. Hence, Nietzsche perceived his task as creating new values, meanings, and goals by which modernity could live:

> What alone can be *our* doctrine. That no one *gives* man his qualities—neither God, nor society, nor his parents and ancestors, nor he himself. . . .
>
> One is necessary, one is a piece of fatefulness, one belongs to the whole, one is in the whole; there is nothing which could judge, measure, compare, or sentence our being, for [it] would mean sentencing the whole. . . . That nobody is held responsible any longer . . . that the world does not form a unity either as a sensorium or as "spirit"—that alone is the great liberation; with this alone is the innocence of becoming restored. The concept of "God" was until now the greatest objection to existence. We deny God, we deny the responsibility in God: only thereby do we redeem the world.[92]

2

Zarathustra's World
contra the Sister's

My existence is a terrible burden. I'd long ago have
chucked it were it not for my having done the most illumi-
nating psychological and moral research in just this state of
suffering and almost absolute renunciation. My joyous
thirst for knowledge brings me to heights where I can triumph over all torment and despair. . . . And yet!—constant
pain, a feeling much like seasickness several hours each
day, a semi-paralysis which makes speaking difficult and,
for a change of pace, furious seizures (the last involved
three days and nights of vomiting; I lusted for death).[1]
What a life! And I'm the great affirmer of life!![2]

After breaking off his relationship with Wagner, renouncing Schopenhauer's
philosophy because it was too pessimistic, and officially retiring from the university in 1879, Nietzsche received a modest pension from Basle and spent
the remainder of his life as an obscure author, wandering throughout Europe
with only a trunk of clothes and paper to write on, in search of a place and climate that was conducive to his sensitive health. After publishing two short
sequels to *Human* (*Mixed Opinions and Maxims*, 1879, and *The Wanderer and
his Shadow*, 1880), Nietzsche produced two additional aphoristic works: *Daybreak* (1881) and *The Gay Science* (1882). These years constitute what is generally regarded as Nietzsche's positivistic phase, wherein he is particularly
concerned with how higher human attributes and characteristics evolve out of
the lower. The question of God continued to torment him as he came to regard
modern science's notion of infallible truth as the refinement and sublimation of
the Christian conscience, which typically yearns for "intellectual cleanliness at
any price."[3] And the breakup with Wagner also tormented him. In 1880, two
years after the break, Nietzsche confessed that he "suffered horribly" from the
loss of human affection:

Nothing, for example, can replace Wagner's, which the past few years have taken away from me. How often I dream of him, and always as he was in the time of our intimacy. . . . I don't think I ever laughed as much with anyone else. That's all over now. What's the use of my being right on many points? The greatest sacrifices have been required of me by my life and thought. . . . It seems so silly to want to be right at the expense of love.[4]

Meanwhile, in Bayreuth, Wagner disclosed to Cosima that wherever he turned "he heard Nietzsche speaking," but that his judgment on Beethoven and the Jews was a disgrace.[5]

Nietzsche first conceived of *Zarathustra* in August 1881 when he was walking through the woods along the lake of Silvaplana, and again the following winter in Genoa while strolling along the bay. In the winter of '83, Nietzsche began writing what is now regarded as his magnum opus.

At this time, Nietzsche was fighting the physical illness (migraines, eye disorders, stomach ailments) which had plagued him since childhood, as well as the severe beginning stages of tertiary syphilis which—it is believed—was the cause of his mental breakdown six years later.[6] His mood swings were often extreme—he vacillated from states of euphoria to severe depression—and maintaining a balance required a concentrated effort on Nietzsche's part. He was convinced that he, like his father, would suffer an early and sudden death, remarking that his daily battle with headaches, coupled with the "ridiculous assortment of ills" that plagued him, demanded so much attentiveness that he ran the risk of becoming petty minded.[7] Friends became even more concerned about Nietzsche's health and his wandering disposition, particularly Franz Overbeck, Erwin Rohde, and Peter Gast, whom Nietzsche corresponded with most often.[8]

With the genesis of *Zarathustra*, Nietzsche was not only experiencing waves of depression caused by physical illness, but those caused by turbulent personal relationships, which Nietzsche was extremely sensitive to after his break with Wagner. Nietzsche was currently at odds with his mother, sister, and two close companions: Paul Rée and Lou Andreas-Salomé.

Nietzsche had met Salomé through Rée and von Meysenbug in the spring of '82, and was instantly attracted to the twenty-one-year-old Russian woman's intellectual gifts. He won her friendship and, according to Salomé's memoirs, proposed marriage to her twice that same year.[9] Rée also had a romantic interest in Salomé which was causing an underlying rift between the two men. Salomé however, made it clear to both Rée and Nietzsche at the outset that she did not have a romantic interest in either of them. Although Nietzsche and Salomé's relationship was short-lived it was extremely intense. Nietzsche untypically trusted and shared his innermost thoughts and feelings with her almost at once. Recalling a visit that she and Nietzsche made to Tribschen together in May '82, Salomé reminisces how Nietzsche spoke of his former days at the Wagners' villa: "For a long, long while, he sat silent on the banks of the lake and was deeply immersed in heavy memories; then, while drawing in the moist sand with his cane, he softly spoke of those times past. And when he looked up, he cried."[10]

Nietzsche, Rée, and Salomé liked to describe their triangle as the holy trinity, and they all shared a common interest in discussing questions concerning theology, theodicy, and the origin of morals. In the summer of '82 they made plans to live together as study companions the following winter. Nietzsche's sister Elisabeth, who disliked the Jewish Rée and Salomé, was not only upset because her brother was infatuated with an "unrespectable" woman whom she despised, but also because Nietzsche was outraged by her own new love interest, the notorious antisemite, Bernhard Förster. Förster, a high school teacher and the son of a Protestant pastor, was one of the leaders of the antisemitic movement in the seventies and a member of the German Seven, a group of thinkers and politicians who sought to renew Germany by an exclusion of the Jews. In 1881 he sent a petition to Bismarck, which was signed by 267,000 people, calling for the limitation of Jewish immigration, exclusion of Jews from governmental and teaching positions, and registration of all Jews. Though Bismarck did nothing with the appeal, Förster was proud that the petition, for which Elisabeth collected signatures, was the first antisemitic movement within the *Reich*.[11] Förster's reputation was widespread; he was regarded by *The Times*, in England, as "the most representative Jew-baiter in all Germany."[12]

Nietzsche did not want his sister involved with this self-avowed Christian who believed Jesus was Aryan because God could not have been a Jew. However, Elisabeth preferred Förster's philosophy to her brother's and remained within the Wagner circle, from which Nietzsche had fled six years earlier: "We feast on compassion, heroic self-denial, Christianity, vegetarianism, Aryanism, [and] southern colonies," Elisabeth proclaimed.[13]

In August, Elisabeth informed her mother of Nietzsche's plans to live with Salomé and Rée in the winter, which did not fare well with the family's staunch Lutheran morality. Nietzsche's mother reprimanded her thirty-eight-year-old son for his shameful ideas, and told him that his dead father would turn over in his grave. Nietzsche left his mother's house vowing never to return. In a letter to Overbeck, Nietzsche described the commotion:

Unfortunately my sister has become Lou's deadly enemy, she was full of moral indignation from beginning to end and claims to know

now what my philosophy is all about. She wrote my mother that she had seen my philosophy come to life in Tutenburg and was horrified; that I love evil whereas she loves the good; that if she were Catholic she'd enter a convent and do penance for all the trouble I will cause. . . . There is a real breach between us—At one point my mother herself said something so rash that I had my trunks packed and left for Leipzig early the next morning. My sister . . . commented ironically: "Thus began Zarathustra's descent." In fact, it is a new beginning.[14]

Months later, these sentiments echo in *Zarathustra* when the prophet proclaims that the creators of new values will be called "destroyers" and "despisers of good and evil": "Behold the good and the just! Whom do they hate most? The man who breaks their tables of values . . . yet he is the creator."[15]

In October Rée and Salomé had become closer and Nietzsche was frequently excluded from their company. Salomé was uneasy with the philosopher's shocking ideas and his eccentricity; Rée simply did not appreciate his admiration for Salomé. The following month, when Nietzsche said goodbye to them at a Leipzig railroad station, he had doubts that they would live together as planned. He was right: he would never see the two of them again. To avoid a face-to-face confrontation with Nietzsche, Rée and Salomé assured him that the plans were still intact; however, they actually planned to spend the winter in Berlin with Rée's mother acting as a chaperon. When Nietzsche's sense that he had been slighted became more intense, he wrote to Salomé and asked her to calm his fears: "A solitary suffers terribly from suspecting the few people that he loves."[16] Rée wrote to Nietzsche, attempting to explain the state of affairs in a more reasonable light. In November, Nietzsche replied by confessing that he himself was indeed a demanding person, and that Rée had the right to treat him "somewhat coldly" because of his affection for Salomé:

> Think of me as well as you can, dear friend, and ask Lou to do the same. I belong to you both from the heart. . . . We shall see each other from time to time, won't we? Don't forget that as of this year I'm suddenly low on affection, and hence very much in need of it. Write me . . . about what . . . concerns us most,—what "has come between us," as you say.[17]

The following month, after brooding over the summer events and coming to the realization that he had lost Salomé and his longtime friendship with Rée, Nietzsche fled to Italy in bitter anger and disappointment. He trusted no one. In mid-December, less than a month before penning *Zarathustra* I, Nietzsche wrote to Rée and Salomé after taking an "enormous quantity of opium":

Don't be too upset by my fits of "megalomania" or "wounded vanity."
And even if some emotional disturbance should happen to drive me to
suicide, there wouldn't be all that much to mourn. . . . Do bear in
mind, you two, that at bottom I'm sick in the head and half-insane,
completely confused by long isolation. . . . It's much harder to forgive
one's friends than one's enemies.[18]

By the end of December he had stopped corresponding with his mother and
refused to answer the sister's letters. Elisabeth, who had no idea of her brother's
ordeal, interpreted his silence as evidence that he was living in sin with his two
friends.

At this point Nietzsche had no significant relationships, virtually no connection with the outside world, and letter writing had become a substitute for
human contact. Nietzsche would remark years later that the whole of *Zarathustra* was a "dithyramb on solitude" and the "*redemption* from nausea."[19]

In January, the philosopher was a recluse residing in Rapallo, combatting
one of the most excessively cold winters he had ever experienced. Because
his stove was defective and did not heat his abode, he was suffering its effects
first-hand. In an essay entitled "Nietzsche," the Jewish libretto Stefan Zweig
recreates the framework in which *Zarathustra* was composed: "Wrapped in
his overcoat and a woolen scarf . . . his fingers freezing, his double glasses
pressed close to the paper, his hurried hand writes for hours—words the dim
eyes can hardly decipher. For hours he sits like this and writes until his eyes
burn."[20] Nietzsche, who was now three-quarters-blind, and whose eyes allowed
him only an hour-and-a-half of vision a day, nonetheless wrote for ten hours,
under the most unfavorable conditions, in the midst of migraines, chills, stomach cramps, night-sweat, nausea, and insomnia.

Regardless, in a letter to Gast, Nietzsche described those ten days as
"bright" and "bracing" and said that "the incredible burden of the weather
transformed itself into thoughts and feelings of frightful intensity."[21] Though he
was still succumbing to periods of illness and deep depression, *Zarathustra*
served as a light in the midst of darkness; it kept him occupied, productive
and sane. However, after the therapy had ceased, Nietzsche wrote to Overbeck that darkness had closed in on him again: "For a short time I was completely in my element, basking in my light. And now it's over. . . . Thus I
haven't been able to forget, even for an hour, that my mother called me a disgrace to the grave of my father."[22] The main recurring theme in *Zarathustra* is
the frustration of aloneness ("Yesterday, in the stillest hour, the ground gave
under me. . . . The hand moved, the clock of my life drew a breath; never had I
heard such stillness around me: my heart took fright")[23] and of not being heard
("Must one smash their ears before they learn to listen with their eyes?").[24]

C. G. Jung, who dedicated a seminar to the psychological aspects of *Zarathustra* (from which a two-volume work resulted), viewed the work as the fluctuation between Nietzsche and his own alter ego, Zarathustra. Nietzsche himself declared that *Zarathustra* contained the most sharply focused image "as I am *after* I have thrown off my whole burden."[25] Thus paradoxically, one cannot understand Nietzsche without reading *Zarathustra*, and one cannot understand *Zarathustra* apart from its biographical and historical context.

In the first part of *Zarathustra*, the prophet proclaims the death of God and the coming of the *Übermensch*. He describes the greatest experience one can have: the "hour of the great contempt" in which persons realize the despicableness of their own human condition: "The hour when you say, 'What matters my happiness? It is poverty and filth and wretched contentment.'"[26] His primary social concerns are with Christianity ("Once the sin against God was the greatest sin; but God died and these sinners died with him. To sin against the earth is now the most dreadful thing")[27] and Darwinism ("Man is a rope, tied between beast and overman—a rope over an abyss. . . . What is great in man is that he is a bridge and not an end").[28]

Zarathustra speaks against the New Idol, German nationalism ("State is the name of the coldest of all cold monsters. . . . On earth there is nothing greater than I: the ordering finger of God am I"),[29] and against Christians and anti-semites ("And this parable too I offer you: not a few who wanted to drive out their devil have themselves entered into swine").[30] He speaks of friendship ("Our faith in others betrays in what respect we would like to have faith in ourselves. Our longing for a friend is our betrayer"),[31] love ("But let this be your honor: always to love more than you are loved, and never to be second"),[32] and grace: "I forgive you what you did to me; but that you have done it to *yourself*—how could I forgive that?"[33]

Most notably, Zarathustra's public proclamations ("But if you have an enemy, do not requite him evil with good, for that would put him to shame. Rather prove that he did you some good"),[34] echo Nietzsche's private life: "What do these Rées and Lous matter! How can I be their enemy? And even if they have harmed me, I have surely derived enough profit from them . . . in this I find . . . a reason for feeling grateful to them both."[35] In a notorious one-liner (which incidentally became Hitler's most-recited Nietzsche quote decades later), Nietzsche cries: "You are going to women? Do not forget the whip"![36]

This misogynist passage reflected an earlier incident and perhaps was a secret message directed at Rée and Salomé. Months earlier the holy trinity were photographed at a studio. Nietzsche and Rée pretended to haul a cart in which Salomé knelt, holding a whip in her hand.[37] The allusion to the whip reflected this past experience and his bitterness at the now dissolved trinity. The failed relationship with Salomé and the loss of his seven-year friendship with

Rée, helps to explain why Nietzsche's attitude toward women changes after the *Gay Science*.[38]

Nietzsche's remarks about women become very negative after his experience with Salomé. The Rée-Salomé episode, coupled with Nietzsche's revolt against Elisabeth's involvement with Förster, resulted in the full-fledged misogyny that surfaced during this time. Elisabeth's antisemitism was extremely upsetting and painful to Nietzsche. He complained to Gast that Elisabeth was "maltreating him" with antisemitic letters, and her anti-Jewish sentiments served as "the reason for a radical break between me and my sister," as he wrote to Overbeck on the second of April 1884.[39] At the height of the break, he told von Meysenbug that there could "be no question of reconciliation with a vengeful anti-Semitic goose."[40] Even so, when reflecting on Elisabeth's notorious role in the Rée-Salomé incident the previous summer, Nietzsche added that much of Elisabeth's abusive behavior toward him was done out of love. This complex of factors is not to suggest that Nietzsche's misogyny is excused by a heart-breaking relationship or by his lifelong struggle for independence from a dominant mother and sister. It is only highlighted here to illustrate that Nietzsche's comments on any subject cannot be severed from his life experiences. What appears general in Nietzsche's writing is always deeply personal.

Nietzsche wrote that the image one has of women is derived from one's mother and determines whether he will respect, despise, or be indifferent to them.[41] Assuming this to be true in Nietzsche's case, it is quite likely that Nietzsche's misogyny was formulated when he was in his teens—at the latest. Nietzsche's mother resented him for challenging and questioning the Christian faith, and for not fulfilling the family's expectations. And Nietzsche resented his mother for shunning his accomplishments and his natural free-thinking spirit. Initially, Nietzsche's revolt against religion could be more indicative of his contempt for his mother and Elisabeth, and less indicative of his contempt for Christianity per se.

Although Nietzsche has positive things to say about women before *Zarathustra*, from this work on virtually all of Nietzsche's remarks about women are derogatory. He often describes females as weak, vengeful, clever "like cats," shallow, superficial, selfish, dependent, and he claims that they are incapable of true friendship. One could hypothesize that this shift is consistent with the general harshness typical of Nietzsche's later works. One could also argue that Nietzsche was merely disguising, or overcompensating for, his true feelings in his earlier writings. Although both of these assertions are accurate to a certain degree, in large measure, the reason for the drastic shift in Nietzsche's perspective comes as a result of his experience with Salomé and his anger at Elisabeth. Even so, Salomé was not the *cause* of Nietzsche's misogyny, but rather, the occasion *for* it.

Nietzsche's negative experience with Salomé simply allowed his preexisting, underlying resentment, to surface. Not only does his resentment *surface*, Nietzsche comes to project his own repressed weaknesses onto women. In the process of his lifelong endeavor to become a superior type of human being who frees himself from feelings like vengeance, Christianity and women become objective symbols for those feelings. Women, whom Nietzsche regards in his last work as "the underprivileged whose most fundamental instinct is revenge," become a generic symbol for those human traits and characteristics Nietzsche regards as unhealthy.[42] And Christianity, the religion of *ressentiment*, serves as a universal symbol to which "sick, domestic, herd animals," both male and female, cling.

The finishing touches on *Zarathustra*'s prologue coincided with the death of Richard Wagner. Nietzsche, although he had closed off personal contact with Wagner seven years earlier, was never able to cut his intense emotional ties.

When Wagner died of heart failure on the thirteenth of February, Nietzsche was in the process of preparing *Zarathustra* I for publication. On the fourteenth, after reading of Wagner's death in the newspaper, Nietzsche's initial reaction was three days of violent illness. Upon recuperating, Nietzsche then responded by consoling himself: "I'm better now, and I even think that Wagner's death is the most substantial relief I could have been granted. It was hard having to be, for six years, the opponent of the man I had respected most."[43] Nietzsche immediately wrote to Wagner's wife to express his condolences, and Wagner remained on his mind during the months that followed. Years later, in his final work, Nietzsche would again speak devoutly of Wagner ("I'd let go cheap the whole rest of my human relationships"), but would firmly restate his reasons for breaking off their friendship a decade earlier: "'Christian love' as well as anti-Semitism, the will to power (to the *Reich*) as well as the *évangile des humbles* [Gospel of the humble]. —Such a failure to take sides among opposites! Beyond a doubt, the Germans are idealists."[44] In contrast, Wagner's sentiments toward Nietzsche remained wholly antagonistic from the time of their break. On at least one occasion, legend has it that when Nietzsche's name was mentioned Wagner furiously stormed out of the room. Ten days before his death, according to Cosima, Wagner remarked that "Nietzsche had no ideas of his own, no blood of his own. What flowed into him was other people's blood."[45]

When Nietzsche sought to publish *Zarathustra* I, he ran into a number of ironic complications. Its publication was delayed by the printing of 500,000 Christian hymnbooks; it was held up a second time due to the constant journeyings of his publisher, Ernest Schmeitzner, whose commitment to anti-Jewish agitation had led him to neglect his business. Nietzsche remarked in exasperation: "It really is too ludicrous; first the Christian obstruction . . . and now the anti-Semitic obstruction—these are truly experiences for the founder of a religion."[46] Nietzsche came to the realization that his association with an anti-semitic publisher was damaging his reputation. In April he wrote to Overbeck: "The accursed anti-Semitism is ruining all my chances for financial independence, pupils, new friends, influence; it alienated Richard Wagner and me; it is the cause of the radical break between myself and my sister etc., etc., etc."[47] Nietzsche entered a long legal struggle against Schmeitzner to obtain payment for the book, and was relieved when his former publisher, Ernst Fritzsch, offered to buy the copyright from Schmeitzner and republish Nietzsche's previous works.

After the book was published hardly anyone took notice. A Christian anti-semite, from his prison cell, wrote an unfavorable review of what he regarded as the "antichrist's work." The book's rejection further shattered Nietzsche and sent him into deeper despair and self-doubt:

> My dear friend. . . . Deep down, a motionless black melancholy. And fatigue. Mostly in bed—that is the best thing for my health. . . . But the worst thing is: I no longer see *why* I should live for another six months— . . . I forgo and suffer too much. . . . It is too late to make things good now; I shall never do anything that is good any more. What is the point of doing anything?
> That reminds me of my latest folly—I mean *Zarathustra*. . . . I am curious to know if it has any merit; this winter I am incapable of making a judgment, and could be most crassly wrong either way. . . . Only my general fatigue has stopped me . . . from telegraphing to cancel the whole printing.[48]

Nietzsche described the year of 1883 as that which goaded him on to a "class of feelings" which he had believed that his will had mastered: resentment and revenge. And he also remarked that the first unfavorable review of part one of *Zarathustra* gave him courage, for the article written against him was constructed in terms of an either/or: "Aut Christus aut Zarathustra!" Nietzsche writes to Gast: "Ludicrous as it may sound to you . . . at this point I heard for the first time from outside that which I have heard from within . . . namely that I am the most terrible opponent of Christianity."[49]

A Jewish man by the name of Dr. Paneth had read *Zarathustra* and arranged several meetings with Nietzsche. The day after Christmas, in 1883, Paneth wrote home to his wife that there was "not a trace of false pathos or any pose of the prophet about him, despite what I had feared from his latest works," describing Nietzsche's manner as completely inoffensive and natural: "Then he told me, but without the slightest affectation, and quite un-self-consciously, that he always felt himself to have a mission and that now, as far as his eyes would allow it, he wanted to work out what was in him."[50] Nietzsche's task, as he perceived it, was to "cross the Rubicon" as an official enemy of Christianity: "I have taken the decisive step," he wrote to von Meysenbug. "Do you want a new name for me? The church has one: I am—the *Antichrist*. Let us not forget how to laugh!"[51] When Elisabeth saw the letter she indignantly wrote to her mother about the terribleness of Nietzsche's new name, stating that she wished that her brother shared Förster's views. According to Elisabeth, Förster had ideals that would "make people better and happier" if they were promoted and carried through: "You will see that someday Förster will be praised as one of the best Germans and a benefactor of his people."[52] Nietzsche's mother agreed with her son that Elisabeth should pursue a better choice for a husband; however, her primary concern was for Elisabeth to be married.

After learning of Elisabeth's engagement to Förster, Nietzsche continually tried to prevent the marriage from occurring. And though he wished them well and gave them a wedding gift, he nonetheless refused to give Elisabeth away or to attend the ceremony in 1885, which, as a tribute to Wagner, took place on May 22nd, the date of the Master's birthday. The following year Elisabeth and Förster brought fourteen German families to the jungles of Paraguay to establish a new Germany. This utopian colony, which they hoped would one day cover all of South America, was devoted to Aryan racial purity and the colony's human breeding technique that would serve to free them from the influence of Jewish capitalism. The project failed and Förster's suicide four years later left Elisabeth a widow.

The whole of *Zarathustra* was completed by the spring of 1885. By that time Nietzsche had long since ceased to be on speaking terms with his family; however, their relationship would become even more antagonistic thereafter. His mother continued her attempts to convert her son; Nietzsche, who described her letters as "dissertations on Christianity," asked her to stop directing them to his address: "The atmosphere in which you live," Nietzsche wrote, "among these 'good Christians,' with their one-sided and often presumptuous judgments, is as opposed as it possibly can be to my own feelings and most remote aims."[53]

Living in virtual solitude, Nietzsche wrote six short books after *Zarathustra* which also went unacknowledged.[54] He collapsed on 3 January 1889 in Turin while attempting to reprimand a coachman who was flogging his horse. He threw his arms around the horse's neck and collapsed in the street; he was carried home and recovered consciousness. That day, and a couple of days after, he scribbled notes to Gast ("Sing me a new song: The world is transfigured and all the heavens are joyous"), signing it the Crucified One;[55] to Cosima

Wagner ("Ariadne, I love you. . . . The heavens rejoice that I am here. . . . I have also hung on the cross"), signing it Dionysus;[56] and to Jacob Burckhardt, signing it Nietzsche: "I too was crucified last year by German physicians in a protracted fashion. Wilhelm, Bismarck, and all antisemites abolished."[57] In another note he combined all of the themes above: "The world is transfigured, for God is on earth. Do you not see how all the heavens rejoice? I have just now taken possession of my kingdom, am casting the Pope into prison, and am having Wilhelm, Bismarck, and Stöcker shot."[58] Nietzsche also sent notes to others, including Overbeck ("I am just having all anti-Semites shot"),[59] the King of Italy, and the Vatican Secretary of State, all which contained the same recurring themes—which reechoed Psalm 96: "O sing to the Lord a new song. . . . Let the heavens be glad, and let the earth rejoice. . . . He will judge the world with righteousness, and the peoples with his truth." Overbeck came to Turin, took Nietzsche to Basle for an examination, and Nietzsche was committed to a mental institution in Jena where he spent the remainder of that year. After his release from Jena, Nietzsche remained under the care of his mother and then the sister at home until his death a decade later on 25 August 1900. (Ironically, this would have been the 30th wedding anniversary of Cosima and Richard Wagner.) Elisabeth put Nietzsche to rest amid the accompaniment of church bells and hymns sung by the church choir. In an obvious disregard for her brother, his coffin displayed a sparkling silver cross on its lid. Mourners—most of whom only knew Nietzsche in the distorted form that Elisabeth had presented him—recited passages from *Zarathustra* as a special sign of reverence. The iconoclast was buried next to his father's grave at the churchyard next to the parsonage.

Around 1892 Nietzsche's writings started to become popular, due to the lectures given at the University of Copenhagen by Georg Brandes, a Danish Jew who corresponded with Nietzsche during his last productive years and who was one of Nietzsche's few loyal readers during Nietzsche's prolific life. Overbeck and Gast supervised his literary estate until Elisabeth, upon returning from Paraguay after Förster's suicide, created the Nietzsche-Archive and began to gain control. As she collected her brother's documents, notes and papers from his correspondents to gather them in the Archive, a bitter legal feud between Elisabeth and Overbeck occurred over Nietzsche's private letters which he refused to relinquish to her.[60] These letters contain many of Nietzsche's negative remarks against Elisabeth, Wagner, and antisemitism.

Elisabeth remained within the Wagner circle, which eventually led to National Socialism, until her death at the age of eighty-nine. After Wagner's death in 1883, among the most prominent members of the circle who promoted Wagnerian principles were Cosima Wagner (d. 1930) and Elisabeth Förster-Nietzsche (d. 1935); the Wagner's son Siegfried and his wife Winifred;

Wagner's son-in-law, Houston Stewart Chamberlain; Dietrich Eckart; Joseph Goebbels; Alfred Rosenberg, who was eventually appointed as the official philosopher of National Socialism and who also served as a spokesman for Nietzsche; and, after 1923, Adolf Hitler, whom Elisabeth revered and who was extremely close to Winifred Wagner. The Nietzsche-Archive in Weimar, under Elisabeth's direction, became a propaganda center for National Socialism as she circulated Nietzschean cult products and promoted her own fascist political program.

The Nazis used two methods to put Nietzsche to the service of political philosophy. First, they flagrantly misquoted and altered his published works, particularly his comments regarding Judaism and the Jews. Rosenberg often invented his own Nietzsche quotes; others, such as Alfred Bäumler, were a bit more scrupulous and occasionally qualified their statements with phrases such as "These words could have been spoken by Nietzsche," or, "This sounds as though it came from the *Genealogy of Morals*."[61] Second, they supported their views with a handful of Nietzsche's unpublished notes on race and breeding, which were compiled by Elisabeth in a work she promoted since the turn of the century as her brother's final "synthesizing" book, "The Will to Power." However, as one of Elisabeth's biographers observes: "The simple fact is that Nietzsche did not write a book entitled *Will to Power*, Elisabeth did."[62] With Elisabeth's help, during the 30s the Nazis created pamphlets out of scraps of Nietzsche's notes which deceived people into thinking that Nietzsche advocated positions of National Socialism.

That Nietzsche opposed German nationalism, antisemitism, and the Germanic-Aryan race, the three doctrines crucial to National Socialism, is now common knowledge in Nietzsche studies. But initially in the 40s when Nietzsche scholars, such as Kaufmann, quoted Nietzsche's published works to refute Nazi claims that Nietzsche supported these doctrines, the Nazis retorted that Nietzsche's published works were "masks of ideas" and that the "true Nietzsche" was not to be found in his publications.[63] Hence, one should ask *why* the Nazis "wanted" Nietzsche and why they went to the trouble of misquoting, distorting, and ripping his texts out of context, which they undeniably did. One should also ask why Elisabeth, from 1892 onward, heavily censored and controlled Nietzsche's published works, *why* she rushed to compile and promote *The Will to Power* (1901) as Nietzsche's last great "synthesizing" work, and why she forged, altered, or destroyed Nietzsche's documents to cover up his negative remarks concerning Wagner, herself, Christianity, and antisemitism. I will expound on the relevance of Elisabeth's mythmaking of Nietzsche in the conclusion. However, prior to what would fast become Nietzsche's erratic rise to fame in Germany, the subtle eye will nonetheless see two dominant traditions initially in conflict, represented by Elisabeth and Brandes. One tradition goes from Wagner to Elisabeth and then to Hitler. The other from Nietzsche to Brandes/Overbeck and then to émigrés such as Kaufmann who, like other Nietzsche scholars, refused to relinquish Nietzsche in whole or in part, to Nazi manipulations. Other commentators, such as Brinton with his 'half a Nazi half an anti-Nazi' stance, fell into a middle position. The first (Nazi) tradition claimed a few of "Nietzsche's" (1901) notes as authentic, stating that Nietzsche really did not mean what he said in his texts. The second tradition appealed to the corpus of Nietzsche's writings, and has used the *Nachlass* responsibly. The third tradition, over time, failed to recognize that the Nazis demeaned Nietzsche's works, thus confusing issues by uplifting random quotes from his publications to "show" Nietzsche was compatible with Nazism. Regardless, since the turn of the century, the general strategy of Elisabeth and then the Nazis was to divert readers *away* from Nietzsche's publications. This crucial point is almost always overlooked.[64]

Whereas Nietzsche was an outspoken cultural critic of Christianity, anti-semitism, and Wagnerism; Elisabeth professed allegiance to the Christian religion, Aryan racial supremacy, and, decades after her brother's death, an allegiance to Hitler and the Nazi party. It is thus no mystery as to how Nietzsche ended up in Hitler's hands. And the strife concerning antisemitism that originated between Nietzsche and Wagner, and was then taken up after Wagner's death by Nietzsche and Elisabeth, should not be undermined. Hitler probably never read a word of Nietzsche; however, he was a Wagner enthusiast since youth and was undoubtedly aware of Nietzsche's sentiments toward Wagner, the Wagner family, Elisabeth, and contemporary Jewry. It is very doubtful that Hitler approved. While Wagner spoke of Jewish "elimination"; Nietzsche, in *Daybreak*, wrote of the "inhumaneness" of former times in which "Jews, heretics and the extermination of higher cultures" was done out of a lust for power and with a good conscience: "The means employed by the lust for power have changed, but the same volcano continues to glow . . . what one formerly did for the 'sake of God' one now does for the sake of money."[65] In the very next aphorism, Nietzsche asserts that the coming century is an invitation to decide the future of European Jews, stressing that unless they become the masters of Europe they will lose it. Whereas Elisabeth created her blond-haired, blue-eyed Aryan breeding colony, Nietzsche expressed disgust and his grave concern: "I'm uneasy about my sister's future. I don't quite believe in Dr. Förster's return to Paraguay. . . . I've as yet managed to mount little enthusiasm for 'the Germanic essence,' and even less for keeping this 'glorious' race pure. On the contrary, on the contrary. . . ."[66]

Many assume that because the Nazis used Nietzsche they "liked" him and/or that Nietzsche's philosophy somehow *led* to (or "influenced") Nazism. The stark evidence, however, points to the contrary. Instead of assuming that

Nazi leaders liked Nietzsche, one should assess his texts to see what Elisabeth and the Nazi leaders did *not* like. Historically, two irreconcilable facts are at work: One fact is that Nietzsche was not an antisemite. The other is that the Nazis claimed that he *was,* all the while knowing he was not. That Nazi leaders exploited terms such as the "superman" and the "blond beast" to deceive millions into thinking that Nietzsche hated the Jews; that they frightened many (well intentioned) people *away* from his works and virtually destroyed his reputation while committing their heinous crimes in his name, should thus be *highly* suspect.[67]

Hitler was gripped by a pathological hatred for the Jews, whom he regarded as devil incarnates who defiled the pure Germanic blood. To quote Hitler's own words: "Whoever wishes to comprehend National Socialism must first know Richard Wagner."[68] Nietzsche would have agreed, and that is precisely why he left the Bayreuth festival to begin with:

> *What had happened?* —Wagner had been translated into German! The Wagnerian had become master over Wagner. *German* art! The *German* maestro! *German* beer! . . . We others . . . were beside ourselves when we found Wagner again, draped with German 'virtues.' . . . I think I know the Wagnerians; I have experienced three generations of them. . . . Not a single abortion is missing among them, not even the anti-Semite. —Poor Wagner! Where had he landed!— If he had at least entered into swine! But to descend among Germans![69]

In recent years, definitive historical studies on the intellectual origins of the Third Reich have stated that Nietzsche was no intellectual forerunner of National Socialism and that the Germanic ideology was formed decades before his works appeared. Several historians have even noted that Nietzsche, in his own lifetime, opposed the actual forbearers of the Third Reich.[70]

The irony is that since Nietzsche's fame ultimately "arrived" with the advent of the Nazi regime during World War II, his *texts* have been a battlefield in which they are judged by the incredibly odd standards forcefully imposed by a few Nazi "scholars" who knowingly and intentionally butchered his writings. Thus, in the midst of the debate over which, if any, elements of Nietzsche are compatible with Nazism, the central issue as to *why* the Nazis perverted his texts, goes unaddressed. If commentators do confront the question, the explanation given is that the then infamous Nietzsche could provide the Nazis with a respectable philosophical justification that their intellectual forebears, such as Adolf Stöcker, Arthur Gobineau, Paul de Lagarde, Eugen Dühring, Chamberlain, and even Wagner, could not.[71] Perhaps another explanation is tenable: taking into account that Nietzsche was a fierce critic of the precursors of National Socialism, and that he opposed doctrines crucial to the Nazi program, it could be that the Nazis harbored a personal vendetta against one who defected from the Wagner circle—and that they sought to discredit and silence him.

After demonstrating *how* Nazis twisted and distorted Nietzsche's texts, Rudolf Kuenzli in "The Nazi Appropriation of Nietzsche" (1983), is dumb-founded as to why the denazification of Nietzsche has taken so long. He proposes that Nietzsche's lingering "mad Nazi" stigma serves as a defense mechanism, it is our strategy and excuse for not having to deal with Nietzsche and face his works. Nietzsche questioned ideals sacred to Western culture, such as democracy and Christianity. It is easier for those who uncritically uphold these ideals to stigmatize a non-Christian elitist as a "fascist," than it is to confront his critique of culture and Christianity as antisemitic. Conversely, in regards to the Nazis, a close reading of Nietzsche's texts in part 2 of this work may further reveal why they had such a stake in distorting them. The dawdling Nazi myth has thus historically consisted of two major strands: The first involves the Nazis' blatant misuse of his philosophy and a highly questionable use of unpublished notes compiled by Elisabeth (1891 onward). The second consists of interpreters writing after the Nazi era who possessed strong religious and ideological commitments (1945-present). What is needed today are political expositions of Nietzsche that attempt to ground his views in the context of *their time* (1844-89). Nietzsche was no liberal egalitarian, but he was by no means a fascist. Perhaps the philosopher's words in "We homeless ones" should serve as a guiding principle: "No, we do not love humanity; but on the other hand, we are not nearly 'German' enough, in the sense in which the word 'German' is constantly being used nowadays, to advocate nationalism and race hatred. . . ."[72] It is my contention that Nietzsche had something very important to say about German culture and its revolt against European Jewry, something that Elisabeth and other political and religious authorities did not (and still *do* not) want the world to hear. One should thus attempt to get beyond an enormous amount of powerful propaganda in an effort to evaluate Nietzsche's works *before* he became a ruthless "Nazi." In a word, Nietzsche's politics *have* to be taken on their own terms, not the National Socialists'.

In 1894, shortly after Nietzsche started becoming popular and well before political renditions of his works prevailed in Germany, Lou Salomé, who became well known for breaking the hearts of many prominent male authors and artists throughout Europe, wrote a book about Nietzsche. The opening page shows the photograph of Salomé holding the whip behind Nietzsche and Rée. In her book she describes Nietzsche, as do most all Nietzsche biographers, as a solitary, soft-spoken, mild-mannered "effeminate" man; an intensely religious person who continually tried to overcome his physical and emotional suffering and exert his will to recovery. Salomé writes of Nietzsche: "Every passage outward always led back to the depth of his self, which ultimately had to become God and world and heaven and hell; every passage took him farther into his final depth and his decline." "But," she adds, "that has made Nietzsche the philosopher of our time. His person typifies the underlying inner dynamics . . . : the anarchy within instincts." She concludes: "In Nietzsche's spiritual nature was something—in heightened dimension—that was feminine."[73] Wagner's biographer, Newman, makes the same point somewhat more crudely: "One sometimes wonders whether Nietzsche's was not a woman's personality . . . incarnated in a male body. There is so much that is . . . feminine about his naive faith in his 'intuitions,' his weathercock veerings, his petty spitefulness when his vanity was hurt."[74]

Nietzsche's often symbolic and metaphorical language regarding "the feminine" is ambivalent.[75] Nonetheless, misogynist passages such as those found in *Beyond Good and Evil* make clear Nietzsche's contempt: "In revenge and in love woman is more barbarous than man. . . ."[76] At this time, however, in a personal letter to his mother (and/or sister), Nietzsche writes how he introduced a woman friend to Helen Zimmern, a writer who translated *Beyond*:

> I had the privilege of introducing this 'champion of women's rights' (Frl. von Salis) to another 'champion' who is my neighbor at meals, Miss Helen Zimmern, who is extremely clever, incidentally not an Englishwoman—but Jewish. May heaven have mercy on the European intellect if one wanted to subtract the Jewish intellect from it.[77]

This letter is a jab at Elisabeth and her husband's antisemitism. It also reflects the perplexing nature of Nietzsche himself. Nietzsche publicly condemns women's rights; privately commends them; associates with, and is attracted to, strong-spirited women—some of whom are leaders of feminist movements; but nonetheless generally regards women as weak. Taking Salomé's cue concerning Nietzsche's "anarchy within instincts," serves to illuminate why Nietzsche wrote in *Daybreak* that misogyny was a form of self-hatred. Months before his breakdown Nietzsche scribbled in the *Nachlass*: "One-half of humankind is weak, typically sick, changeable, inconstant—she needs a religion of weakness that glorifies being weak."[78]

This one remark reveals the philosopher's resentment towards his mother, the sister, their religion, half the human race, and finally, himself. For Nietzsche was weak, typically sick, changeable, inconstant, and in need of a religion which glorified strength and health. Nietzsche was both for and against his own nature and temperament. He owned a disposition that fought against submission and sought to overcome itself continually.

Nietzsche's misogyny and his critique of Christianity as the religion of *ressentiment* is interwoven with the repressed side of himself which refused to accept his own physical, emotional, and spiritual frailties. Nietzsche's painful experience with Salomé, coupled with the sense of betrayal provoked by Elisabeth's marriage to Förster, propelled Nietzsche's hostility towards women and Christianity. However, his abandonment by Rée did not cause Nietzsche to despise "all men" in general, nor did it destroy his opposition to antisemitism which, largely because of Rée, compelled him to leave the Wagner circle years before. At the time of *Zarathustra*, the fracture of these significant relationships and the grief caused by Wagner's death, resulted in Nietzsche's reclusiveness that remained intact until his final breakdown. Overall, the split with Wagner in '76 and then Elisabeth in '84, together with the milieu in which Nietzsche lived, allowed Nietzsche to strongly link antisemitism with Christianity, both of which he loathed throughout his adult life. The concept of "women" functions as a psychological symbol representing weakness; "Christianity" (and "Christian") generally functions as a cultural symbol representing sickness and vengeance under which both sexes are classified.

3

Christianity, Culture, and the *Volk*

This is my last day here, dear friend. All the birds have
flown. The fall sky is gloomy. It's getting cold. So 'the her-
mit of Sils-Maria' has to be on his way. . . . In Germany it
is always as if hostile winds were blowing at me, but I feel
neither tempted nor obliged to blow back. . . . Judging by
the Wagnerians I've met so far, present-day Wagnerizing
strikes me as an unconscious drift towards Rome, tending
to do from within what Bismarck does from without. . . .
Only a "church militant" needs intolerance; and faith
deeply at peace and sure of itself has room for skepticism,
for mildness towards other people and other things.[1]

Nietzsche critiques Christianity primarily as an ethicist, not as a metaphysician
making truth claims about the existence or non-existence of God. When
Nietzsche assails the Judeo-Christian tradition, his primary targets are Christianity's notions of morality, its eschatology, and the related notion of a punitive
or an all-good (meek and submissive) God, exemplified by the masses' understanding of Jesus Christ as the Redeemer. The philosopher is also preoccupied with the Lutheran-state church, nationalism, and Christianity's role in the
rampant antisemitism of his time. These themes recur throughout Nietzsche's
writings, and will be addressed briefly in order to demonstrate how they are
major obstacles to healthy cultures and to the cultivation of free spirits. A more
comprehensive analysis of these themes will be provided in the following
chapters.

Nietzsche combines cultural critique with his philosophy of nature. The
human spirit, according to Nietzsche, was not pure and separate from the
senses, from the nervous system, or from the environmental realm. Rather,
spirit and body were a unity, intimately related to climate and geographical
location. The salvation of humankind, Nietzsche wrote, was not dependent
"upon any kind of quaint curiosity of the theologians, but the question of *nutriment.*"[2]

According to Nietzsche, divinity had been erroneously sought in the concepts of God, soul, the Beyond, truth and eternal life, whereas the basic things:
nutriment, place, and climate had been ignored: "All questions of politics, the

ordering of society, education have been falsified because contempt has been taught for the little things, which is to say for the fundamental affairs of life."[3] Moreover, moral valuations were not—and could not—be based on notions of reason or rationality, as Kant and other Enlightenment thinkers assumed, but on natural human instincts. Whereas the ancient Greeks celebrated and regulated their evil passions and natural inclinations within the usages of society and religion, Nietzsche claimed that Christianity repudiated natural drives and thus cut off the roots of life itself. As a consequence, these repressed instincts were not destroyed or converted into virtues—quite the contrary. They manifested themselves in alternative and often more destructive forms: the savage instincts turned humans against other humans (*ressentiment*), against humans themselves (which is the essence of the bad conscience), and often found outlets in abstract theological and philosophical concepts, such as a wrathful god who was separate from the earthly realm and only fully known to humans at the Last Judgment, after death.

Nietzsche presupposes that the concept of a punitive God was the God of Christianity and was merely a psychological projection of human resentment:

What? A God who loves men, provided only that they believe in him, and who casts an evil eye and threats upon anyone who does not believe in this love? What? A love encapsuled in if-clauses attributed to an almighty god? A love that has not even mastered the feelings of honor and vindictiveness? How Oriental this is! "If I love you, is that your concern?" is a sufficient critique of the whole of Christianity.[4]

Consequently, projecting repressed instincts (such as vengeance) onto a god not only humanized the divine; it dehumanized the human. In other words, projection and/or repression does not rid one of natural instincts, it merely prevents humans from recognizing the sinister nature within themselves. The God upon whom these sinister traits are projected is then called "good," when the reverse is actually the case. Christianity then, has not only dedeified nature, it has also reified human nature by repressing desires instead of sublimating them. Hence, Nietzsche attempts to revaluate all values and go beyond the good and evil that currently shapes the image of God, humans, and nature in the Western world.

Nietzsche regards Christianity as essentially antinatural and antihistorical; it has virtually no contact with reality whatsoever. It falsifies history by interpreting all history prior to Jesus as the story of Christ's coming; it falsifies the present by interpreting morality in terms of supernatural consequences; it falsifies the future with the hope of eternal life; and it falsifies reality itself by interpreting God or ultimate reality as static, when in fact life is continually in a process of becoming.[5] Christian eschatology, Nietzsche believes, is the ultimate glorification of nihilism; it is the deification of nothingness, the antithesis of life itself. The hope of personal immortality is essentially nothing but an ego trip, the false worship of the self—not God. In the *Antichrist*, Nietzsche states his case succinctly: "The 'salvation of the soul'—in plain language: 'the world revolves around *me*.'"[6]

Nietzsche desires to create a culture in which human creativity flourishes. The virtues he wants upheld are not the Christian virtues of meekness, pity and humility, but courage, honesty, and truths which are essential to the preservation of life, not death: "Christians have never put into practice the acts Jesus prescribed for them, and the impudent chatter about 'justification by faith' . . . is only the consequence of the church's lack of courage and will to confess the *works* which Jesus demanded. . . . Listen to the speeches of Germany's first statesman on what has really occupied Europe for forty years now—listen to the language, the court-chaplain [Adolf Stöcker] Tartuffery."[7]

Adolf Stöcker (1835-1909) was the court chaplain in Berlin who founded the Christian Socialist Workers' Party in 1878. As a man of the cloth he was a prominent leader in national politics who exploited the existing antisemitism in Germany to legitimize antisemitism as a political force and to buttress the authority of the Christian state. In a speech given before the Christian Social Workers' party on 19 September 1879, Stöcker, whose political rhetoric was usually presented in the form of "equality" and piousness, says that he would like to deal with the Jewish question "in full Christian love but also in full social truthfulness." He declares:

> Sooner or later all immigrants disappear into the people with which they dwell. Not so the Jews. Over against the German essence, they set their unbroken Semitism; against Christianity, their stubborn cult of the law or their enmity toward Christians. . . . The question now is what ought to happen. We think that Jews and Christians must work together so that the right relationship exists between them. . . . Here and there a hatred against Jews, which is contrary to the Gospels, is beginning to blaze forth.

Nonetheless, Stöcker warns, "If modern Jewry continues as before to employ the power of the press and of capital to ruin the nation, then a catastrophe is ultimately unavoidable. . . . The social maladies that Jewry brought with it must be cured by wise legislation."[8]

Nietzsche's critique of cultural Christianity frequently revolves around three broad psychological and sociological themes which are interrelated with one another and with his understanding of power: the notion of faith or belief in relation to praxis, the individual believer in relation to the institutional state-church, and Christianity in relation to the culture at large and to non-Christians, specifically Jews. Nietzsche was repulsed by antisemitism because of its hostility toward spiritual and cultural values: "The struggle against the Jews has always been a symptom of the worse characters, those more envious and more cowardly. He who participates in it now must have much of the disposition of the mob."[9] Contrary to the popular view, Nietzsche regarded the Jews as creative geniuses who made great contributions to morality and culture, naming Heinrich Heine, Jacques Offenbach, and Benedict Spinoza among the most prominent. In reference to the Jews, Nietzsche writes in *Daybreak*:

> For two millennia an attempt was made to render them contemptible by treating them with contempt, and by barring to them the way to all honours and all that was honourable. . . . They themselves have never ceased to believe themselves called to the highest things, and the virtues which pertain to all who suffer have likewise never ceased to adorn them. . . . [W]hat they have experienced in this terrible time of schooling has benefitted the individual to a greater degree than it has the community as a whole. . . . [T]heir courage beneath the cloak of miserable submission, their heroism . . . surpasses the virtues of all the saints.[10]

And while Nietzsche states two aphorisms later that the German too is capable of great things, it is improbable he will do them: "for, as befits a sluggish spirit, he obeys *whenever he can*."[11]

According to Nietzsche, in nineteenth-century Germany "really active people" were inwardly without Christianity. The "euthanasia of Christianity," he says, comes as a result of its falling into the hands of the "moderate intellectual middle-class who only possess an adapted, marvelously *simplified* Christianity."[12] According to Nietzsche, modern Germany's industriousness, which is noisy, time-consuming, and "stupidly proud," prepares and educates people, more than anything else, for unbelief. Industriousness has dissolved the religious instincts; persons have no time left for religion; and the majority are unclear as to whether religion "involves another business or another pleasure":

> They are not enemies of religious customs; when participation in such customs is required in certain cases, by the state, for example, they do what is required, as one does so many things—with a patient and modest seriousness and without much curiosity and discomfort. . . . Those indifferent in this way include today the great majority of German middle-class Protestants.[13]

Elsewhere Nietzsche observes that the fundamental error propagated by Protestant teachers is that all that matters is faith, and that out of faith works will automatically proceed: "This is simply not true: but it has so seductive a sound it has confused other intelligences than Luther's."[14] According to the philosopher, faith cannot provide the strength which is needed for a deed; it is incapable of replacing the mechanism which must first be set in motion if an idea is to translate itself into action: "Works, first and foremost! That is to say, doing, doing, doing! The 'faith' that goes with it will soon put in an appearance—you can be sure of that!"[15]

Nietzsche's condemnation of Christian morality is a denouncement of what he often refers to as the morality of the weak, the morality of custom, or the "morality of the common man [that] has won."[16] This democratic or decadent morality concerned with the "common good" is a contradiction, for, from Nietzsche's radically elitist perspective, that which is common cannot be of any value. Mass morality is characterized by a passive acceptance of those aspects of tradition that manufacture conformity. It elevates modest demands and resignation to the status of godhead, and favors the preservation and enhancement of the community *over* that of the individual. Zarathustra says that when one breaks away from the *Volk* and announces, "I no longer have a common conscience with you, it will be a lament and an agony."[17] The herd will mourn the sheep who is lost and—through means of guilt—attempt to convert them back to their own conventional ways: "He who seeks easily gets lost," the people claim.[18] Although the deviant is initially regarded by society as evil for overthrowing an existing law or custom; history often reverses that judgment and later comes to exalt them for single-handedly protesting that which the majority have deemed to be sacred.[19] From time to time, Nietzsche asserts, the so-called "teachers of the purpose of existence" decree that "there is something at which it is absolutely forbidden henceforth to laugh."[20]

Whereas free spirits question herd morality and use up convictions because they know themselves to be sovereign, Nietzsche says that the opposite type succumb to convictions because they need to be used up. Free spirits struggle and suffer in the midst of uncertainty, the others possess faith. Free spirits have questions, their opposites have answers. The former are solitaires, the latter compose the crowd: "Loneliness can be the escape of the sick," Zarathustra cries, but it can "also be escape from the sick."[21] When one no longer shares a common conscience with the people, one must, says the prophet, pass them by: "Thus spoke Zarathustra, and he passed by the fool and the great city."[22]

In *Human*, Nietzsche combines his dry sense of humor with his pragmatic intellect to portray the free spirit's opposite:

The bound spirit assumes a position, not for reasons, but out of habit; he is a Christian, for example, not because he had insight into the various religions and chose among them; he is an Englishman not because he decided for England; rather, Christianity and England were givens, and he accepted them without having reasons, as someone who was born in wine country becomes a wine drinker. . . . Later, when he was a Christian and an Englishman, he may also have devised some reasons in favor of his habit; even if these reasons are overthrown, he, in his whole position, is not. . . . The habit of intellectual principles without reasons is called faith.[23]

Nietzsche, in his later essays, profoundly analyzes various aspects of Christian morality. In his earlier aphoristic works, although his views are insightful, his approach is more akin to a rhetorical intellectual teasing; he lures the reader into viewing basic Christian principles from unconventional angles. For instance, he turns the second commandment upside down in an aphorism entitled "Hatred of One's Neighbor": "Supposing we felt towards another as he feels towards himself . . . then we would have to hate him if, like Pascal, he found himself hateful."[24] His short and quick excerpts are designed to entice readers into examining themselves and the unconscious processes which underlie conventional moral principles: "To admit a belief merely because it is a custom—but that means to be dishonest, cowardly, lazy! —And so could dishonesty, cowardice and laziness be the preconditions of morality?"[25]

The point is that Nietzsche's task is to facilitate critical and original thinking, which he believes is absent overall in the culture in which he lives: "That there is no longer a single German philosopher—about that there is no end of astonishment."[26]

Nietzsche habitually makes his case against "the subtle comedy of European Christianity."[27] He argues that regarding one religion as the true and only valid perspective is both a transgression *against* one's neighbor and against one's own mind.[28] When Nietzsche condemns common Christian virtues such as pity or neighbor love, he is not advocating ruthlessness ("There is not enough love and kindness in the world to permit us to give any of it away to imaginary beings").[29] Rather, his task resembles that of a surgeon; he dissects the values themselves to uncover what undesirable attributes may lie beneath them:

Strong ages, noble cultures, consider pity, "neighbor love," and the lack of self and self-assurance something contemptible. . . . [And] we moderns, with our anxious self-solicitude and neighbor-love, with our virtues of work, modesty, legality, and scientism—accumulating, economic, machinelike—appear as a weak age. Our virtues are conditional on, are provoked by, our weaknesses.[30]

In *Human*, Nietzsche declares that "good nature, friendliness, and courtesy of the heart" have made much greater contributions to culture than the more famous expressions of the selfless drive, "called pity, charity, and self-sacrifice." Moreover, he adds, "there really is not much about them that is selfless."[31] Elsewhere Nietzsche expounds that when the concept of selfless action is examined closely, it quickly evaporates into thin air: "Never has a man done anything that was only for others and without any personal motivation."[32] In typical fashion, Nietzsche overturns and twists values, demonstrating how they are double-edged. His aphorisms are occasionally conundrums, in which the reader must work to decipher the moral or religious meaning.

Overall, Nietzsche believed that the primary intention behind Christian morality was not for persons to *become* more moral, but rather, to make them *feel* as sinful as possible. To put it simply, in order to be redeemed it is not necessary that one *is* sinful, only that one *feels* sinful.[33] In *Twilight of the Idols*, when comparing the law of Manu with the New Testament, Nietzsche condemns the theologians for using guilt, sin, and punishment to "improve" humankind in their attempts to create a moral world-order—which is by its very means immoral. Using these dreadful coercions to improve humanity, Nietzsche jests, "sounds almost like a joke to our ears."[34] One need only to look in menageries to see that when animals are tamed by means of fear and wounds, they are weakened and made less harmful until they eventually become sick. Nietzsche, most likely with Elisabeth's anti-Jewish, Aryan breeding colony in mind, proclaims it is the task of "we immoralists" to take Christianity's concepts of guilt, sin, and punishment out of the world again:

> The morality of *breeding* and the morality of *taming* are, in the means they employ to attain their ends, entirely worthy of one another: We may proclaim it as the supreme principle that to *make* morality, one must have the unconditional will to its opposite. This is the great, the uncanny problem which I have been pursuing the longest: the psychology of the *improvers* of mankind. Expressed in a formula one might say: *every* means hitherto employed with the intention of making mankind moral has been thoroughly *immoral*.[35]

Nietzsche mocks many tenets central to the Christian faith, particularly its metaphysical concepts of heaven, hell, and supernatural spirits. He ridicules principles which the church has decreed as those which are "absolutely forbidden henceforth to laugh":

"You should play fair even with the devil and pay him what you owe him," said an old soldier after they had told him the story of Faust in a little more detail. "Faust belongs in Hell!"—"Oh, you frightful man!" exclaimed his wife. "How can that be? All he did was to have no ink in his inkwell! To write with blood is a sin, I know, but is that any reason why such a handsome man should burn?"[36]

In his later writings, Nietzsche's tone becomes more serious and resentful, as he expounds his thesis that Christianity has split the world into two halves: the Christian community has placed itself on one side—on the side of truth—and the rest of the world on the other: "This was the most disastrous kind of megalomania that has yet existed on earth: little . . . prigs and liars began to claim for themselves the concepts of God, truth, light, spirit, love, wisdom, life . . . in order to define themselves against the world."[37] This process, claims Nietzsche, is actually the conceit of being chosen playing modesty. Christians regard themselves as the salt, the meaning, and the Last Judgment of all the rest. It is the continuation of the slavish Jewish instinct, he says, which previously defined itself as sovereign against everything non-Jewish. Nietzsche insists that Christianity can only be understood out of the soil of which it grew, which is the Judaism of the Diaspora. He regards the modern-day notion of salvation as born out of weakness, mainly because it preaches the damnation of non-Christians, particularly heretics and Jews, who were called to the "highest things":

The higher man is distinguished from the lower by his fearlessness and his readiness to challenge misfortune. . . . Christianity, with its perspective of 'blessedness,' is a mode of thought typical of a suffering and feeble species of man. Abundant strength wants to create, suffer, go under; the Christian salvation-for-bigots is bad music to it, and its hieratic posture an annoyance.[38]

Nietzsche regards Judeo-Christian morality as possessing a "will to revenge" cloaked beneath the modern Christian's guise of justice: "What do you suppose he finds necessary . . . to give himself . . . the appearance of superiority over more spiritual people? . . . Always *morality*; you can bet on that. Always big moral words. Always the rub-a-dub of justice, wisdom, holiness, virtue."[39] This veil of morality is in contrast to the 'grand style of morality' as represented by the creative culture of European Jewry.[40]

Throughout his writings, Nietzsche attempts to replace Christian imperialism with a pluralistic perspectivism. He views the former as detrimental to individual growth, to German culture, and to international relations: "These

serious, excellent, upright, deeply sensitive people who are still Christians,"
Nietzsche writes in *Daybreak*, owe it to themselves and to their faith to sojourn
in the wilderness and to experiment without Christianity for years on end.
Then they can win for themselves a right to voice an opinion as to whether
Christianity is necessary:

> For the present they cleave to their native soil and thence revile the
> world beyond it; indeed, they are provoked and grow angry if anyone
> gives them to understand that what lies beyond their native soil is the
> whole wide world! that Christianity is, after all, only a little corner.[41]

Essentially, Nietzsche hypothesizes that Christianity has, both publicly
and privately, been reduced to a "phenomenon of the consciousness," and that
by all practical purposes, it has been negated. It has become a religion of the
head which defends itself not by its works, but by its beliefs: "If the uprooting
of Christianity begins in the head then it is obvious where it will first start to
disappear: in precisely the place where it will also defend itself most strenu-
ously."[42] On the one hand, this psychological defense mechanism leads to individual and communal self-interest designed to promote individual and communal happiness: "Now the *belief* that we *love* our enemy, for example—even
when it is only belief, fancy, and in no way a psychological reality (is not love,
that is to say)—undoubtedly makes us *happy* so long as it really is believed."[43]
On the other hand, it leads to religious-bigotry and fanaticism because the
"point of honesty in deception" is that people will believe something is true *if* it
is evidenced that others believe in it firmly ("Christian, too, is a sense of cruelty
towards oneself and all those who think differently; the will to persecute").[44]
Nietzsche regards Christianity as a sense of cruelty towards oneself because the
individual, as subordinate to the institution, is fearful of calling its power in history into question, mainly because the power of the institution lies in its power
to couch its dogmas and doctrines in a manner that promises individual fulfillment. Thus, persons in fear are unable honestly to question themselves or their
religion. As a result, the virtues Nietzsche espouses, such as courage, creativity,
and intellectual freedom, are annihilated.[45]

In the net of this power-play between institution and individual, one hand
simply washes the other: dogmas and doctrines are no longer living expressions
of the individual's religious experience or personal commitment; rather, they
are utilized by the state-church as a means of controlling what Christians should
believe. The church and dogmatic theologians use concepts based on past experiences as measures of what constitutes the identity of the Christian believer, but
they do not communicate or hand down new experiences with these concepts.
Moreover, Christian dogmas and doctrines are not employed in the service of

the society at large; in large measure, they are used to separate the particular believing community *from* the society at large: "Christianity has done its utmost to close the circle and declared even doubt to be sin. —And notice that all this means that the foundation of belief and all reflection on its origin is likewise sinful."[46] Nietzsche tries to break this "circle of dangerous repetition," by pushing towards the other extreme:

> Christianity is not tied to any of the impudent dogmas that have adorned themselves with its name: it requires neither the doctrine of a personal God, nor that of sin, nor that of immortality, nor that of redemption . . . and even less of a Christian 'natural science.'
>
> Christianity is a *way of life*, not a system of beliefs. It tells us how to act, not what we ought to believe. Whoever says today . . . "nothing will serve better to maintain my peace than suffering"—he would be a Christian.[47]

Nietzsche viewed the everyday Christian of his time as "a pitiful figure, a man who really cannot count up to three." He prefaces the statement with, "Assuming that he believes at all."[48] The mass Christianity that Nietzsche opposed, was, he claimed, the total inversion of the gospel of Jesus, which consisted of an existential disposition—not a set of creeds.[49] Christianity, when understood as a system of beliefs, not only resulted in a culture full of repressed individuals; socially, it led to religious-bigotry—particularly to the "dangerous national hostilities" which, Nietzsche wrote in *Human*, consisted of the literary misconduct which led "the Jews to the slaughterhouse, as scapegoats for every possible public and private misfortune."[50] In *Beyond*, Nietzsche wrote that he "never met a German who was well-disposed toward the Jews," and that anti-semitic loudmouths should be expelled from the country.[51] In the *Nachlass*, during his last productive year, Nietzsche continues to insist that Christianity has degenerated into German nationalism with a streak of vengeance: "The Christian takes up again all the activities he has forsworn (—self-defense, judgment, punishment, oath-taking, distinguishing between nation and nation, contempt, wrath—). The church is . . . as much a symptom of the triumph of the anti-Christian as the modern state, modern nationalism— The church is the barbarization of Christianity."[52] Elsewhere Nietzsche reiterates:

> Can one even imagine a spiritually staler, lazier, more comfortably relaxed form of the Christian faith than that of the average Protestant in Germany? . . .
>
> One reminds me that today we also encounter an *immodest* Protestantism—that of the court chaplains and antisemitic specula-

tors; but nobody has claimed yet that any 'spirit' whatever 'moved' on the faces of these waters. —That is merely a more indecent form of Christianity, by no means more sensible.[53]

Nietzsche regards the crisis in cultural Christianity as due to an overall lack of courage, responsibility, freedom of the spirit, and labor, claiming that Christian praxis has been replaced by a complacent religion of the bourgeois middle-class. Moreover, the model for the Christian life, Jesus, has been virtually forgotten. The individual is finding blessedness and complacency through a sociopolitical institution and through their notion of Christ as *their* savior, but they are not engaged in the dangerous practice of leading a Christian life. This dual lack of labor and of faith results in a religion of private concepts, private feelings, private salvation—and in a religion that is socially governed by currently accepted conventions and prevailing beliefs. It results in a lifestyle that Nietzsche regards as opposed to authentic Christianity, which he claims is a way of life which is still possible at any time: "It is false to the point of nonsense to find the mark of the Christian in a 'faith,' for instance, in the faith in redemption through Christ: only Christian *practice,* a life such as he *lived* who died on the cross, is Christian."[54]

Nietzsche appeals to Jesus to support his personal conviction that works, not faith, is the way of the Christian life: "Jesus opposed the commonplace life with a real life, a life in truth."[55] "Jesus' *practice* is his legacy to mankind: his behavior before the judges . . . his behavior on the *cross*."[56] "Jesus said to his Jews: 'The law was for servants—love God as I love him, as his son!'"[57] Thus, whereas conservative Christianity preached that belief in the Son was the way to the Father; the one who proclaimed the death of God argued that Christ-like practice was the way to an inner reality:

> The life of the Redeemer was nothing other than this practice—nor was his death anything else. . . . He knows that it is only in the practice of life that one feels 'divine' . . . at all times a 'child of God.' Not 'repentance,' not 'prayer for forgiveness,' are the ways to God: *only the evangelical practice* leads to God, indeed, it *is* 'God'! . . . A new way of life, *not* a new faith.[58]

In a note recorded in the late 1880s, Nietzsche uses the image of Jesus to justify his own ideal of what constitutes the exemplary life:

> The exemplary life consists of love and humility; in fullness of heart that does not exclude even the lowliest; in a formal repudiation of maintaining one's rights, of self-defence, of victory in the sense of per-

sonal triumph; in faith in blessedness here on earth, in spite of distress,
opposition and death; in reconciliation; in the absence of anger; not
wanting to be rewarded; not being obliged to anyone; the completest
spiritual-intellectual independence; a very proud life beneath the will
to a life of poverty and service.[59]

Nietzsche writes that the institutional church should be opposed to the
state, and that the Germans are not spiritual enough to understand the nature of
a church. Because the church provides a "structure for ruling" that secures the
highest rank for more spiritual people without the use of crude force, Nietzsche
reasons that "the church is under all circumstances a *nobler* institution than the
state."[60] However, because the distinction between church and state has ceased
to exist in Germany, the result is a democratic morality which discourages
eminent human beings and social hierarchy. Nietzsche wants to cultivate culture
for nobles and views the state-church, which descends from Luther's "peasant
rebellion," as a major obstacle:

> The more God has counted as a discrete person, the less faithful one
> has been to him. Men are far more attached to their ideas than they are
> to their most beloved beloved: that is why they sacrifice themselves
> for the state, the church, and also for God—so long as he remains
> their own production, *their idea*, and is not taken all too much for a
> person. In the latter case they almost always wrangle with him: even
> the most devout of men gave vent, indeed, to the bitter exclamation:
> *my God, why hast thou forsaken me?*[61]

Most often, Nietzsche's polemic against early Christianity is directed at Paul,
"the greatest of all apostles of vengeance";[62] his assault on the Christian Middle
Ages is aimed at Luther, who had "all the vengeful instincts of a shipwrecked
priest";[63] and his fury against modern Christendom is unleashed at Wagner,
"the bigot at the top."[64] According to Nietzsche, it is profoundly significant
that the arrival of Wagner coincides with the arrival of the *Reich*: "both events
prove the very same thing: obedience and long legs."[65]

Nietzsche describes Christianity, the principle of democracy, and the state
as interrelated into a powerful unified system. Morality and the concept of divinity has been placed into the hands of the masses, and has subsequently destroyed
the order of rank within society that Nietzsche regards as necessary to fostering
greatness. According to the philosopher, the Lutheran-state has become God—
and its lie is that the people compose it.[66] Individuals have become mediocre,
have conformed to the status quo, and the principle of equality has been elevated
as an absolute, unquestionable, moral tenet in and of itself:

'Equality' as a certain factual increase in similarity, which merely finds expression in the theory of equal rights is an essential feature of decline. The cleavage between man and man, the plurality of types, the will to be oneself, to stand out—that is characteristic of every strong age. The strength to withstand tension, the width of the tensions between extremes, becomes ever smaller today; finally, the extremes themselves become blurred to the point of similarity.

All our political theories and constitutions—and the 'German *Reich*' is by no means an exception—are consequences, necessary consequences, of decline; the unconscious effect of decadence has assumed mastery.[67]

Nietzsche was not concerned with the aspect of democracy which gives the masses electoral power and enables them to challenge the authority of the elite. His concern was to shun the notion of the *Volk* entirely and to elevate the individual above and beyond it: "A free life is still free for great souls. . . . Only where the state ends, there begins the human being who is not superfluous: there begins the song of necessity, the unique and inimitable tune."[68] In the *Nachlass* he writes:

A "Christian state," "Christian politics" . . . are a piece of impudence, a lie, like for instance a Christian leadership of an army, which finally treats the "God of Hosts" as if he were chief of staff. The papacy, too, has never been in a position to carry on Christian politics; and when reformers indulge in politics, as Luther did, one sees that they are just as much followers of Machiavelli as any immoralist or tyrant.[69]

A more detailed discussion of Nietzsche's political views will begin in chapter 5. But it must be stressed that Nietzsche despised democracy, socialism, and Christianity for cultural reasons primarily; he believed that the Lutheran state-church restricted freedom, that it coerced persons into mass-conformity, and that it strongly discouraged the free-thinking of its individual citizens. According to Nietzsche, who described himself as "the last anti-political German," culture and state are antagonists: "All great cultures are ages of political decline: what is great culturally has always been unpolitical, even *anti-political*."[70] Essentially, Nietzsche opposed German nationalism, the Lutheran state-church, and the concept of the *Volk*, who in turn were identified by a uniformity of German blood. He was of the opinion that the democratization of Europe was, as he saw it during the time of Bismarck, "an involuntary arrangement for the cultivation of *tyrants*—taking that word in every sense, including the most spiritual."[71]

If one attempts to critique Nietzsche's views on democracy—as well as aristocracy and socialism—one must attempt clarification of those terms. When Nietzsche interchanges the terms democracy and equality, he most often is referring to mediocrity and sameness among human beings.[72] Typically, he looks beneath the virtue of equality to unmask the instincts which lie beneath it:

> Call that in which the distinction of the European is sought 'civiliza-tion' or 'humanization' or 'progress,' or call it simply. . . . Europe's *democratic* movement: behind all the moral and political foregrounds to which such formulas point, a tremendous *physiological* process is taking place and gaining momentum. . . . The tempo of this process of the *'evolving European'* may be retarded by great relapses, but per-haps it will gain in vehemence . . . the still raging storm and stress of 'national feeling' belongs here, also that anarchism which is just now coming up. But this process will probably lead to results which would seem to be least expected by those who naively promote and praise it, the apostles of 'modern ideas.'[73]

Nietzsche opposes the principle of equality on the basis that it is a detri-ment to healthy cultures. He regards the struggle for equal distribution of polit-ical power as a sickness in and of itself that society should resist. In his later works, it becomes increasingly evident that Nietzsche's anti-egalitarianism, fueled by his misogyny, is rooted in a principle of domination that would sub-jugate women, workers—and most likely even slaves—in the new aristocratic society he envisioned. The rudimentary principle of Nietzsche's political stance is adequately expressed by Zarathustra: "For, my brothers, the best should rule, the best also want to rule."[74] The crucial question that follows is who the best are and what character traits the rulers themselves would possess.

Nietzsche's political views are somewhat perplexing. On the one hand, he abhors the pursuit of wealth as a cultural aim and prided himself on living modestly: "But that is how I have always lived. I had no wishes. A man over forty-four who can say that he never strove for *honors*, for *women*, for *money!*"[75] On the other hand, his politics appear to show little concern for underclasses. However, his contempt for democracy was based on his opposi-tion to the *values* of middle-class Protestantism, as opposed to contempt for actually poor and oppressed peoples. In *Beyond*, Nietzsche writes: "The noble human being, too, helps the unfortunate, but not, or almost not, from pity, but prompted more by an urge begotten by an excess of power."[76] Analogously, it would be presumptuous to simply pronounce that Nietzsche opposes "equal rights" without first noting the contrast he draws between the slave's *demand* for equal rights, which arises from resentment and envy, versus the noble's art of *practicing* (or granting) equal rights, which arises from the spirit of abundance and voluntary sacrifice.[77] Nietzsche is mostly concerned with the psychological dynamics of human motivations, not with abstract political or religious doctrines per se. For Nietzsche, egoism is necessary for recognizing the value and freedom of others, for only those with a firm sense of self can truly enter into natural social relations without feeling hostile or threatened:

> He who cannot command himself should obey. And many can command themselves, but much is still lacking before they also obey themselves. This is the manner of noble souls: they do not want to have anything for nothing; least of all, life. Whoever is of the mob wants to live for nothing; we others, however, to whom life gave itself, we always think about what we might best give in return.[78]

An overall view reveals a fourfold dimension to Nietzsche's most pressing political concerns and visions. (1) Nietzsche's ideal rulers do not appear to be violent ("When the exceptional human being treats the mediocre more tenderly than himself and his peers, this is not mere politeness of the heart—it is simply his *duty*").[79] (2) His apparent disregard for lower classes is less indicative of lack of actual concern for the poor in nineteenth-century Germany, and more indicative of his disdain for the values of Christianity, which he sees as originating amongst the lower classes and as opposed to "aristocratic" values. Nietzsche is simply not a classicist in the economic sense.[80] (3) As time goes on, Nietzsche's abhorrence of the Christian state-church, coupled with his misogyny, evolves into political visions that become more and more hierarchical, as free spirits become fewer and fewer. And finally, his later writings are increasingly marked by a tantalizing praise for modern Jewry over against nationalist Germany: "—Jews among Germans are always the higher race—more refined, spiritual, kind. *L'adorable Heine*, they say in Paris."[81]

When approaching Nietzsche's texts distinctions must be made between democracy understood as the middle-classes' fetishism with mediocrity, and a democratic egalitarianism that would, in fact, liberate women and others deprived of rights to become creative individuals. Nietzsche's primary attack is directed against the former, yet includes the latter. As becomes apparent in his later works, his politics are rooted in a governing principle which has no qualms about subjugating the many to create cultural conditions favorable to the few. Although Nietzsche's ideal rulers are not tyrannical, he embraces a politic that is based on a pathos of distance between masters and slaves.[82] Nietzsche desires to erect a political structure in which the "mediocre"—no matter how defined—would be subservient to exemplars. Whereas Nietzsche condemns Christianity because it is based on faith, not works; the opposite pertains to the noble. Christian faith is first and foremost grounded in the worship of what is heteronomous (God, Jesus, neighbor, state, church, society), whereas *"The noble soul has reverence for itself."*[83] In the final analysis, Nietzsche's psychological need to replace Lutheran notions of justification by faith with self-affirmative values opposed to self-abnegation, unfolds in his social analysis and in his visions of a renewed society which seeks to elevate heroic individuals. Nietzsche explicitly bestows upon the Jews a vital role in the Europe of the future.

On the whole, Nietzsche regards Christianity and the Lutheran state-church as a major obstacle to the advancement of healthy cultures and humans primarily, but not solely, for the following reasons: First, its emphasis on intellectual certainty strangles the intellect and renders the skeptical capacity of human beings impotent—to the point where questioning is regarded as immoral in itself. Second, its emphasis on the afterlife devalues life on earth now. Third, its God—who is vengeful, separate from nature, and only fully known at the time of death is virtually irrelevant (and thus dead) to *life*, and also leads believers to elevate the moment of death as the ultimate goal of life (which is nihilism par excellence). Fourth, the conception of Jesus as a meek Savior who redeems humankind leads to passive acceptance and triumphalism. Zarathustra sighs: "He whom they call Redeemer has put them in fetters. . . . Would that someone would yet redeem them from their redeemer."[84] Fifth, he is very concerned with the concepts of guilt and punishment which have become central to the interpretation of existence. And last but not least, the Christianity of Wagner and Elisabeth, which served as an archetype of cultural Christianity, leads Nietzsche to equate the Christian religion with "the damnable German anti-semitism" and nationalism.[85]

When Nietzsche first proclaimed the death of God in the *Gay Science*, he was not making a theological statement about the reality of God's existence. Nor was Nietzsche killing his human father once again, as Freud and other psychoanalysts theorize.[86] Rather, his proclamation was based on his empirical observation of nineteenth-century German culture. Nietzsche saw the demise of Christianity, the demise of morality, and thus the death of religion as a cultural and existential *fact*. Even though Nietzsche lived in a Christian nation, he saw it as fundamentally immoral and faithless—thus, by all traditional religious standards—irreligious. Albert Camus' remark that Nietzsche "did not form a project to kill God" but "found Him dead in the soul of his contemporaries"[87] illustrates this, as does the *Encyclopedia of Philosophy*: "He [Nietzsche] recognized . . . that as a matter of historical fact, atheism was ushering in an age of nihilism."[88]

In the *Gay Science*, when the madman lights his lantern in "the bright morning hours" and runs to tell the people of God's death, he is making an

empirical observation and an ethical statement. This statement is analogous to
the story of Jesus' preaching in the temple, when he declares that he has come
to bring release to the captives. In opposition to the traditional Christian charge
that rebuked the Jews as agents of the Devil for killing Christ ("His blood be on
us and our children," Mt. 27:24), Nietzsche ascribes the crime of Deicide to
Christians, to the Church, and to himself:

> The madman jumped into their midst and pierced them with his eyes.
> "Whither is God?" he cried; "I will tell you. *We have killed him*—you
> and I. . . . Are we not straying as through an infinite nothing? Do we
> not feel the breath of empty space? Has it not become colder?
>
> "How shall we comfort ourselves, the murderers of all murderers?
> What was holiest and mightiest of all that the world has yet owned has
> bled to death under our knives: who will wipe this blood off us? What
> festivals of atonement, what sacred games shall we have to
> invent?" . . .
>
> Here the madman fell silent and looked again at his listeners;
> and they, too, were silent and stared at him in astonishment. At last he
> threw his lantern on the ground, and it broke into pieces and went
> out. "I have come too early," he said then; "my time is not yet. This
> tremendous event is still on its way. . . . This deed is still more distant
> from them than the most distant stars—*and yet they have done it
> themselves.*"
>
> It has been related further that on the same day the madman
> forced his way into several churches and there struck up his *requiem
> aeternam deo*. Led out and called to account, he is said always to
> have replied nothing but: "What after all are these churches now if
> they are not the tombs and sepulchers of God?"[89]

Here Nietzsche concedes his religious tradition as totally and hopelessly
corrupt. Nietzsche's endeavor is paradoxical: He seeks to replace and destroy
Christianity—which he claims in principle does not even exist—but in reality
still remains. Nietzsche insists: "When Christianity is once destroyed, one will
become *more appreciative of the Jews.*"[90]

Generally speaking, in Nietzsche's early writings he has a strong and
healthy sense of a mission. With the approach of his insanity, he possesses an
inflated sense of self-importance which borders on delusions of grandeur. In his
fortieth year, a letter to von Meysenbug perhaps illustrates a transitional stage
between these two poles: "My task is enormous, my determination no less so.
This much is certain: I wish to force mankind to decisions which will determine
its entire future."[91]

According to Jung, Nietzsche was an extremely sensitive and religious person who collided with his shadow. This in turn resulted in a dissociation of personality because he could no longer project the divine image: Nietzsche was no atheist, but his God was dead; thus, Nietzsche himself became a god.[92] Jung states that once God died, the considerable psychic energy that Nietzsche had invested into the reality of God's existence did not appear under the guise of a new name, for example, atheism, the state, of which people believe and expect just as much as they formerly did of God. Jung reasons: "Happily enough for the rest of mankind, there are not many individuals as sensitive and as religious as Nietzsche"; for if dull people lose the idea of God nothing happens immediately or *personally*. "But," Jung adds, "socially the masses begin to breed mental epidemics, of which we have now a fair number."[93]

Jung's observations, recorded in 1938, are accurate. Nietzsche perceived himself as a specimen who embodied the overall climate of German culture: he declared that his own personal experience of nihilism (the death of God which signifies the exhaustion of all meaning) would be the fate of generations to come: "The story I have to tell" Nietzsche proclaimed, "is the history of the next two centuries. For a long time now our whole civilization has been driving . . . towards a catastrophe . . . like a mighty river desiring the end of its journey, without pausing to reflect. . . . Where we live, soon nobody will be able to exist."[94] In the *Gay Science* Nietzsche reiterates:

The greatest recent event—that God is dead, that the belief in the Christian god has become unbelievable—is already beginning to cast its first shadows over Europe. For the few at least, whose . . . *suspicion* is strong . . . enough for this spectacle . . . trust has been turned into doubt. But in the main one may say: The event itself is far too great, too distant, too remote from the multitude's capacity for comprehension. . . . Much less may one suppose that many people know as yet *what* this event really means—and how much must collapse now that this faith has been undermined because it was built upon this faith, propped up by it, grown into it; for example, the whole of our European morality. This long plenitude and sequence of breakdown, destruction, ruin, and cataclysm that is now impending—who could guess enough of it today to be compelled to play the teacher and advance proclaimer of this monstrous logic of terror, the prophet of a gloom and an eclipse of the sun whose like has probably never yet occurred on earth?[95]

Before turning to Nietzsche's mature writings, a brief profile of his life until the time of *Zarathustra* (1883) reveals that he encountered many losses, some of which were initiated by Nietzsche, others which were not. The most traumatic incidents were the loss of his father and brother at an early age; his loss of the Christian faith, which began in his teens and was intermingled with his misogyny; the break with his surrogate father, Richard Wagner, who, when referring to their initial contact, Nietzsche regarded as "the first great breath of my life";[96] the loss of Rée and Salomé; and finally, the loss surrounding Elisabeth's involvement with the viciously antisemitic Förster, which was basically a replay of the painful Wagner scenario. The latter two incidents snapped Nietzsche, resulting in his personal and intellectual isolation that began when he left the Wagner circle, and then reached its fruition with the seclusion that consumed Nietzsche for the last five years of his rational life. Although these traumas involved a multitude of factors, Christianity, Judaism, and/or antisemitism were central elements in each. Although political antisemitism deeply affected Nietzsche personally, he remarked in the early 80s that he did not want to enter a public debate over the Jews, for he had more important things on his mind.[97] Prior to, and including *Zarathustra*, Nietzsche's writings are generally regarded as apolitical, whereas those thereafter mark a definite shift. Even so, vengeful enemies, whom Nietzsche often regards in *Zarathustra* as the "good and the just" and "the preachers of equality," frequently appear throughout the entire work and most likely refer to Christians and/or antisemites.

Nietzsche's private letters occasionally serve to compliment his published works; however, they do not, as one English translator notes, reveal the psychological motives which directed his thoughts, nor are they wrought with self-revelations.[98] Although the letters are "signals of his presence," Nietzsche's legacy and the complexity of his mind are to be found in his books, which became his life from *Zarathustra* onward:

And that is how it is, friend, with all the people I love: everything is *over*, it is the past, forbearance; we still meet, we talk, so as not to be silent; we still exchange letters, so as not to be silent. But the look in the eyes tells the truth; and this look tells me (I hear it often enough!), "Friend Nietzsche, you are completely alone now!"
And that is really where I have arrived.[99]

Part II

The Mature Writings, 1883-1888

Nietzsche opened another attack on the dominant culture
and its pretensions to enlightened, autonomous self-consciousness. With an arsenal of explosive, unmasking aphorisms, with an insistence upon the metaphorical truth of the
will to power driving all our "higher" states of reflection,
with Dionysiac laughter and dancing on the grave of our
cultural illusions, with an insistent and radical perspectivism beyond the half-hearted attempts of all liberal
humanism, with a wrenching of all ordering principles to
expose the chaos, the no-thing which is their nonground,
with an exposure of the *ressentiment* which may define our
"nobler" instincts of self-sacrifice and egalitarianism, with
a denunciation of the half-awake, timid, lazy, self-indul-
gent tone of much humanism, with a genealogical
hermeneutics of suspicion upon all moral and religious
codes, with a recall of the reality of body over spirit prolep-
tic of Freud's later rehabilitation of eros, pleasure and sex-
uality, with an insistence upon wit and self-overcoming,
upon laughter and dance not in spite of, but because of the
good news that God is dead and we have killed him,
Nietzsche performed his art, his magic, his explosive, radical hermeneutics of suspicion upon the entire Western cultural heritage.

—David Tracy *The Analogical Imagination*

4

Thus Spoke Zarathustra:
Creation, Redemption, and the
Birth of a Dancing Star

My dear old friend Gersdorff. . . . The period of silence is
over. My *Zarathustra*, which will be sent to you in a week
or so, will perhaps show you to what lofty heights my will
has soared. Do not be deceived by the legendary character
of this little book. Beneath all these simple but outlandish
words lie my whole philosophy and the things about which
I am most in earnest. . . . I know perfectly well that there is
no one alive who could create anything like this *Zarathustra.*[1]

It is a kind of abyss of the future—horrible, above all in its
rapture. Everything in it is me alone, without prototype,
parallel, or precedent; anyone who ever *lived* in it would
come back to the world a different person.[2]

Thus Spoke Zarathustra consists of four parts, and was composed between
January 1883 and February 1885. The first three parts were each published by
Nietzsche separately, the fourth public edition was added later. It is an under-
statement to say that it was written in bursts of inspiration; the first three parts
were composed in about ten days each. The book, which is full of parables, stories, and metaphors, is difficult to classify. It is not a novel, nor strictly an
autobiography. It is part fiction and part nonfiction. It has been described as a
philosophical work inasmuch as the philosopher's main ideas, such as the will
to power, the eternal recurrence, and the *Übermensch* are presented. It has
been described as a literary accomplishment in that it is presented in story
form and the character of Zarathustra is a constant throughout. It has been
described as a religious exposition, since it is rich in Biblical symbolism, and
Zarathustra emerges as the prophet of a new age who challenges Christianity.

And it has been described as Nietzsche's autobiography, because Zarathustra's experiences often resemble Nietzsche's.[3]

The book is pivotal to Nietzsche's critique of Judeo-Christianity, for his overarching goal is to replace traditional Christian concepts with new ones. The text is multilayered and inexhaustible in meaning. But broadly speaking, the will to power replaces God as the ground of creation; the *Übermensch* signifies the historical Messiah who has yet to appear; and the eternal return dislodges the doctrine of personal immortality. In large measure, the work can be viewed as a polemic against the idea of the Creator understood as a metaphysical principle. Nietzsche favors an anthropological view which posits humans, not god(s), as the creators, sustainers, and redeemers of the earth. He especially polemicizes against redemption, understood as life beyond death. Nietzsche believes that redemption, understood as individual immortality demeans the body, the earth, and is essentially triumphalist. Zarathustra's critique of "the beyond" and the Last Judgment sows the seeds for his psychology of *ressentiment*, which is further developed in the *Genealogy* and the *Antichrist*.

As a personal treatise, *Zarathustra* conveys Nietzsche's solitary journey as a misunderstood loner; one who possessed insights no one recognized or wanted to hear. The motifs which originated in childhood—a consciousness of being different, the difficulty in conforming, and the need for a higher and more purposeful mission—persist in *Zarathustra*, whose subtitle reads: "A Book for All and None." Nietzsche firmly insists that readers will not understand his writings unless their experiences resemble his and continues to search for kindred souls: "Behold," the prophet cries in the prologue, "I am weary of my wisdom, like a bee that has gathered too much honey; I need hands outstretched to receive it."[4]

In *Ecce Homo*, which Nietzsche began writing on his forty-fourth birthday as a gift to himself, Nietzsche said of *Thus Spoke Zarathustra* that he had given humanity its "greatest gift so far."[5] He also conveyed that when he looked into his *Zarathustra*, he walked around in his room for a half an hour, "unable to master an unbearable fit of sobbing."[6] These remarks suggest Nietzsche's immanent mental collapse and the abysmal depth of his pain, more than his critical ability to assess the book's relevance. Even so, many persons have indeed received the book as a gift. The past century reveals that Nietzsche's *Zarathustra* has been a powerful force in shaping and changing human lives.

In theological circles, Karl Barth, Dietrich Bonhoeffer, Martin Buber, and Paul Tillich are among those captivated by Nietzsche's religious observations. Barth did not view Nietzsche or Zarathustra positively; Bonhoeffer, Buber, and Tillich did. Tillich first read *Zarathustra* in a foxhole during World War I and regarded this occasion as a conversion experience. It was then that he realized the idea of God had to change in the modern world.

The book begins with the tale of Zarathustra's solitary retreat into the mountains at the age of thirty, accompanied only by his friends: an eagle and a serpent. Ten years have passed and the prophet has now decided to crawl out of his cave to share his wisdom with others. As he descends alone from the mountain he encounters an old saint in the forest who observes that Zarathustra has changed. The old man says to Zarathustra:

"You lived in your solitude as in the sea. . . . Alas, would you now climb ashore?" . . .
Zarathustra answered: "I love man."
"Why," asked the saint, "did I go into the forest and the desert? Was it not because I loved man all-too much? Now I love God; man I love not."
Zarathustra answered: "Did I speak of love? I bring men a gift."
"Give them nothing!" said the saint. "Rather, take part of their load and help them to bear it. . . . And if you want to give them something, give no more than alms, and let them beg for that!" . . .
"No," answered Zarathustra. "I give no alms. For that I am not poor enough."

The saint laughs at Zarathustra and tells him to stay in the forest far away from human beings, "Go rather even to the animals," he says. Zarathustra asks the saint what *he* is doing in the forest. The saint responds that he makes songs and sings praises and hymns to God. When he asks Zarathustra *what* he brings as a gift, the prophet bids the saint farewell:

"What could I have to give you? But let me leave lest I take something from you." And thus they separated, the old one and the man, laughing as two boys laugh. But when Zarathustra was alone he spoke thus to his heart: "Could it be possible? This old saint in the forest has not yet heard anything of this, that *God is dead*!"

Undaunted, Zarathustra proceeds into the marketplace and speaks to the people about what is most contemptible: the last man: "Alas, the time of the most despicable man is coming, he that is no longer able to despise himself." Zarathustra warns the people that the earth is getting smaller, and that the time is getting nearer when the last man will make everything small. They will "invent" happiness, will no longer question their private beliefs or tradition ("Becoming sick and harboring suspicion are sinful to them"); will possess a technical rationality which will deceive them into thinking they are all-knowing, and there will be "no end to derision." Works will no longer be works, but forms of entertainment; no one will want to rule, no one obey—because both require too much exertion. True friendship, creativity, and hope will be annihilated: "'What is love, what is creation, what is a star?' thus asks the last man, and he blinks."

Zarathustra tells the people there is still time for humanity to set itself a goal and to plant the seed of its highest hope before it is overcome: "Behold, the time is coming when man will no longer shoot the arrow of his longing beyond man, and the string of his bow will have forgotten how to whir"! If the human race does not set a common goal, modern technology and evolutionary thinking will dominate; and individuals, in all their uniqueness, will perish, giving way to a robotic way of human functioning with no model for living: "No shepherd and one herd! Everybody feels the same, everybody is the same, whoever thinks differently goes voluntarily into a madhouse." According to Nietzsche, one misunderstands great human beings when viewing them from the miserable perspective of some public use; that one cannot put them to any use, that in itself may belong to greatness.[8]

Zarathustra is interrupted by the clamor and delight of the crowd who shout and laugh at him: "Give us this last man, O Zarathustra! Turn us into these last men!" The prophet becomes sad and realizes that he cannot speak to the many, but only to the few. He says to his heart: "They do not understand me: I am not the mouth for these ears. [T]hey think I am cold and I jeer and make dreadful jests. And now they look at me and laugh: and as they laugh they even hate me. There is ice in their laughter."[9]

The last men, or the "masses of barbarian force" were exemplified by Nietzsche's philosophical and political nemesis, Eugen Dühring, who was a ferocious antisemite.[10] In the *Nachlass*, Nietzsche reechoes Zarathustra's confrontation with the crowd in the marketplace, with Dühring at the center:

> Germany, rich in clever and well-informed scholars, has lacked great souls, mighty spirits . . . ; and today mediocre and quite ill-constituted men place themselves in the market square almost with a good conscience and without any embarrassment and praise themselves as great men and reformers, as, e.g., Eugen Dühring does—indeed a clever and well-informed scholar, but one who nevertheless betrays with almost every word he says that he harbors a petty soul and is tormented by narrow, envious feelings. . . . Today when the mob rules, when the mob bestows the honors![11]

The stories of the saint in the forest and the last men, which both occur in different sections of the Prologue, set the tone for the entire work: the saint represents Christianity, the last men represent the mediocre bourgeois culture of

Nietzsche time, particularly antisemites. The term "last men" is also a play on words referring to the generational line of Adam, the "first man": Christians.

Nietzsche sees Christianity as the greatest objection to earthly survival primarily because of its fetishism with the afterlife. In *Daybreak*, Nietzsche makes his point clearly and succinctly in an aphorism entitled, "We gods in exile!":

> Men have become *suffering* creatures as a consequence of their moral-
> ities: what they have purchased with them is, all in all, a feeling that at
> bottom they are too good and too significant for the earth and are
> paying it only a passing visit. . . . For the present, the 'proud sufferer'
> is still the highest type of man.[12]

This obsession with otherworlds pits humans against history, against nature, against others, and against themselves. Nietzsche refers to proponents of orthodox eschatology throughout *Zarathustra* as the despisers of life, the after-worldly, the world-weary, the preachers of death, the gravediggers, the good and the just, the priests, the tarantulas, and the poison-mixers, to name a few. He incessantly preaches that otherworlds are extremely dangerous concepts and attempts to bring the focus and purpose of life down to earth: "I beseech you . . . remain faithful to the earth, and do not believe those who speak to you of otherworldly hopes! Poison-mixers are they, whether they know it or not. Despisers of life are they, decaying and poisoned themselves, of whom the earth is weary: so let them go."[13]

The afterworldly, Nietzsche suspects, have invented hell out of resentment toward finitude, and they are unconcerned with the earth's survival because it is demeaned as a stomping grounds for human trial and error— which god will judge at the end times ("Oh my brothers, who represents the greatest danger for all man's future, is it not the good and the just"?)[14] Because Zarathustra wants to create meaning for the earth, the unhealthiness of Christianity's otherworlds, which has dominated Western culture for centuries, must be exposed and abolished.

According to Zarathustra, the believers of the true faith have not only invented afterworlds to comfort themselves and threaten others, they have invented them to compensate for incapacities "experienced only by those who suffer most deeply."[15] Zarathustra admits that he too once cast his delusion beyond man; however, he later gave up his conception that the world was cre-ated by a suffering and tortured god: "This god whom I created was man-made and madness . . . and only a poor specimen of man and ego." The prophet pro-claims that he sacrificed the god of immortality and that others should follow: "I overcame myself, the sufferer; I carried my own ashes to the mountains; I invented a brighter flame for myself . . . now it would be suffering to believe in such ghosts."[16]

The prophet sees the desire for heaven as the essence of Christianity—the hook on which believers are caught. This hook, however, is meaningless and detrimental to life ("Verily, it is a beautiful catch of fish that Zarathustra has brought in today! Not a man has he caught but a corpse. Human existence is uncanny and still without meaning.").[17] Moreover, because the preachers of death are obsessed with right believing, as opposed to right action, justice too has been stripped from the earthly realm and attributed to God after death—at the Final Judgment:

> Such maxims I heard pious afterworldly people speak to their conscience—verily, without treachery or falseness, although there is nothing falser in the whole world, nothing more treacherous:
>
> "Let the world go its way! Do not raise one finger against it!"
>
> "Let him who wants to, strangle and stab and fleece and flay the people. Do not raise one finger against it. Thus they will learn to renounce the world."
>
> "And your own reason—you yourself should stifle and strangle it; for it is a reason of this world; thus will you yourself learn to renounce the world."
>
> Break, break, O my brothers, these old tablets of the pious. Break the maxims of those who slander the world.[18]

In *Ecce Homo*, Nietzsche provides commentary on the quoted section above (15) and on section 26 of "On Old and New Tablets." In reference to the Social Darwinist Herbert Spencer, Nietzsche writes: "To demand that all should become 'good human beings,' herd animals, blue-eyed, benevolent, 'beautiful souls'—or as Mr. Herbert Spencer would have it, altrusitic—would deprive existence of its *great* character and would castrate men." The "good," Nietzsche continues, are actually "the last men," "the beginning of the end"; they are the most harmful type of man because "they prevail at the expense of *truth* and at the expense of the *future*."[19]

Zarathustra continually speaks his word against "the good and the just." In turn, they call him the danger to the multitude for calling into question the concepts of eternal life and eternal damnation, and the related conception of God as avenger and Judge: "And now are you angry with me because I teach that there is no reward or paymaster? With their virtue they want to scratch out the eyes of their enemies, and they exalt themselves only to humble others."[20]

Zarathustra's polemics against Christian eschatology and absolute truth are ruthless and unceasing throughout *Zarathustra*. He perceives that eternal punishment is not a device in the hands of a just god, but merely a human tool of projection and revenge: "Verily, you fill your mouth with noble words; and are we to believe that your heart is overflowing, you liars? . . . Behind a god's mask you hide from yourselves, in your 'purity'; your revolting worm has crawled into a god's mask."[21]

Because Christians are concerned with presenting themselves as pious, and view raw human instincts as vulgar, they mask their underlying impulses and repress those traits which, in fact, have severed them *from* their bodies. Nietzsche expounds this theme (of *ressentiment*) in the *Genealogy*, which will be discussed in the following chapter. As Michel Foucault notes in his clever essay, "Nietzsche, Genealogy, and History," Nietzsche's genealogy is "situated within the articulation of the body and history. Its task is to expose a body totally imprinted by history and the process of history's destruction of the body."[22]

In *Zarathustra's* "On the despisers of the body," Nietzsche anticipates Freudian and Jungian psychology with his observation that behind the ego is a self, a "mighty ruler" which is in control of the ego: "Always the self listens and seeks; it compares, overpowers, conquers, destroys. . . . In your body he dwells; he is your body."[23] Because the despisers of the body turn away from their true nature, they are incapable of creating themselves. Consequently, they unknowingly become hostile to their bodies, to others, and to the earth: "An unconscious envy speaks out of the squint-eyed glance of your contempt."[24]

One of the most powerful passages on eschatology in relation to the body and history occurs in the prologue to book one. A tightrope walker is performing on a rope stretched between two towers over a crowd of people. He has been tripped up by a jester and is falling to the ground amidst the shrieking of the crowd who scurry to get out of the way. Unlike everyone else, Zarathustra does not move and the body, which is "badly maimed and disfigured but not yet dead" lands next to him. When the man recovers consciousness he finds Zarathustra kneeling beside him. He tells the prophet that the devil tripped him and that he fears the devil will drag him to hell. He asks Zarathustra: "Will you prevent him?" Zarathustra assures him that all he fears does not exist: "There is no devil and no hell. Your soul will be dead even before your body: fear nothing further." The man becomes suspicious: If Zarathustra is correct that he loses nothing when he loses his life—it follows that he is little more than a beast. "By no means," Zarathustra replies. "You have made danger your vocation; there is nothing contemptible in that. Now you perish of your vocation: for that I will bury you with my own hands." After these words, the dying man is silent. He moves his hand as if he were seeking Zarathustra's hand in thanks.[25]

This passage is strikingly similar to the story of a tightrope walker that Wagner conveys in his autobiography, *Mein Leben*, that Nietzsche had edited and was thus familiar with. Wagner, recalling his childhood stay at the home of his stepfather's younger brother, writes:

> We lived in the market-place which often offered strange sights—for example, the performances by a troupe of acrobats who appeared on a rope stretched from tower to tower over the square, which for a long time gave me a passion for such feats. I even went so far as to do the same thing myself with a balancing-pole on a rope of twisted cords which I rigged up in the yard.[26]

It is very likely that the jester (the devil) who trips up and thus kills the tightrope walker in *Zarathustra* is in reference to Wagner. The jester, alluding to Zarathustra's public speech in the market square that day, and to the corpse Zarathustra now carried on his back, sneaks up to Zarathustra in the evening and whispers in his ear:

> "Go away from this town Zarathustra, there are too many here who hate you. . . . It was your good fortune that you were laughed at . . . it was your good fortune that you stooped to the dead dog; when you lowered yourself so far, you saved your own life for today. But go away from this town, or tomorrow I shall leap over you, one living over one dead." And when he had said this the man vanished; but Zarathustra went on through the dark lanes.[27]

Nietzsche rejects the separation of the soul from the body, as well as the Christian view that history is preordained toward a metaphysical end. His primary target is to expose sacralized hatred that lurks beneath the Christian conceptions of hell—and the corresponding triumphalist doctrine that Jesus Christ is the only way to salvation. He combats revenge theology throughout his writings, challenging Christian claims that they alone possess the truth ("'This is my way; where is yours?'—thus I answered those who asked me 'the way.' For *the* way—that does not exist.")[28] To believe in eternal life denies the body; to believe in flawless truth denies the mind. Nietzsche reiterates again and again throughout his writings that the value of truth and the "will to truth" are themselves in need of critique: "*Who* is it really that puts questions to us here? *What* in us really wants 'truth'? We asked about the *value* of this will. Suppose we want truth: *why not rather* untruth? and uncertainty? even ignorance?"[29] In the *Genealogy*, Nietzsche reiterates:

It is still a *metaphysical faith* that underlies our faith in science—and we men of knowledge of today, we godless men and anti-metaphysicians, we, too, still derive *our* flame from the fire ignited by a faith millennia old, the Christian faith, which was also Plato's, that God is truth, that truth is divine.

—But what if this belief is becoming more and more unbelievable, if nothing turns out to be divine any longer unless it be error, blindness, lies—if God himself turns out to be our *longest lie?*[30]

Nietzsche's critique of truth is clearly interwoven with his contempt for the perdurable Christian emphasis on the alleged words of Jesus as recorded in the gospel of John: "I am the way, the truth and the life. No one comes to the father except through me" (Jn 14:6). In *Zarathustra*, the prophet satirizes the creation account of the monotheistic God who spoke the world into existence (Genesis I), with his own tale of how *all* the gods died when this occurred. According to Zarathustra, the old gods laughed themselves to death when one of the gods among them spoke the "godless word": —that he alone was the only god to be worshipped. This "jealous, old grimbeard of a god thus forgot himself" (grew old and died); and all the other gods "laughed and rocked on their chairs" crying: "Is not just this godlike that there are gods but no God?" Then they too, died from laughter. Zarathustra concludes: "He that has ears to hear, let him hear!"[31]

Elsewhere Nietzsche humorously stresses that Christianity does not graciously "offer" salvation through Christ, but rather *demands* it. This is apparent when Zarathustra, hoisting the corpse, approaches a stranger's house for refreshment. In a spinoff on the infamous Biblical diction, "Ask and it will be given to you; seek and you will find; knock and the door will be opened" (Mt. 7:7, Lk. 11:9), an old man comes to the door and proceeds to offer Zarathustra *and* the corpse bread and wine. The old man says to the prophet: "[B]id your companion, too, eat and drink; he is wearier than you are." Zarathustra muses: "My companion is dead; I should hardly be able to persuade him." The man then becomes agitated: "I don't care," he says peevishly. "Whoever knocks at my door must also take what I offer. Eat and be off!"[32]

Throughout his works, Nietzsche does not explicitly seek to elaborate upon what differentiates the human species from animals. However, comments scattered throughout his writings reveal that he believes humans are the animals capable of making promises; they are the most timid of all creatures; the creatures who suffer most; and the animals who are capable of laughing. They are the most *interesting* creatures who possess the unique capacity to sublimate their animalistic instincts. In *Zarathustra*, Nietzsche regards humans as the cruelest animals, for they have invented hell, which is often, for them, a type of heaven on earth: "At tragedies, bullfights, and crucifixions he has so far felt best on earth."[33]

Believers view heaven as a state of bliss in which their souls (and perfected bodies) are unified with God. Non-believers' souls are separated from God, and their bodies will be tortured eternally. Nietzsche's main opposition to the concept of eternal life is not that "the sick and decaying" have invented the heavenly realm *because* they suffer ("Zarathustra is gentle with the sick. Verily, he is not angry with their kinds of comfort and ingratitude").[34] Rather, he is angry because they invented the realms of heaven and hell at the expense of the body, history, and earth. The afterworldly, claims Zarathustra, hate the youngest of all the virtues, which is called honesty. They transport themselves from their bodies to paradise (in the imagination), without realizing that they owe this heavenly transposition to their earthly bodies in the first place. Nietzsche views the imaginative concepts of eternal life and eternal death as psychologically grounded in a state of repression. By visualizing utopic otherworlds, or lusting for vengeance against others in the beyond, persons are negating their physical construction:

> Verily, it is not in afterworlds and redemptive drops of blood, but in the body, that they too have most faith. . . . But a sick thing it is to them, and gladly would they shed their skins. *Therefore* [emphasis mine] they listen to the preachers of death and themselves preach afterworlds.[35]

Paradoxically, Nietzsche seems to imply that Christians not only believe in redemption to escape their wretched bodies; they must first despise their bodies before they can believe. It is the latter issue that is Nietzsche's main concern. Nietzsche maintains that profound suffering makes noble; it separates higher human beings from the lower. To regard bodily suffering as a total disgrace, or as a means to an ascetic or transcendental end, constitutes nihilism: "For pay heed to this," Nietzsche commands in *Ecce Homo*, "it was in the years of my lowest vitality that I *ceased* to be a pessimist."[36] According to Zarathustra, not afterworlds but *creation* is the "great redemption" from suffering and the means to enlightenment: "But that the creator may be, suffering is needed and much change. Indeed, there must be much bitter dying in your life, you creators."[37]

Although Zarathustra overturns the ascetic ideal as the goal and purpose of humanity, he does not succumb to nihilism; he admonishes people to hold holy their highest hopes.[38] At bottom, the goal Zarathustra espouses is anthropocentric: it is to prepare plant, animal and earth for the coming of the *Übermensch*. It is elitist, based on an order of rank rooted in the spirit and power to transform human nature. The will to power in union with the capacity for sublimation is what

Nietzsche views as that which distinguishes humans from animals. That central theme pervades his writings. Free spirits are the inventive and artistic beings who are able to overcome themselves and rise above the all-too-human mass.

Although Nietzsche promotes reciprocal relationships between humans and the environment, his main concern is not with saving the planet per se. Rather, it is with saving the dignity, spirit, and worth of individuals—which Christianity has traditionally upheld and Darwinism has called into question. In addition, whereas Christianity preaches that all persons are of equal worth in the eyes of the Creator, Zarathustra exposes this as a fallacy, for the concept of "the chosen" and the related notions of heaven and hell presupposes superiority and inequality among presumably equal souls. Ultimately, this ranking is based on the notion of doctrine, or correct belief: "Thus I speak to you in a parable—you who make souls whirl, you preachers of *equality*. To me you are tarantulas, and secretly vengeful. But I shall bring your secrets to light."[39] In contrast to the preachers of equality, Nietzsche's approach is spiritually, not racially—or religiously—aristocratic. Some human beings, Nietzsche holds, *are* nobler than others and should serve as models for humanity.

In *Human*, Nietzsche regards the noblest human being as Jesus of Nazareth. However, in the following work, *Daybreak*, he questions Jesus' psychological disposition:

> He who sets such store on being believed in that he offers Heaven in exchange for this belief, and offers it to everyone, must have suffered from fearful self-doubt and come to know every kind of crucifixion: otherwise he would not purchase his believers at so high a price.[40]

As evidenced from the passage above, Nietzsche concedes that Jesus *did* teach heaven and hell—the antihistorical, antinatural doctrines Nietzsche abhors. However, in *Zarathustra*, Nietzsche defends Jesus by attributing his erroneous teachings to his youth: "Believe me, my brothers! He died too early; he himself would have recanted his teaching, had he reached my age. Noble enough was he to recant."[41] Because Jesus has failed to hold holy the love of life and earth— and has forsaken it for death and the beyond—Zarathustra offers himself as a sacrifice: "Thus I want to die myself that you, my friends, may love the earth more for my sake; and to earth I want to return that I may find rest in her who gave birth to me."[42] Nietzsche would continue to struggle with the historical Jesus and his relation to Christian eschatology until his final collapse. While in his forties, Nietzsche wrote in the *Nachlass*:

> Jesus opposed the commonplace life with a real life, a life in truth: nothing was further from him than the stupid nonsense of an eternal

personal survival. What he fights against is this exaggerated inflation of the 'person': how can he desire to eternize precisely *that*?

In the same way he fights against hierarchy within the community . . . how can he have meant punishment and reward in the beyond![43]

Nietzsche attacks Christian eschatology for the following reasons: As a concept in modern Christendom it has been reduced to individual immortality; this is incompatible with his conception of Jesus as one who opposed self-inflation. As a public teaching, it has been made into an exclusivist concept within the Christian community itself: Christians are saved and non-believers, particularly Jews, are not. Moreover, not only are the godless not saved, they are condemned to the domain of a tortured and endless death because they are not complying with the Christian worldview—regarded as the sole Truth. Nietzsche struggles with these views because they are incompatible with his sense of justice. And finally, Nietzsche believes that life after death demeans life in the body (and history) *before* death. The construction of these after-worldly concepts arise from human suffering and from death denial. Preaching eternal life is, Nietzsche holds, essentially the same as preaching death: "They would like to be dead, and we should welcome their wish. Let us beware of waking the dead and disturbing these living coffins!"[44] When one imagines the cessation of one's personal history (or when one thinks of the body as clinically dead), one not only wrongfully imagines that one *has* a soul, but also that the soul severs itself from the body and history to escape that fatal moment. This "problem of personal immortality," as Rosemary Ruether describes in her classic work in feminist theology, *Sexism and God Talk*, "is created by an effort to absolutize personal or individual ego as itself everlasting, over against the total community of being."[45]

Nietzsche, in contrast to Ruether, is hardly concerned with establishing an egalitarian community of human beings. Rather, he seeks to reach a small and select group of spiritual elites. However, he nonetheless views individuals as those who should recognize themselves as unified with history, with nature, with their bodies, and with (significant) others. Although he holds the individual in high esteem, it is notable that he does not immortalize them or view them as the crown of creation, nor does he accept the Christian god who is severed from the created realm.[46]

As stated before, the ideas of the *Übermensch* and the will to power publicly come to the forefront in *Zarathustra*. Although these terms have political overtones, philosophers and theologians tend to view Nietzsche's praise of the will to power as an existential-psychological concept which signifies the principle life-force underlying all creation, denoting spiritual development.[47]

Although Nietzsche describes the desire for power and control—in the social sense—as a human phenomenon, in *Zarathustra*, he promotes the use of this will not as domination and mastery over others, but as mastery over oneself. In this manner, he converts a natural desire for power into virtues which are born from an excess of strength, not from weakness or pity. In other words, he contends that we have creative and destructive capacities; we are creators as well as creatures. The *Übermensch* represents the ideal human being who strives to exert one's will to excellence, self-mastery, and self-control. Nietzsche writes in *Ecce Homo* that the word overman, which is used to designate a "type of supreme achievement, [is] opposed to 'modern men,' to 'good men,' [and] to Christians and other nihilists." The *Übermensch* is an "'idealistic' type' of a higher kind of man, [who is] half 'saint' and half 'genius.'"[48]

Übermenschen are not human beings whose primary goal is to rule over others through exploitation, greed, and revenge. The reverse is true ("Is it my fault that power likes to walk on crooked legs?").[49] They are higher than the beasts precisely because they have transcended the "teachers of virtue," who, Zarathustra claims, are the primary carriers of power and vengeance. The virtuous are those who have hitherto lied retribution, punishment and reward into the foundation of things:

> For *that man be delivered from revenge*, that is for me the bridge to the highest hope and a rainbow after long storms. The tarantulas, of course would have it otherwise. . . . But thus I counsel you, my friends: Mistrust all in whom the impulse to punish is powerful. Mistrust all who talk much of their justice! . . . And when they call themselves the good and the just, do not forget that they would be pharisees, if only they had—power.[50]

The *Übermensch* and the will to power are central to Nietzsche's views on creation. The former gives birth to new values; the will to power, as a cosmic principle, underlies nature—including human nature itself. It is important to note that Nietzsche is not concerned with cosmology or cosmogony. He simply does not speculate on metaphysical issues concerning the creation of the world, nor does he desire to construct a scientific account of the universe. Rather, creation is a human phenomenon; we are the animals who are capable of integrating our natural instincts and of creating something above and beyond ourselves.[51]

Nietzsche's first long discussion on the will to power occurs in the section, "On Self Overcoming." Nietzsche endorses three central tenets in this section: Whatever lives, obeys. Those who cannot obey themselves are commanded. And commanding is harder than obeying. His remark that "Even in the will of those who serve I found the will to be master" is most likely an allusion to the Christian praise of self-sacrifice which, beneath the humble notion of Christ as savior, actually conceals the will to truth and to domination. In stark contrast to the Christian view that the Messiah sacrificed himself so that we might be saved in the beyond, Zarathustra teaches that we must sacrifice ourselves for the earth and the coming of the *Übermensch*. He states that the creator must annihilate external commands traditionally given by God (Thou shalt), and become an internal commander and law giver unto themselves (I will). In order to possess this capacity to generate values, however, one must first overcome a sinful nature, one's own devils: "And life itself confided this secret to me: 'Behold,' it said, 'I am *that which must always overcome itself.*' Indeed, you call it a will to procreate or a drive to an end, to something higher, farther, more manifold: but all this is one, and one secret."[52]

The will to power constitutes the attempt at self-mastery by sublimating natural instincts—including those of punishment and revenge—as well as overcoming the human desire for absolute and unconditional truth, which Nietzsche views as the hallmark of modern science and of Christianity. The will to truth is crude in contrast to the will to create, which characterizes the will to power of genuine philosophers.[53] The will to power also expresses Nietzsche's longing for a return to a pre-Christian era, particularly to his idealistic view of the ancient Greeks, who did not repress natural instincts, but assimilated them positively in a social context. The will to power is also a cosmic principle underlying nature and the whole of creation. It differs from Schopenhauer's view. Schopenhauer's cosmic will denotes a chaotic force which drives the universe. Nietzsche's cosmic will is neither chaotic nor orderly, it is simply free: it denotes life's inexhaustible struggle for more power. This anthropological view of the will revises the metaphysical principle that Schopenhauer espouses. "I say unto you," Zarathustra cries, "one must first have chaos in oneself in order to give birth to a dancing star . . . you still have chaos in yourself."[54]

Whereas Schopenhauer views the will as an endless, striving force which ultimately desires death because it can never be satisfied, Nietzsche regards the will as an endless striving force which desires more vitality and an abundance of life. Hence, he avoids the death wish that he believes Schopenhauer, Buddhism, and Christianity inherently possess. Nietzsche regards both Buddhism and Christianity as nihilistic religions.[55] Even so, he says that the former is nobler than Christianity, for Buddha "does not ask his followers to fight those who think otherwise: There is nothing to which his doctrine is more opposed than the feeling of revenge, antipathy, *ressentiment* ('it is not by enmity that enmity is ended')."[56]

In *Zarathustra*, the inversion of the cosmic will occurs in an obvious reference to the Genesis I creation account, wherein Nietzsche transforms "and

God saw that *it was* good," into anthropological categories: "To redeem those who lived in the past and to recreate all *'It was'* into a 'thus I willed it'—that alone should I call redemption."[57] In this sentence alone, Nietzsche not only transforms Schopenhauer's will, he also subsumes Christian eschatology *into* creation. Creation and redemption are synonymous. Redemption is not an occurrence beyond death or after life; it is the "innocence of becoming" now. Later in the section, the point is emphasized further, as Nietzsche reiterates that hell—and a god of hell—is an evil and insane human projection: "'Can there be redemption if there is eternal justice? Alas, the stone *It was* cannot be moved: all punishments must be eternal too.' Thus preached madness."[58]

Brief mention must be made of Nietzsche's antithesis to Christian immortality: the infamous eternal recurrence, in which life lived on earth will recur in the exact same sequence, unconditionally and eternally. It is debatable whether Nietzsche regarded this concept literally; however, it is clear that the notion was meant to stress faithfulness to the earth and to ground the meaning of life in history. The idea was also used as the supreme conqueror of Time, in contrast to Eugen Dühring's theory.[59] More than anything, the eternal recurrence signified the ultimate affirmation of the whole of life; it was not used by Nietzsche to immortalize the ego or the human being. He essentially used the notion symbolically to stress personal transformation, and that one should live differently now. In the *Gay Science*, Nietzsche writes of the concept hypothetically:[60]

> What if a demon were to steal after you into your loneliest loneliness and say to you: "This life as you now live it and have lived it, you will have to live once more and innumerable times more; and there will be nothing new in it, but every pain and every joy and every thought and sigh and everything unutterably small or great in your life will have to return to you, all in the same succession and sequence. . . ." Would you not throw yourself down and gnash your teeth and curse the demon who spoke thus? Or . . . would you have answered him: "You are a god and never have I heard anything more divine." If this thought gained possession of you, it would change you as you are or perhaps crush you. The question in each and every thing, "Do you desire this once more and innumerable times more?" would lie upon your actions as the greatest weight.[61]

Whereas Nietzsche, in the *Antichrist*, regards Christianity as "the hatred of the *senses*, of joy in the senses, of joy itself";[62] Zarathustra esteems the eternal recurrence as the joy "that wants the eternity of *all* things, *wants deep . . . deep, eternity.*"[63] This joy includes pain, and the affirmation of every woe. Human pain is the deepest pain, which courage must overcome. The eternal recurrence is the point at which two infinite paths meet in contradiction, "they offend each other face to face"; and the gateway at which they meet is inscribed with the word, Moment: "'All that is straight lies,' the dwarf murmured contemptuously. 'All truth is crooked; time itself is a circle.'"[64] Elsewhere, Nietzsche baptizes this idea with the symbol of Dionysus, who represents a faith that the Crucified did not: a model for life, not death; a way of justice, distinct from revenge; and universal redemption, embracing the whole of creation:

> Such a spirit who has *become free* stands amid the cosmos with a joyous and trusting fatalism, in the *faith* that only the particular is loathsome, and that all is redeemed and affirmed in the whole—he does not negate anymore. Such a faith, however, is the highest of all possible faiths; I have baptized it with the name of *Dionysus.*[65]

The eternal return was Nietzsche's antithesis to the Christian notion of individual immortality, conceived as a futuristic realm where souls reside in peace or eternal torment. But it was not used in antithesis to a historical or universal conception of redemption, which seeks to remain faithful to the earth—and which sanctifies, to paraphrase Tillich—the Eternal Now.

Overall, the concepts of creation and redemption as formulated in *Thus Spoke Zarathustra* should be read in light of Darwinian evolution, Schopenhauer's influence, and Nietzsche's disillusionment with nineteenth-century German Christianity. The work is in large measure a polemic against the eschatological concepts of heaven and hell, the conception of God as Hangman and Judge, and it preaches the coming of the *Übermensch*. The theme underlying the entire work is that human beings must be the new creators now that God is dead and that Darwinism has eliminated the divine *from* nature and from history. In this sense, power becomes ultimate in the Nietzschean scheme of things, and humans are to draw upon that power in meaningful and creative ways:

> Creation—that is the great redemption from suffering, and life's growing light. But that the creator may be, suffering is needed and much change. Indeed, there must be much bitter dying in your life, you creators. . . . Willing liberates: that is the true teaching of will and liberty—thus Zarathustra teaches it. . . . Away from God and gods this will has lured me; what could one create if gods existed?[66]

Some scholars have noted that Nietzsche's *Übermensch* was incompatible with the eternal return, for if all things will recur on earth continually, the coming of the *Übermensch* (whom Nietzsche said had not yet appeared) would be an impossibility. Kaufmann argues that these interpreters find logical problems because they regard the advent of Nietzsche's *Übermensch* literally, whereas he was simply using this term symbolically in *Zarathustra* to illustrate ideal types of free spirits. He states that although Nietzsche inclined toward viewing the eternal recurrence as scientifically provable, the *Übermensch* is not incompatible with that view, for Nietzsche does not view *Übermenschen* as products of evolution, but as those spirits who are dispersed throughout different generations (hence, *Übermenschen* would appear over and over again).[67]

If we adopt the widely accepted view that *Übermenschen* represent ideal free *spirits* (in the plural), and Kaufmann's notion that Nietzsche tended to view the eternal recurrence as scientifically true, then he has apparently resolved the dilemma. Nonetheless, his solution is untrue to Nietzsche's text. In the infamous passage, Zarathustra speaks of the *Übermensch* in the singular (hence, if the *Übermensch* has not yet come, and the eternal recurrence is understood literally, then it *would* be impossible historically). Nietzsche writes: "Never yet has there been an overman. . . . Verily, even the greatest I found all-too-human."[68] Kaufmann states that this passage, which symbolizes a "Goethe become truly perfect" matters little.[69] However, in fact, here Nietzsche is referring to Jesus of Nazareth (the noblest human being), and is boldly stating the traditional Jewish contention that the Messiah has not yet appeared in history—as Christianity teaches—and that Christ is human not divine.[70] It should be remembered that the two rare persons who initially took an interest in this work were a Christian antisemite (from his prison cell), and Paneth, a Jewish man. The former denounced Nietzsche ("Aut Christus aut Zarathustra!"); the latter viewed the author as somewhat prophetic.[71] The social and political implications of Nietzsche's religious views should therefore be kept in mind. Since the first century, Christendom condemned the Jews as Christ killers and for rejecting the divinely revealed truth of Jesus as the Messiah. And despite severe persecution throughout the ages, including the mass murder of Jews in Europe during the Crusades, the Jews held that the Messiah, as foretold by the Hebrew prophets, had not yet appeared.[72] The Jews' continued existence and their self-identity as God's chosen people served as an irritant to Christian antisemites who tried to usurp the Jews for God's favor. This sibling rivalry fueled the Jewish-Christian conflict and the antisemitism inherent within Christian theology itself, in which Christendom claimed to be the new Israel now that the "stubborn" Jews had rejected and indeed murdered, the Father's only begotten Son. However, as one contemporary Jewish thinker observes, because Jesus was Jewish, the "Christian problem" stems from the fact that there can be no church without Judaism and Jews; yet neither Christianity nor its teachings are integral to the ongoing life of the Jewish people or to the Jewish faith. This serves as a threat to those Christian antisemites who view themselves as the younger brother who has bested the older brother, and who find it difficult to grasp that the Jews have their own history that not only predates, but post-dates the rise of Christianity.[73]

Most interpreters would agree that the conundrum between the eternal recurrence and the *Übermensch* is less a logical problem, and more typical of Nietzsche's paradoxical mind and his masterful skill to engage his readers. For these reasons alone, the apparent incongruity will never be solved. Traditionally however, nearly all of Nietzsche's ardent readers address the paradox and offer their solutions—without exception here. In my view, the *Übermensch* signifies the Messiah who has not yet come; *Übermenschen* represent free spirits throughout history, including Jesus, who was fully *human* (in the *Antichrist*, Nietzsche says one could call Jesus a free spirit, "using the expression somewhat tolerantly").[74] Furthermore, Nietzsche indeed believes in the eternal recurrence as a truth, but *not* in the literal sense that it is an absolute and unchanging fact of time, space, or history.[75] Truth, for Nietzsche, is contingent upon whether one adopts and appropriates a tenet existentially as one's own, *as if* it were absolutely and unconditionally true. One must adopt this doctrine wholeheartedly, as literally, historically, and even scientifically true, all-the-while knowing it is false (or mythical). It was precisely this subjective, existential understanding of truth that Nietzsche believed that mass Christianity (and, to a lesser degree, modern science) did not attain. Nietzsche recognized untruth as a necessary condition of existence. The important issue for him was not the truth or falsehood of a claim, but how that claim promoted or detracted from life.[76] This interpretation sheds some light on resolving the apparent riddle. Although Nietzsche does refer to the eternal recurrence in his notebooks as "the most scientific of all possible hypotheses,"[77] the eternal recurrence, however understood (scientifically, literally, historically, symbolically) remains an *hypothesis*—not a truth.

The solution to the riddle offered here leads us back to the riddle itself. By enticing his readers into the paradox, Nietzsche finally drives us to the point where we no longer ask if the doctrine of the eternal recurrence is objectively true. But rather, why *we* ourselves want truth (why not rather untruth? and uncertainty? even ignorance?), and to what extent our truths enhance our lives.

Zarathustra's insistence that individuals should serve as a bridge to the *Übermensch* and sacrifice themselves for the earth, signifies a future hope as well as a bonding thread which weaves throughout past and present history. This fragmented and motley group is one in which free spirits befriend and instruct each other how to survive amidst cultural decline. The flamboyant themes which permeate *Zarathustra* also run—though less conspicuously—throughout Nietzsche's early meditations. In the second meditation, Nietzsche writes of individuals who, in contrast to the masses, "form a kind of bridge across the turbulent stream of becoming."[78] In the third, he states that culture demands of exemplars not only inward experience, "but . . . above all an act . . . a struggle on behalf of culture and hostility towards those influences, habits, laws, institutions in which he fails to recognize his goal: which is the production of the genius."[79]

Nietzsche indeed desires that free spirits inherit the earth, but knows that society must be radically transformed if this is to occur. Generally, he believes that cultural conditions must be established if exemplars are to flourish, and that the latter must simultaneously create themselves along with cultural conditions favorable to this flourishing.[80] The philosopher incessantly grapples with the dilemma that life *is* the will to power, and this will permeates the whole of creation. Sociologically, he regards a certain degree of exploitation as inevitable.

Paradoxically, in contrast to Social Darwinism, Nietzsche views strong exemplars as the victims of society. The masters have been crushed by the slavish masses who acquire strength in numbers, not in loftiness of soul: "The human beings who are more similar, more ordinary, have had, and always have, an advantage; those more select, subtle, strange, and difficult to understand, easily remain alone . . . and rarely propagate."[81] Nobles should therefore self-actualize the will to power in an effort to cultivate themselves spiritually—if not socially—over against the reigning mob: "In all kinds of injury and loss the lower and coarser soul is better off than the nobler one: the dangers for the latter must be greater; the probability that it will come to grief and perish is actually . . . tremendous."[82]

Until culture is transformed, Zarathustra admonishes his friends to flee into their solitude—away from the "buzzing flies in the market-place" and their "invisible revenge": "[T]hey sting in all innocence. But you . . . deep one, suffer too deeply even from small wounds; and even before you have healed, the same poisonous worm crawls over your hand." In contrast to what he understood to be Christianity, Zarathustra does not teach revenge or passive submission. He teaches escape as a means of self-cultivation: "No longer raise your arm up against them. Numberless are they, and it is not your lot [in life] to shoo flies."[83] In this sense, Barth is absolutely correct to describe Nietzsche as "the prophet of humanity without the fellow man."[84] Even so, in Zarathustra's scheme the lonely creators "of today" who have chosen themselves, will someday emerge as a chosen *people*, out of whom the *Übermensch* will then arise: "Verily, the earth shall yet become a site of recovery. And even now a new fragrance surrounds it, bringing salvation—and a new hope."[85] The chosen ones will be redeemed from the past (from birth, sex, race, nationality, and religion), their distinction will come through the courage to create new tables of values, and visions for the future: "Not whence you come shall henceforth constitute your honor, but whither you are going! Exiles shall you be from all father-and forefather-lands! Your *children's land* shall you love—the undiscovered land in the most distant sea."[86]

Nietzsche sought to remake the image of human beings—and the image of God, nature, and society—throughout his writing career. His philosophical enterprise, including his polemic against Christianity and his concepts of the will to power, the *Übermensch*, and the eternal recurrence, were efforts designed to render sacred a desacralized world, and were deeply rooted in his response to Darwinism and to Christianity, which he believed both contributed to the earth's desacralization. The former reduced the children of God to the status of animals and took away human dignity and worth. Christianity created a chasm between God and humans, God and nature, and humans and nature, which made it possible for Darwinism to flourish. Both resulted in the loss of divinity.

Zarathustra is the work of a solitary eccentric and was written during the most desperate, lonely and tormenting period of Nietzsche's life. But it nonetheless conveys profound spiritual depth, joy, vision, and hope. As an autobiographical account it is powerful; as an exposition on creation and redemption it is rich in myth and symbolism; and as an ethical critique of nineteenth-century German Christianity and culture and Darwinism, it is perceptive. As an overall work, it is ingenious. Throughout, it creates vital ways of viewing creation and redemption, particularly by its denial of Christianity's otherworlds. All in all, *Zarathustra's* radical this-worldliness and its insistence that creation is a human power, elevates history as the arena in which the sacred resides.

Zarathustra marks the beginning of what is regarded as mature Nietzschean thought, for it is here that his major philosophical ideas begin to crystallize. In particular, Nietzsche's notion of *ressentiment* (revenge), which is expounded in the *Genealogy*, is related to punishment, guilt, and redemption: "The *spirit of revenge*, my friends, has so far been the subject of man's best reflection; and where there was suffering, one always wanted punishment too. For 'punishment' is what revenge calls itself; with a hypocritical lie it creates a good conscience for itself."[87] The work towers as a psychological critique of Christianity, especially how repressed human nature and suffering relate to the ego, resentment toward non-believers, and the construction of heaven and hell. However, as will become evident in the next chapter, the work is by no means apolitical. Although Zarathustra shies away from public involvement—and invites his friends to do the same—in the work of the following year, *Beyond Good and Evil*, Nietzsche emerges as a controversial political force begging to be reckoned with, voicing his opposition to antisemitism and German nationalism. Nietzsche wrote in a letter to Burckhardt that *Beyond* "says the same things as *Zarathustra*, but differently, very differently."[88]

Perhaps Zarathustra's veiled rhetoric was partially based on the fear of articulation. This is implied when Zarathustra encounters the "foaming fool" at the gate of the "great city," which the fool regards as a hell for hermits thoughts: "Don't you smell the slaughterhouses and ovens of the spirit even now? Does not this town steam with the fumes of slaughtered spirit?," says the fool. Wanting to be rid of the prophet, the fool (similar to the jester) warns Zarathustra, telling him to spit on the city and turn back. Zarathustra puts his hand over the fool's mouth and replies:

> "Stop at last . . . your speech and your manner have long nauseated me . . . I despise your despising; and if you warned me, why did you not warn yourself? . . . For all your foaming is revenge, you vain fool; I guessed it well."
>
> "But your fool's words injure me, even where you are right. And even if Zarathustra's words *were* a thousand times right, still *you* would always *do* wrong with my words."
>
> Thus spoke Zarathustra; and he looked at the great city, sighed, and long remained silent.[89]

At the beginning of *Zarathustra*, the prophet speaks to the saint in the forest who warns him not to go to humanity ("Go rather, even to the animals"). Determined, Zarathustra confronts the crowd in the market place and warns them about the last men. They reject his teachings and at dark the jester tells him to leave ("Go away from this town, Zarathustra . . . there are too many here who hate you. You are hated by the good and the just; you are hated by the believers in the true faith, and they call you the danger of the multitude").[90] The prophet begins to withdraw again and speaks only to kindred souls ("An insight has come to me between dawn and dawn. . . . Companions the creator seeks. . . . No shepherd shall I be, nor gravedigger. Never again shall I speak to the people: for the last time have I spoken to the dead").[91] In the end, as in the beginning, Zarathustra's animals are the ones he feels most akin to, as evidenced that they preach Zarathustra's doctrine that eternity begins now; eternal life is life lived on earth:

> "O Zarathustra," the animals said, "to those who think as we do, all things themselves are dancing; they come and offer their hands and laugh and flee—and come back. Everything goes, everything comes back; eternally rolls the wheel of being. Everything dies, everything

blossoms again; eternally runs the year of being. Everything breaks, everything is joined anew; eternally the same house is being built. Everything parts, everything greets every other thing again; eternally the ring of being remains faithful to itself. In every Now, being begins; round every Here rolls the sphere There. The center is everywhere. Bent is the path of eternity."[92]

5

Toward the Genealogy of Morals:
The Dionysian Drama of the
Destiny of the Soul

Dear Friend:

    I am enjoying a great blessing this morning: for the first time a 'fire-idol' stands in my room; a small stove—and I confess that I have already pranced round it once or twice like a good heathen. . . .

    All those who have been in need of 'moral dignity' . . . have been among the admirers of Rousseau, even down to our darling Dühring. . . . And I suspect that there is something of the resentment of the mob to be found at the bottom of all Romanticism.[1]

On all sides the chasm has become too great, and I have to have recourse to every possible kind of chastening influence in order not to descend among the men of resentment myself. The sort of *defensive attitude* towards me taken up by all those people who were once my friends has something annoying about it which is much more mortifying than an attack. "Not to hear and not to see"—that seems to be the motto. . . .

    I am industrious but melancholy, and I have not yet recovered from the state of vehement irritation into which the last few years have thrown me. I am not yet "sufficiently impersonalized."[2]

Toward the Genealogy of Morals: *A Polemic* consists of three essays and was published in November 1887. It was written as a supplement to Nietzsche's previous aphoristic work, *Beyond Good and Evil* (1886), which immediately followed *Thus Spoke Zarathustra*. When referring to these works in *Ecce Homo*,

Nietzsche describes *Zarathustra* as "far sighted," *Beyond* as a "focus on the age," and he alludes to the *Genealogy* as that which seeks beginnings: "Dionysus is, as is known, also a god of darkness."[3] It appears that—intentionally or not—the *Genealogy* in its search for origins completes a literary trinity in reverse. This process begins with the heights of the future as envisioned by the prophet Zarathustra; it moves to the present as a critique of modernity; and explores the past through the symbol of Dionysus. Zarathustra is a creator; Dionysus destroys. Nietzsche makes reference to no god(s) to characterize the modern era.[4]

With *Beyond Good and Evil*, Nietzsche's writings take on a political tone characterized by an uninhibited bitterness and a hard edge ("For I am beginning to touch on what is *serious* for me, the 'European problem' as I understand it, the cultivation of a new caste that will rule Europe").[5] From this point on, Nietzsche's works vigorously solicit public response: "The time for petty politics is over: the very next century will bring the fight for the dominion of the earth—the *compulsion* to large-scale politics."[6] More than anything, his later writings reveal the pain, cynicism, but also the utmost seriousness of a frustrated author who desperately sought an audience. As one commentator puts it, Nietzsche, who prided himself on standing apart was, "like every great thinker . . . less isolated, more indebted, and more in need of response than he often admits."[7]

In an aphorism from the section "Peoples and Fatherlands" in *Beyond*, Nietzsche identifies the European problem as "nationalistic nerve fever"; the anti-French, anti-Polish and specifically, the anti-Jewish sentiments expressed by the Christian romantics, the Wagnerians, the Teutons, and the Prussians (especially the "wretched historians" Sybel and Treitschke).[8] In an obvious allusion to the Wagner circle in which he himself once travelled, Nietzsche writes:

> Forgive me, for during a brief daring sojourn in very infected territory I, too, did not altogether escape this disease and began like everyone else to develop notions about matters that are none of my business: the first sign of the political infection. For example about the Jews: only listen!
>
> I have not met a German yet who was well disposed toward the Jews; and however unconditionally all the cautious and politically-minded repudiated real anti-Semitism, even this caution and policy are not directed against the species of this feeling itself but only against its dangerous immoderation . . . about this, one should not deceive oneself. . . .[9]

In this lengthy passage—which the Wagnerites would have viewed as shocking—Nietzsche regards the Jews as "the strongest, toughest, and purest race now living in Europe" and states that it might be "useful and fair to expel the anti-Semitic screamers from the country." He states that the Jews, if they wanted to, "could have a stranglehold on all of Europe but that they have no plans of the kind"; argues in behalf of Jewish assimilation; and ends the passage by stating that the Jews will partake in the cultivation of his "new caste that will rule Europe." This excerpt would have especially offended Nietzsche's sister Elisabeth and her husband Förster, who were just recently married (May 1885) and were championing a Germanic-Aryan race. Their marriage was most likely decisive in prompting the philosopher's political involvement. Five months after the wedding, he and Förster reluctantly granted Elisabeth's request and met on Nietzsche's forty-first birthday. The first meeting, which was also the last, went without incident. The two men were cordial to each other and managed to avoid political arguments. Nietzsche wrote to Overbeck that there was something sincere and noble in Förster's character, but that their values were certainly different. Förster was surprised and relieved at the contrast between Nietzsche's gentle disposition and the fierce tone of his writings. He regarded his half-blind, physically frail brother-in-law as an invalid to be pitied rather than feared.[10]

Beyond Good and Evil is thus marked by Nietzsche's political involvement, and his sharp threefold categories of Jews. Nietzsche exalts original Israel and contemporary Jewry; he attributes the slave revolt in morality to priestly-prophetic Judaism, that strand of the Jewish tradition that Christian antisemites claimed as their ancestor.[11]

The *Genealogy* is characterized by a maturity of Nietzsche's thought and a seriousness unequaled in his other works. Yet it also shows an increasing loss of inhibition and an unusual tendency to ramble at length in essay style. In general, whereas the first two essays are untypically impersonal and somber in tone, the third returns to Nietzsche's early mentors Schopenhauer and Wagner, scathing Christianity as never before and frequently bordering on juvenile ranting (particularly sections 22ff.). In the essays, Nietzsche puts forth key ideas concerning resentment, the bad conscience, and ascetic ideals. According to Nietzsche, the first essay deals with the origin of Christianity out of the spirit of revenge, a great rebellion against noble values; the second with the psychology of conscience as an "instinct of cruelty" and not as "the voice of God in man"; and the third with the ascetic ideal as an ideal of annihilation and decadence, "a will to the end." Overall, Nietzsche continues in *Ecce Homo*, "This book contains the first psychology of the priest."[12] I will briefly sketch the structure of each essay. Then I will discuss them within the historical and political setting of antisemitism, and within the wider framework of Nietzsche's philosophy.

In the preface to the *Genealogy*, Nietzsche states that the subject of his polemic is "on the origin of our moral prejudices" (2), particularly the "unegoistic instincts" of pity, self-abnegation, and self-sacrifice, which he regards as dangerous and in need of critique (5).

The first essay, "Good and Evil, Good and Bad," begins with a discussion of the utilitarian theories of "these English psychologists," including Spencer, who decree that originally unegoistic actions were considered good from the point of view to whom goodness was shown. Nietzsche rejects this interpretation, viewing it as a modern democratic prejudice toward all questions of origin (1-4). The creation of values, he states, initially had nothing to do with utility or unegoistic actions. Rather, on the basis of self-affirmation and the pathos of distance, the noble rulers established themselves as the good "in contradistinction to all the low-minded, common and plebeian" (2).

Nietzsche states that within warrior-aristocracies, the terms "good and bad" originally denoted social classes, character traits, and a powerful physicality reveling in power, courage, war, and adventure. The priestly caste, embodying the most "deeply repressed priestly vengefulness," inverted these values, contending that the weak, poor, and suffering were the good; the noble aristocratic souls, the evil (7).

The slave-revolt in morality originated with priestly Judea and was inherited by Christianity (7); it is now the victorious (Judeo-Christian) morality of modernity (9). What is peculiar to slave morality is the notion of justice in relation to vengeance. Whereas "good and bad" originally denoted class distinctions between nobles and slaves, "good and evil" came into the world when resentment itself gave "birth to values." Natures that were denied the true reaction of deeds compensated themselves with an imaginary revenge (10). The basic distinction between noble and slave morality is that the former is self-affirming; the latter must first create an evil enemy before it can affirm itself (10). The German of today who assumes a position of power, Nietzsche declares, arouses a deep and icy mistrust. He is an echo of that "inexhaustible horror with which Europe observed for centuries, that raging of the blond Germanic beast" (11).

Through his parable of the lambs and the birds of prey, Nietzsche demonstrates that the weak and impotent hold the strong accountable, or guilty, for expressions and manifestations of spontaneous strength (13). They themselves, in their passiveness, regard weakness as a merit and find joy and pleasure in seeing others suffer and in leaving eternal vengeance to God (13ff.). Nietzsche supports his view by quoting three famous Christians and their bloodthirsty visions of hell: Dante, Tertullian, and Thomas Aquinas, "the great teacher and saint" (15): "'Beati in regno coelesti,' he says, meek as a lamb, 'videbung poenas damnatorum, ut beatitudo illis magis complaceat'" [The blessed in the kingdom of heaven will see the punishments of the damned, in order that their bliss be more delightful for them].[13]

He concludes the first essay by stating that the two value frameworks, "good and bad" and "good and evil" are represented by Rome and Judea, the latter (Judeo-Christianity) of which has "won for the present." Nietzsche regards three major epochs of world history as being opposed to aristocratic values: the slave revolt of Judeo-Christianity, the Reformation, and the French Revolution (16). The appearance of Napoleon as a synthesis of the inhuman and superhuman, seems to represent, for Nietzsche, the resurgence of aristocratic and imperial morality of Rome (which upheld the supreme rights of the few), in the midst of the revolt of the rabble represented by the French Revolution (which upheld the supreme rights of the majority).[14] Nietzsche concludes that it should be abundantly clear that the aim and slogan of his previous work, *Beyond Good and Evil* does *not* mean "Beyond Good and Bad" (16-17).

The second essay, "'Guilt,' 'Bad Conscience,' and the Like" traces the origin and characteristics of the conscience and that "other somber thing," the bad conscience. Nietzsche writes that the conscience, or "the memory of the will" is characterized by the capacity to remember and make promises, as well as by the "positive faculty of repression," which has the capacity to forget (1). In prehistoric times memory was created by, and originated within, the instinct which realized that pain is the most powerful aid to mnemonics. In a certain sense, Nietzsche states, the whole of asceticism belongs here (1-3).

The bad conscience is characterized by a sense of guilt, punishment, and duty, which originated in the sphere of legal obligations between creditor and debtor (4-6). It was also here that the intertwining of guilt and suffering became inseparable, for suffering itself was used to balance debts or guilt. Punishment, Nietzsche writes, was not initially associated with guilt, but with indebtedness (4-6, 8).

Nietzsche traces four stages of justice in relation to punishment, concluding that the justice of the "most powerful man" is mercy (9-10). True justice, writes Nietzsche, is not based on revenge but is a positive attitude (11).

Nietzsche returns to the origin (the procedure) and the purpose (the meaning) of punishment (12-15), stressing that distinctions must be made between the two. In prehistory, punishment had nothing to do with an interiorized guilt; it was an objective retaliation against one who had caused injury by which the injured expressed their anger. Only later stages of history used punishment for the main purpose of evoking feelings of guilt (bad conscience, 12-15), but this is a falsification of psychology. Punishment, Nietzsche argues, actually does not evoke guilt but the sting of alienation (14). He concludes that although punishment tames humans, it does not make them better (15).

The bad conscience came into existence when humans found themselves within the walls of society and peace. Instincts that were not discharged were turned inward, and developed into what was later regarded as the "soul." The bad conscience began in the state, wherein the instinct for freedom (the will to power) was made latent by the rulers. The joy and the will to self-maltreatment provided the conditions for the "unegoistic" values (selflessness, self-denial, self-sacrifice) which are tied to cruelty (16-18). The bad conscience developed in the state, evolved through religion (through consciousness of being in debt to the deity), and culminated with Christianity's theory of atonement (19-21). With the Christian concept of guilt before God, self-torture, repression, and projection reached its pinnacle (22). In contrast to the Christian God, Nietzsche writes that the Greek gods are nobler, for they took upon themselves not only the punishment, but also the guilt. He claims that moderns are the heirs of the "conscience-vivisection and self-torture of millennia"; they have an evil eye for natural inclinations, and have become inseparable from the bad conscience itself. The "man of the future" must redeem moderns not only from the reigning ideal but from the will to nothingness and liberate the will again (24).

Nietzsche final essay, "What is the Meaning of Ascetic Ideals," has no clear progression of thought. It starts out trying to distinguish between various types of asceticism: the artist, the scholar, the priest, and the saint, but then it deteriorates into an overall rant against a declining vitality throughout Europe in which Nietzsche attacks democracy, socialism, feminism, German nationalism, and antisemitism.

In this essay, Nietzsche views asceticism as a sublimation for the purpose of focusing energy on creativity. It can be hypocritical (in Wagner and Schopenhauer), but it has a role in philosophy (1-10). That the ideal has many meanings, expresses the basic fact that the human will needs a goal; it would "rather will *nothingness* than *not* will" (1).

Nietzsche's serious diatribe is against priestly asceticism, in whom *ressentiment* rules without equal. The priest, who appears out of the slave revolt and belongs to no one race or class, possesses a power-will that wants to dominate life itself (11), and have dominion over the suffering (15). The priest, "who is the savior, shepherd and advocate of the sick herd" seeks a cause for suffering, a guilty agent onto which he can vent his affects. Through vengeance, he also seeks a cure, in an effort to deaden pain (11-15). The ascetic priest, Nietzsche writes, seeks a sociological or psychological cause to explain suffering, and reinterprets suffering in terms of fear, guilt, sin and punishment. Consequently, life-denying concepts such as redemption and hell arise (20). The otherworldly goals of the ascetic priest represent sickness par excellence.

Nietzsche questions modern science and historiography as sources for alternative goals (23-26). All science fails because it still has a metaphysical faith in absolute truth, derived from Christianity and Plato, that stands or falls with this ideal (24). It creates bad values which presently dissuades "man from his former respect for himself" (25). Historiography, although it claims to reject teleology, is self-deceived in believing it adheres to a purely descriptive method. The so-called "objective" and "contemplative" modern (antisemitic) historians, Eugen Dühring and Ernst Renan, Nietzsche charges, are "historical nihilists" who pose as ascetics and priests but are really only tragic buffoons, "*comedians* of the Christian-moral ideal" (26). Atheism too is driven by the will to truth and is thus not the antithesis of the ascetic ideal but its later evolution (27). Christian morality must end by drawing an inference against itself, which will happen when it poses the question as to the meaning of all will to truth. The will to truth must gain self-consciousness, regard itself as problematic, and overcome itself (27).

Nietzsche concludes by stating that suffering itself was not the initial problem confronting the human animal; the problem arose when humans suffered from the problem of meaning. The interpretation of suffering by ascetic priests brought fresh suffering with it, "deeper, more inward, more poisonous, more life-destructive suffering," by placing it under the perspective of guilt (28).

Nietzsche's *Genealogy*, which he wrote in twenty days and described as "a small polemical pamphlet," was designed to clarify *Beyond Good and Evil*: "Everybody has complained that I am not understood," Nietzsche wrote to Gast, "I think [the *Genealogy*] sharply focuses the problem of my last book." Nietzsche, having paid for printing costs over the past three years, simply could not negotiate a publishing contract: "One undeniable fact emerges—no German publisher *wants* me (even if I do not claim an honorarium)."[15] Even so, in the midst of his obscurity Nietzsche claimed that Jews viewed him favorably: "Whoever reads me in Germany today has first *de-Germanized* himself thoroughly, as I have done: my formula is known, 'to be a good German means to de-Germanize oneself'; or he is—no small distinction among Germans—of Jewish descent."[16]

Nietzsche's "pamphlet" appeared in an age which historians have called "the incubation" of antisemitism (1870-1914).[17] Through his early association with Wagner, he became more exposed to, and influenced by, the contempt for Jews that was gaining social force throughout German culture in the latter third of the nineteenth-century.

From the late Middle Ages to the eighteenth century the Jews had been ghettoized in Europe, given only very restricted rights to settlement, marginalized economically and politically. The French Revolution emancipated the Jews in France, and this was carried into Germany by Napoleon, who gave the struggle for Jewish emancipation its greatest advance. After the French Revolution, the gradual process of emancipation was carried on by Prussian leaders. Napoleon's downfall brought antisemitic reaction and the rise of anti-Napoleonic nationalism in Germany, reaching a point of violence in many German cities in 1819. Full emancipation came in 1848 when the Jews were admitted to the legislative assemblies after that year's revolution.[18] It was only between 1848 and 1870 that the ghetto was disbanded and the Jews generally attained full citizenship in western Europe.

Although it is difficult to discern precisely what transpired during the incubation period, it is clear that German society was an incubator of antisemitism and that the Lutheran church and its idea of the Christian state played an instrumental role.[19] Many Protestants believed that the Jews were foreigners alien to a Germanic Christian land, that they were a people within a people, and a state within a state. The Jews, who composed only 1 percent of the population, were blamed for the economic crash of 1873, as the visible urban group were, on average, more prosperous than the Christians. There were (proportionally) ten times as many Jewish university students as Protestants, and fifteen times as many as Catholics. Around 1885 (the year Nietzsche finished penning the fourth book of *Zarathustra*), one out of every eight students in German universities was Jewish.[20]

The rapid advance of Jewish emancipation brought a reaction in national antisemitic movements in Germany. One historian, in a manner sounding similar to Nietzsche's letter at the beginning of this chapter, describes the 1880s as a time in which "the attack came from all sides": from the left, the right; from aristocrats and populists; from industry, from farms; from the academy and from the gutter; from music, literature, and, not least, from science.[21] The tense religious and political climate is reflected throughout the course of Nietzsche's writing career. In 1878, the year of his formal break with Wagner, Nietzsche writes of what he regards as the "dangerous *national* hostilities":

> Incidently, the whole problem of the *Jews* exists only within national states, inasmuch as their energy and higher intelligence, their capital of spirit and will, which accumulated from generation to generation in the long school of their suffering, must predominate to a degree that awakens envy and hatred; and so, in the literature of nearly all present-day nations (and . . . in proportion to their renewed nationalistic behavior), there is an increase in the literary misconduct that leads the Jews to the slaughterhouse, as scapegoats for every possible public and private misfortune.[22]

Antisemitism in nineteenth-century Germany has been described as a bifurcated movement which was expressed in two forms: Christian antisemitism and anti-Christian antisemitism. The former, rooted in Christian theology, usually distinguished some positive element in ancient Judaism which was carried on and perfected in Jesus, from a deformed Israel which is made antithetical to Jesus and Christianity. The latter was found in French philosophies such as Voltaire and Holbach. It consisted in an attack on Jews and Judaism as well as Christianity itself, including its Biblical Jewish sources, its eschatological conception, and its ethical theological elements.[23] Nietzsche firmly opposes both forms of antisemitism. But he despises the concepts of election and the antinatural notions of justice and eternal vengeance that he regards as originating with the ancient Jewish religion. He believes Christianity adopts these ideas; regard themselves as God's chosen people; and then apply against the Jews that which the Jews previously applied against their enemies—the Last Judgment.[24] Thus, while Nietzsche derides certain elements of Judaism as a religion, particularly those elements that Christian antisemites honored, he nonetheless remains steadfast in his praise for contemporary Jewry, as demonstrated biographically and throughout his texts.

The defense of the Christian state was a high priority for the antisemitic court preacher and pastor, Adolf Stöcker, who was Förster's ally and perhaps the most well-known among German Protestants. Stöcker, who represents Christian antisemitism, preached that the Jewish "problem" could not be solved unless the Jews renounced their faith and ceased to "live in the flesh."[25] His popularity soared in the eighties, as he opened his ultraconservative, antisemitic campaign to the economically strapped middle-classes and began distributing antisemitic propaganda. He denounced the capitalistic power of modern Jewry; publicly expressed his fear that "the cancer from which we suffer" [the German spirit becoming Judaized] would impoverish the German economy, and pleaded for a return to Germanic rule in law and business.[26] His fundamental political theology was that because the Jews rejected the message of salvation in Christ, Christian-Germans were the true inheritors of God's election. Because the Jews crucified Christ, they committed the "unpardonable sin" and brought upon themselves the curse of everlasting abhorrence.[27] Stöcker claimed that his intention was to deal with the Jewish question "in full Christian love but also in full social truthfulness."[28] And the "truth," Stöcker held, was that Israel had to give up its desire to become master in Germany or a catastrophe was ultimately unavoidable.[29] In this fashion, Stöcker exploited the existing hatred of the Jews to shore up the authority of the Christian state.

Nietzsche makes occasional reference to Stöcker in his notes and in his writings (the most famous is his mad note that he wants "Wilhelm, Bismarck, and Stöcker shot").[30] In the early 1880s, Nietzsche became disturbed by Stöcker's anti-Jewish sentiments and regarded the Christian Social Workers' movement as one which grew out of resentment and cowardice.[31] By the late 1880s, Nietzsche is even more alarmed and preoccupied with Stöcker's rhetorical revival of the Christian state.[32] He writes of the homeopath of Christianity, "that of the court chaplains and anti-Semitic speculators."[33] Regarding Christian antisemites as "little, good-natured, absurd sheep with horns" who posed as judges and possessed "little herd animal virtues"; Nietzsche, while grieving the death of Friedrich III, announced in a personal letter in the summer of '88 that "the age of Stöcker had begun."[34] Elsewhere, in the *Nachlass*, Nietzsche compares and contrasts "morality as a means of seduction," tracing it through the logic of the apostle Paul to Luther and to Rousseau, noting the historical connection between the religious and political contempt for Jews: "In the case of *Christ*, the rejoicing of the people appears as the cause of his execution; an anti-priestly movement from the first. Even in the case of the *anti-Semites* it is still the same artifice: to visit condemnatory judgments upon one's opponent and to reserve to oneself the role of *retributive justice*."[35] Although the Jews indeed profited from the liberal ideas of political equality from the middle of the nineteenth century onward, a latent movement of hostility towards the complete social equality of the Jews nonetheless existed. The persistent reluctance on the part of the Christian upper and middle-classes to treat "the helot [Jew] of yesterday as the equal of today," especially became manifest in the open anti-semitic movements of Stöcker and von Treitschke, who felt professionally threatened by the Jewish minority, yet superior to them.[36]

The most radical representative of anti-Christian antisemitism during the 1880s was the anarchist Eugen Dühring, whom Nietzsche refers to as the "Berlin apostle of revenge" and who appears as Nietzsche's chief political opponent in the second and third essays of the *Genealogy*.[37] Dühring opposed the Christian-state and sought a new state that would serve a free and individualistic society.[38] Dühring, who was a favorite author to the members of the Executive Committee of the People's Will in the 1880s, preached a particular and peculiar democratic socialism. He drew upon John Stuart Mill's *Utilitarianism* ("these English psychologists") in attempting to establish the doctrine of punishment upon the instinct of retaliation.[39]

Dühring sought national self-sufficiency in a controlled economy. He wanted this limited national socialism to be based on the enthusiasm of the masses and on a general will of the Germanic *Volk*.[40] His central position was that the *Volk* possessed a unity of interests that were engaged in the struggle against the Jews who opposed the "common good" and the *Volk's* general will.[41] His theological position was that the Germans should reject the Old Testament, that the Jews were not people of God, and that Christ was an Aryan and an antisemite.[42] He opposed mixed marriages in order to protect the German people from blood contamination, and assailed Christianity as incompatible with the Nordic spirit.[43] According to historians, Dühring went farther than most in his fundamental stance to deny the right of Jewish existence. He is therefore regarded as the first proto-Nazi, a "sinister and embittered figure" whose obscure followers later became prominent members of the SS after his death in 1921. The year after Wagner's death, Dühring's convert and pupil,

Heinrich von Stein, visited Nietzsche and tried to coax him back into the Wagner circle. Nietzsche refused. He instead attempted to lead the young academician out of the "morass" that Dühring and Wagner had plunged him—to no avail.[44]

Dühring, whom historian Peter Gay describes as a "bombastic, shallow, and confused writer," was most famous for his general will or "equal wills" theory which was rooted in the notion of altruistic human nature.[45] On the one hand, morality is based on the notion of equal wills who abstain from hurting each other; this, Dühring says, is the ground of all ethics. On the other hand, history begins with force and consists of oppression and slavery; it does not begin in the economic system. History sees oppression and inequality; morality, freedom and equality. Contradictions between force (oppression) and will (freedom) must be resolved to reshape history, and this will come in the "socialitary system." Because the Jews manipulate the economy, they oppose the common good and must thus be eliminated.

In the second essay of the *Genealogy*, Nietzsche seeks to repudiate attempts such as Dühring's which seek the "origin of justice in the sphere of *ressentiment*."[46] Nietzsche argues against Dühring's view of altruistic human nature, stating that life operates essentially through injury, assault, and exploitation; it cannot be conceived without this character. He contends that "wherever justice is practiced and maintained one sees a stronger power seeking a means of putting an end to the senseless raging of *ressentiment* among the weaker powers that stand under it—by taking the object of *ressentiment* out of the hands of revenge."[47] He concludes that Dühring's principle of equal wills is a principle hostile to life, "an agent of the dissolution and destruction of man, an attempt to assassinate the future of man, a sign of weariness, a secret path to nothingness."[48]

Dühring adopts an oversimplified Rousseauian view that human nature is essentially good and that social institutions are corrupt. Once the revolution removes the corruptions, which Dühring regards as the Jews, natural humanity—or the German *Volk*—will once again emerge victorious, pure, and in harmony with the universal common good. Nietzsche partly inverts this position by contending that humans are by nature savage, cruel, and tyrannical, but in a pre-moral way.[49] Throughout his writings and notebooks, Nietzsche affirms the human beast and elevates the *Übermensch* (the free-spirit) as the product and goal of true humanity: "Man is beast and superbeast; the higher man is inhuman and superhuman: these belong together."[50]

Nietzsche writes that Dühring has a bad conscience (characterized by a cruel sense of guilt and punishment), whereas stronger and nobler types have a "better conscience" and a "freer eye." The philosopher reasons: "The active, aggressive, arrogant man is still a hundred steps closer to justice than the reactive man; for he has absolutely no need to take a false and prejudiced view of the object before him in the way the reactive man does and is bound to do."[51]

Nietzsche first became aware of Dühring during his Leipzig years. According to Bergmann, the *Übermensch* provided a collective goal for the sovereign individual Nietzsche sought. This was in contrast to the future society of higher beings envisioned by Dühring, who was also an individualist.[52] So that Nietzsche's *Übermensch* would not be confused with "the masses of barbarian force"; the philosopher locked his *Übermensch* in conflict with his ultimate antagonist, the subman of mass society, *the last man*.[53] In the 1880s, Nietzsche returned to Dühring's works to "comprehend the mysteries of the new terrorism."[54]

Nietzsche writes that there is a "perfect equation" between Christians and anarchists. Their aims and instincts are directed only toward destruction. In the *Antichrist*, Nietzsche states that the socialist rabble weakens the acceptance of labor by the workers, and teaches them to desire revenge against their betters: "The source of wrong is never unequal rights but the claim of equal rights. What is *bad*? But I have said this already; all that is born of weakness, of envy, of *revenge*. The anarchist and the Christian have the same origin."[55] In *Twilight* he repeats that the former seek others to blame for their suffering; Christians blame themselves as well. Both instincts are rooted in resentment: "The Christian and the anarchist are both decadents. . . . The 'last judgment' is the sweet comfort of revenge—the revolution, which the socialist worker also awaits, but conceived as a little farther off. The 'beyond'—why a beyond, if not as a means for besmirching *this* world?"[56] In the *Genealogy*, when combating Dühring, Nietzsche reiterates: "To the psychologist who would like to study *ressentiment* close up for once, I would say this plant blooms best today among anarchists and anti-Semites . . . where it has always bloomed." According to Nietzsche, it is no surprise to see a "repetition in such circles of attempts often made before—to sanctify revenge under the name of justice."[57] It is clear that although Nietzsche rants against several political groups, his specific targets are Christians and anarchists, the latter of which Dühring represents. Nietzsche associates both groups with *ressentiment*, bad conscience, and antisemitism. The philosopher's three essays in the *Genealogy*, which are preoccupied with Judeo-Christianity and resentment; systems of guilt and punishment in relation to Christ and the state-church; and with suffering in relation to sin, sublimation, and ascetic ideals, should thus be read in the context of the political climate in Germany, by which Nietzsche was deeply affected:

> For this is the rub: one needs guilty men. The underprivileged, the decadents of all kinds are in revolt on account of themselves and need victims so as not to quench their thirst for destruction by destroying

themselves. . . . To this end, they need an appearance of justice, i.e., a theory through which they can shift the responsibility for their existence . . . on to some sort of scapegoat. This scapegoat can be God . . . or the social order, or education and training, or the Jews, or the nobility, or those who have turned out well in any way. . . .[58]

The instinct of revenge and *ressentiment* appears here in both cases as a means of enduring. . . . Hatred of egoism, whether it be one's own (as with Christians) or another's (as with socialists), is thus revealed as a value judgment under the predominating influence of revenge; on the other hand, as an act of prudence for the self-preservation of the suffering by an enhancement of their feelings of cooperation and solidarity. . . . In both cases we are in the presence of invalids who feel better for crying out, for whom defamation is a relief.[59]

Broadly speaking, Christian antisemites sought to convert "stubborn" contemporary Jews to Christianity and usually distinguished noble Jews of the priestly-prophetic era from corrupt scribal/rabbinic Judaism (original Israel). Nietzsche's position is thus the exact opposite of theirs. Anti-Christian antisemites abhorred the whole of Judaism and disdained Christianity as well. Even so, Stöcker and Dühring's respective positions were not incompatible. Both groups viewed Jews as morally inferior despite their opposing views toward Christianity.[60]

For Nietzsche, the fundamental problem of morality did not reside in social institutions or in civilization per se, as it did for Rousseau, Stöcker, and Dühring. The crux of the problem was in the conception of morality itself.[61] Within the Christian scheme, those who accepted Christ would partake in the Kingdom of God; those who did not (Jews, the godless) were consigned to eternal damnation which would occur at the Last Judgment (I, 14ff.). In the case of Dühring's anarchic-socialism, atonement through the socialitary system was the ideal; the Jews were the obstacles needing to be removed (II, 11). Christian antisemites sought eternal vengeance—or what they regarded as the "triumph of justice"—in God; anti-Christian antisemites sought victory on earth in the coming revolution, which justified any means to reach its utopic end. Nietzsche views these groups as morally inferior to the Jews, whose "psychological and spiritual resources are extraordinary."[62]

Zarathustra says he is "weary of the words reward, retribution, punishment and revenge in justice."[63] In what was likely an allusion to Christians and anarchists, he describes how the "preachers of equality" speak to each other: "'We shall wreak vengeance and abuse on all whose equals we are not'—thus do the tarantulas-hearts vow. 'And will to equality shall henceforth be the name for virtue.'" The prophet says that it is not the heart that fires them, but revenge: "What was silent in the father speaks in the son; and often I found the son the unveiled secret of the father."[64]

As stated, throughout his writings, Nietzsche's views toward ancient Judaism in relation to Christianity are intricate. In the *Genealogy* alone, he makes the five following assertions: (1) ". . . all honor to the Old Testament! I find in it great human beings, a heroic landscape, and something of the very rarest quality in the world . . . ; what is more, I find a people."[64] (2) "It was the [priestly] Jews who . . . dared to invert the aristocratic value-equation and to hang on to this inversion with . . . the teeth of the most abysmal hatred. . . ."[66] (3) He speaks derogatorily of Jesus as the "seduction and bypath to . . . *Jewish* values and new ideals"[67] (4) He rants against the "anti-Semites, who today roll their eyes in a Christian-Aryan bourgeois manner,"[68] and (5) in praise of European Jewry, he writes: "one only has to compare . . . the Chinese or the Germans, for instance—with the Jews, to sense which is of the first and which of the fifth rank."[69]

Contrary to appearance, there is a consistent logic to Nietzsche's stance toward Judaism throughout this and other writings. Nietzsche praises the ancient Hebrews, primarily Joshua and Kings (pre-8th century period) and modern Jewry (1 and 5 above). He is ambivalent towards historical Judaism which encompasses the period from the prophets and priests of the Old Testament through Pharisaic-rabbinic Judaism (8th century onward), which Christian antisemites claimed as their ancestor (2 and 3). He despises Christian and anti-Christian antisemitism, as well as German nationalism (4 and 5). And he frequently refers to Jesus and Christians as Jews (3). A careful reading of his works is therefore required to discern which Jews Nietzsche is referring to. Nietzsche often sets up positive Jews (noble heroes and modern Jews) over against negative Jews (Christians, whom he regards as the contemporary heirs of the chandala morality of Judeo-Christianity).[70]

Nietzsche views original Israelites as a heroic people using power in a straightforward way, and regards the European Jews as remnants of a great race. Christianity is the ultimate continuation of slavish Judea, which has become the modern-day Christian religion of *ressentiment*, responsible for creating the religion of guilt, punishment, and revenge that attacks all those systems of power that are aristocratic and noble, especially the Roman Empire (*GM* I, 16). Just as ancient Judaism is the countermovement to original Israel, Christianity, in its inheritance of negative Judea, is the slave-revolt against original Israel. In modern Germany, Christianity is the revolt against the nobles, including Jews and philosophers. The Christian state, in its opposition to contemporary Jewry, is a form of the bad conscience; the will to self-hatred and self-maltreatment as manifest in its resentment of, and reaction against the Jews who were, in fact, related to the *Volk* and to German Christians:

What they hate is not their enemy, no! they hate 'injustice,' they hate
'godlessness'; what they believe in and hope for is not the hope of
revenge . . . but the victory of God, of the *just* God, over the godless;
what there is left for them to love on earth is not their brothers in
hatred but their 'brothers in love.' —Enough! Enough![71]

Nietzsche wants to overthrow the Lutheran state-church and all political forms
of socialism and democracy; he seeks to integrate elements of original Israel
and other ancient cultures to form his aristocratic master race that will rule
Europe.

In *Human*, Nietzsche's desire to create a model society contain the main
elements of Greece and Israel: "If Christianity did its utmost to orientalize the
West, it is Judaism above all that contributed mainly to occidentalize it again;
that is, it made Europe's history and task into a *continuation of the Greek.*"[72]

It is difficult to discern the racial, class, and cultural meaning of nobles and
slaves as presented throughout the *Genealogy* and Nietzsche's other works;
his terms vacillate between spiritual and social meanings, and his primary critique is as a psychologist of morals. However, by focusing on the racial element; cultural, class, and ethical characteristics of nobles and slaves will
become more apparent.

In the *Genealogy's* first essay, Nietzsche traces the development of Aryan
humanity from its ancient roots to modern Europe, locating the slave revolt in
morality as exemplified in the Judeo-Christian tradition. Here, Nietzsche first
mentions the notorious "blond beast," a term which Elisabeth and the Nazis
later would exploit. His anti-Judaic streak reaches its pinnacle in section seven
with his description of the *priestly* value system rooted in *ressentiment*.
Although Nietzsche's text was eventually misquoted by the Nazis to support
their war against European Jewry, it needs to be read in the total framework of
Nietzsche's views of the Jews. By attacking the priestly strand of Judea,
Nietzsche was deriding an element of Judaism that Christian antisemites and
Aryan racial supremacists, such as Elisabeth, claimed as a noble descendent.

When contrasting slave and noble morality in the first essay, Nietzsche
traces the origin of the word *good* to the self-identification of the warrior-aris-
tocracy. He describes this aristocracy as the Aryans, who were the conquerors
of inferior indigenous people of Europe, as well as elsewhere ("One may be
quite justified in continuing to fear the blond beast at the core of all noble
races").[73] In contrast, the inferior indigenous people who were conquered by this
race are characterized by coloring, a shortness of skull, "perhaps even in the
intellectual and social instincts."[74] The Greek noble class, the "rich," the "pos-
sessors" (which is the meaning of *arya*) applied to themselves the term good
(warriors) and also defined themselves in terms of character traits, regarding

themselves as the true (*esthlos*). Greece exemplifies the noble-aristocracy. Judea became the exemplar of the priestly-slave nation after its conquest by other empires, and Christianity inherits this work of Judea in constructing a morality of revenge against the conquerors. Originally, Nietzsche holds, good and bad were terms for different social classes.

From the root of priestly-Jewish hatred, "the profoundest and sublimist form of hatred," Israel attained the ultimate goal of its vengefulness through the bypath of the Redeemer, who was "the ostensible opponent and disintegrator of [original] Israel," and who served as a "dangerous bait" for the world to adopt the priestly-value system. This, Nietzsche contends, was part of the "secret black art of truly *grand* politics of revenge."[75]

Nietzsche's adoption of the myth that nobility originates with the Aryans, and that priestly Judea is the root of slave morality, appears to undermine his stern opposition to a Germanic-Aryan race specifically designed to exclude Semites. However, a close reading will show that Nietzsche is actually opposing the Germanic-Aryan myth that was prevalent during his time. References to the blond beast will not only shed light on his racial views, but also on his highly unpopular political position which upheld the Jews over-against Germans.

The term blond beast occurs five times throughout Nietzsche's writings (three times in the first section of the *Genealogy*, once in the second section, and once in *Twilight of the Idols*). When Nietzsche's first reference to the blond beast appears in the *Genealogy*, he states that the beast is at the bottom of all "noble races," including "the Roman, Arabian, Germanic, Japanese nobility, the Homeric heroes, and the Scandinavian Vikings" who "all shared the need to prowl about avidly in search of spoil and victory."[76] In the one instance where Nietzsche specifically refers to the beast as German, he quickly adds that the Aryan of antiquity is *distinct* from the Germans of today (". . . between the old Germanic tribes and us Germans there exists hardly a conceptual relationship, let alone one of blood").[77] It should be noted that Nietzsche also refers to the state as "some pack of blond beasts of prey." (Although he does not name Germany, he does not say it is not.)[78] In *Twilight*, the final reference to the blond beast is used in reference to the Teutons that the Christian Church 'tamed' in the early Middle Ages.[79]

Nietzsche's idealization of the past "Aryan race" of antiquity consists of many races and is thus distinct from Aryan racial mythologies in Germany that excluded Jews. Even so, Nietzsche's version of the master race nonetheless demeans "negroes" and others (Nietzsche states that "the descendants of every kind of European and non-European slavery, and especially of the entire pre-Aryan populace, represent the *regression* of mankind").[80] Hence, one could also infer that his ideal master race of the future, although European, including the Jews and other peoples, would also be based on a principle of slavery and exclusion.[81]

It appears that Nietzsche's principle of slavery would prevail in the higher caste of Europe that he envisions. Due to the circumstances surrounding his historical milieu, commentators often assume that because Nietzsche was not an antisemite, he was not a racist. However, it needs to be stated that racism need not necessarily be antisemitic. Even so, Nietzsche's ideal master race, in which he describes prehistoric physical characteristics such as skull size, was not principally designed to denigrate one race or another. It was rather constructed to rebut contemporary Aryan racial theorists, such as Dühring, who writes: "The Jewish skull is no thinker's skull—all the time the Lord God and business affairs have claimed all the space in it."[82]

Nietzsche expounds his views on the Aryan race in *Twilight*. Although he deems racial breeding in the law of Manu as superior to Christian taming, he nonetheless regards both as immoral and inadequate for creating civilized moralities in modern culture. Nietzsche clearly condemns the Germanic-Aryan race with his remark that "Aryan humanity and the concept of 'pure blood' is the opposite of a harmless concept." However, at the end of the passage he praises Aryanism when stating that Christianity is the "revaluation of all Aryan values . . . the *anti-Aryan* religion *par excellence*."[83] This has traditionally confused interpreters who rightly assume that Nietzsche abhorred both Christianity *and* the Germanic-Aryan race. However, the contradiction is only apparent. As Golomb notes, in this passage Nietzsche is stating that Christianity is the countermovement to the positive morality of original Israel, as is the Judaism of the diaspora from which Christianity arose. Nietzsche writes: "Christianity, sprung from Jewish roots and comprehensible only as a growth on this soil, represents the counter-movement to any morality of breeding, of race, of privilege: it is the *anti-Aryan* religion par excellence." By upholding his Aryan ideal to include the Jews and other peoples, Nietzsche is opposing Aryan racial theories that affirmed Aryan-Christian-Germans over against contemporary Jewry and original Israel, such as those promoted by Wagner, Elisabeth, Louis Jacolliot and Ernst Renan. Jacolliot, supported by the apocryphal "laws of Manu" which he claims to have discovered, wrote that Moses derived from Manu and Jesus from Zeus. He ascribed Biblical origins to Asia, "proved" that Jesus Christ came to regenerate the new world, and regarded the Old Testament as a collection of superstitions. Jacolliot, whom Nietzsche read just prior to *Twilight*, regarded the Jews as a degraded and stupid people, and Moses as a "fanatical slave charitably educated at the court of Pharaohs."[84] Nietzsche overturns Jacolliot's position. He ascribes an "affirmative" Aryan religion to Manu and an affirmative Semitic religion to the law-book of Mohammed and to the older parts of the Old Testament. He ascribes the "negative" Semitic religion to the priestly-caste and the New Testament, and the negative Aryan religion to Buddhism.[85] Analogously, whereas the antisemitic Renan demeaned original Israel and contemporary Jewry, praising the priestly-prophetic element of Judea, Nietzsche inverts that position. Nietzsche upholds original Israel and contemporary Jewry, ascribing *ressentiment* to Judeo-Christianity and to modern-day antisemitism.

In the *Genealogy's* third essay, Nietzsche refers to Renan in connection with Dühring and just prior to stating that he does not like the "anti-Semites, who today roll their eyes in a Christian-Aryan bourgeois manner." According to historians, Renan was the chief scientific sponsor of the Aryan myth in France who later became an almost official ideologist of the Third Reich.[86] Renan also appears in the *Antichrist* as Nietzsche's chief theological opponent, which will be addressed in the following chapter.

In *The Aryan Myth*, Poliakov writes that Nietzsche's thought, including terms such as the blond beast and the master race, was exploited in fascist and racist propaganda. Yet, Poliakov states that the disconcerting aspect of Nietzsche was that he "seemed to assign the first place to the Jews" and "wished his German contemporaries the strongest possible injection of Jewish blood." Poliakov's assertion is presumably based on Nietzsche's remark that the Jews were the purest race: "Indeed," the historian writes, "some of the veteran anti-Semites were not in the least deceived. Eugen Dühring insinuated that Nietzsche was a Jew, and Theodor Fritsch warned youthful students against the 'insolent Pole.'" Poliakov wisely ends the brief discussion: "But one could go on forever about Nietzsche."[87]

Although Poliakov's observation that Nietzsche was an advocate for contemporary Jews is well taken, he misses the core of Nietzsche's philosophy which assigned to the Jews a privileged status not on a biological basis, but on the basis of psychology and history. As Golomb demonstrates, the Jews' capacity to transform "the long school of their suffering" into creativity, not resentment, were the primary characteristics Nietzsche admired about the Jewish people.[88]

In a lengthy aphorism in *Daybreak*, Nietzsche describes the Jews as those who take revenge against their oppressors; however, he does not condemn them. This is because their revenge does not "go too far," it is born out of self-respect and spiritual strength, not weakness (*ressentiment*). Nietzsche writes that Israel, because they have inherited a good deal of spiritual and bodily demeanor, will transform its revenge into an "eternal blessing for Europe." He continues to say that the Jews are justifiably heading toward mastery of Europe; that this process will not consist of an act of conquest or violence; and that they will be sufficiently noble to rule. Those they dominate will not be ashamed to have them as their masters: "Then there will again arrive that seventh day on which the ancient Jewish God may *rejoice* in himself, his creation and his chosen people—and let us all, all of us, rejoice with him!"[89]

As evidenced in the third essay, the dialectic of suffering is central to Nietzsche's thought; his personal and philosophical quest is to find a way to affirm suffering, without glorifying, denying, or resenting it. Suffering is the origin of resentment as well as its product, which becomes manifest in reactions that are rooted in the envy of all that is noble, healthy, and powerful ("He has conceived 'the Evil One,' and this in fact is his basic concept, from which he then evolves . . . a 'good one'—himself!"). Conversely, "profound suffering" is also the root of nobility, separating higher human beings from the lower. Through the discipline of "great suffering," Nietzsche writes, creator and creature are united: "in man there is material, fragment, excess, clay, dirt, nonsense, chaos; but in man there is also creator, formgiver, hammer hardness, spectator, divinity, and seventh day: do you understand this contrast?"[90] On the one hand, Nietzsche views his political opponents as those who seek comfortableness; they want to abolish suffering and demonstrate shared *pity* for the "creature in man." On the other hand, they perpetuate suffering by flailing the creators, whom Nietzsche typically regards as the "genuine philosophers," among which he numbers contemporary Jews. In contrast to the slaves of *ressentiment*, nobles revere the instinctual beast, create out of their suffering, and are "incapable of taking their enemies, accidents, or misdeeds seriously for very long": "Here alone genuine 'love of one's enemies' is possible—supposing it to be possible at all on earth!"[91] As Golomb shows in "Nietzsche's Judaism of Power," it is because of the Jews' long-suffering, and hence their superior ability to create, that Nietzsche bestows upon them positive power (*Macht*), as opposed to pure brute political force (*Kraft*), and esteems them as the strongest, toughest, and purest race residing in Europe.[92] The Jews are esteemed by Nietzsche because of their capacity to sublimate political force (*Kraft*) with spiritual power (*Macht*), the latter of which the Germans lack:

> Germany today is connected with the undeniable and palpable stagnation of the German spirit; and the cause of that I seek in a too exclusive diet of newspapers, politics, beer, and Wagnerian music, together with the presuppositions of such a diet; first, national constriction and vanity, the strong but narrow principle *"Deutschland, Deutschland über alles,"* and then the *paralysis agitans* of 'modern ideas.'[93]

Nietzsche's views of nobles and slaves as presented in the *Genealogy* can be summarized as follows. He thinks of there as having been an original prehistoric nobility that had innate characteristics; vitality, guilt-free use of power and domination. He calls them Aryans and the Blond Beast; for Nietzsche they

seem to be the original nobles of all major ancient cultures who had a unique
"spirit." In contrast, the dark-headed peoples are natural slaves subjugated by
the nobles, and who have no capacity to rule but only to serve. With the emergence of the prehistoric human being into political society, a judicial system of
punishment and reward arose with the bad conscience, wherein natural instincts
were internalized, viewed as guilty, and the corresponding notion of a "guilty
agent" arose. This system was projected into the theological realm wherein
God became the Judge to whom the guilty ones were indebted, and for whom
Christ became the payment. Christ, however, does not relieve guilt, for Christianity continues its condemnation of natural instincts, and finds non-Christians (pagans, Jews) guilty and deserving of punishment. He deems the Greek
gods as nobler. In the first essay, Nietzsche thus traces a noble morality from
Aryan humanity to Greece and then to Rome. The slave morality goes from
slaves to priestly Judea and then to Judeo-Christianity, the current European
morality of *ressentiment*.

Nietzsche seems to want a society that is beyond the law and beyond the
Christian nation, wherein noble individuals reign sovereign in matters of justice,
which is rooted not in punishment but in mercy. The sovereign individual
emerges as the "ripest fruit" in history who is the "master of a free will." The
emancipated individual has the capacity to make promises and to forget, is
aware of the privilege of responsibility, and has power over oneself and one's
fate. The master is "liberated from morality of custom, autonomous and
supramoral" [beyond conventional morality]. They possess the "dominating
instinct" which is called "conscience."[94]

In the Nietzschean society, the beast of human nature is not to be repressed
or vengefully projected onto external objects (such as God or nobles) but self-
actualized in a process of sublimation. This process transforms suffering into
creativity, not resentment, fusing the Nietzschean psychological principles of
the Apollonian and the Dionysian. Analogously, Nietzsche seeks an aristocratic society based on subliminal principles of *Kraft* and *Macht*.

The ancient Hebrews, who initially had an aristocratic national life like the
ancient Aryans, were subjugated and used its intelligence and energy forged in
suffering to construct a religion of revenge which revolted against the noble
imperial ruling class (Rome). Christianity carries this revenge religion to a new
generalized stage, taking it out of the national context of Jewish rebellion and
organizing the subjugated slaves of the empire. In this form Christianity com-
municated the religion of *ressentiment* to all Europe, conquering Rome and
subverting the original nobility. At bottom, Nietzsche's distinction between
slaves and nobles does not appear to be contingent upon race or nationality.
However, his opposition to feminism strongly suggests that women, at this stage
in his writings, are to be subjugated in a culture which is dominated by males.[95]

Historically, the myth of the Germanic-Aryan race was formed and promoted by racial theorists such as Gobineau, Wagner, and Renan well before the *Genealogy* appeared. Nietzsche was entering the political dialogue of his time, presenting an alternative version of the Aryan master race; a version that would have inflamed anti-Jewish racists. In the text, Nietzsche severs the Germanic bloodline *from* Aryan humanity (". . . between the old Germanic tribes and us Germans there exists hardly a conceptual relationship, let alone one of blood"), proclaims mixed races instead (the blond beast is at the bottom of all "noble races," including "the Roman, Arabian, Germanic, Japanese nobility, the Homeric heroes, and the Scandinavian Vikings"),[96] and exalts the Jews over the Germans ("one only has to compare similarly gifted nations—the Chinese or the Germans, for instance—with the Jews, to sense which is of the first and which of the fifth rank").[97] His praise of the Jews, however, was not based on blood, but on their strong capacity to create in the midst of suffering. Although decades later the Nazis uplifted terms like the "blond beast" to create the illusion that Nietzsche supported Aryan racial supremacy—and even that they derived the concept from *him*—Nietzsche was, in fact, opposing the actual precursors of the Third Reich, which Nazi leaders were well aware. Initially, Nietzsche used the term "blond beast" when referring to the state and the Christian church of the Middle Ages.

In the preface to the *Genealogy*, Nietzsche speaks of the moral past of humankind, stating that cheerfulness will come "on the day when we can say with all our hearts, 'Onwards! our old morality too is part *of the comedy!*'" "Then," he continues, "we shall have discovered a new complication and possibility for the Dionysian drama of the destiny of the Soul."[98] By the middle of the third essay, Nietzsche is ranting mercilessly against the whole of modern Germany, including Dühring, Renan, and Christianity. He crucifies the "worms of vengefulness and rancor" that swarm on the soil of modern Europe, describing antisemites as "moral masturbators," "hangmen," and as those who represent the "will to power of the weakest": "They are all men of *ressentiment*, physiologically unfortunate and worm-eaten . . . inexhaustible and insatiable in outbursts against the fortunate and happy."[99]

In 1887, Nietzsche's works were attacked in the *Antisemitische Correspondenz* (an antisemitic newsletter), depicted as "eccentric," "pathological," and "psychiatric."[100] The philosopher welcomed the small, but growing number of negative reviews of his last two works (*BGE* and *GM*), for the public disapproval appeared to him a sign that he was becoming somewhat of an "influence" in Germany: "You can guess that [Dr. Förster] and I have to exert ourselves to the uttermost to avoid treating each other openly as enemies. . . . The anti-Semitic pamphlets shower down wildly upon me (which pleases me a hundred times more than their earlier restraint)."[101] Even so, Zarathustra's fear of articulation—as expressed in his encounter with the "foaming fool at the city gate"—appears justified. Although his opponents assailed his ideas; toward the end of the year, they retaliated by assimilating his unconventional rhetoric to support their own. In an impassioned letter to his sister on Christmas 1887, Nietzsche expressed frustration at not being able to do anything about it: "That in every Anti-Semitic Correspondence sheet the name Zarathustra is used has already made me almost sick several times."[102] The ironic twist is exemplified in a suppressed letter written at that time in which Nietzsche complained: "Nothing stands more in the way of my influence than for the name Nietzsche to be associated with such anti-Semites as E. Dühring."[103] According to Theodor Lessing, a controversial German-Jewish philosopher who was a Nietzschean writing in the early 1920s, Zarathustra's "foaming fool" is Dühring.[104]

The Genealogy's story of the human's emergence into society as a political animal is analogous to Nietzsche's own story. The philosopher's preoccupation with, and opposition to antisemitism, which separated him from Wagner years before and now served to alienate him from Elisabeth and Förster, profoundly shaped his emergence as a national heretic in the latter half of the 1880s: "Thus spoke Zarathustra and laughed for the second time. But then he recalled his friends whom he had left; and . . . soon it happened that he who had laughed wept; from wrath and longing Zarathustra wept bitterly."[105]

Nietzsche, although widely ignored and ill-received by antisemites, did have a handful of loyal readers with whom he corresponded in his last productive years. These included the French historian Hippolyte Taine, a liberal who wrote extensively about the French Revolution; and Georg Brandes, a Danish Jew who advocated the cause of Jewish assimilation and later disputed the merits of Zionism with Theodor Herzl.[106] Brandes, an eminent Scandinavian critic of his time and an influential teacher at the University of Copenhagen, became a champion of Nietzsche's political and philosophical views toward the end of 1887. With Brandes' support Nietzsche felt confident that antisemites would know exactly where his thought was "centered":[107] "In Germany there's much complaining about my eccentricities," Nietzsche remarked. "Likewise, I now regard my having been a Wagnerian as eccentric. It was a highly dangerous experiment; now that I know it didn't ruin me, I also know what significance it had for me—it was the most severe test of my character."[108] Brandes first lectures on Nietzsche began in Copenhagen in 1888, at which time Nietzsche's name began to spread quickly. Although Nietzsche knew of, and was pleased about, the lectures, by the time his fame started to become a reality, he was unaware of his surroundings.

Before turning to the following chapter, which will compare the Genealogy with the Antichrist, the main points are as follows: (1) Nietzsche opposes Christian and anti-Christian antisemitism. He regards modern Jews as people with

positive qualities that need to be integrated into European society. (2) He despises certain elements of the Jewish religion, particularly the notions of election and retributive justice that he believes Christianity (and the Germanic *Volk*) has inherited and has subsequently applied against modern Jewry. (3) He views Christians and anarchists as those who exemplify resentment and the bad conscience, polemicizing against the egalitarianism and antisemitism common to both. Overall, the *Genealogy* conveys Nietzsche's persistent campaign against utilitarianism, the "democratic prejudice" which upheld "the nonsense of the greatest number" fostered by "socialist dolts" and "flatheads," such as Spencer, Dühring, and Renan.[109] Nietzsche locates resentment as originating within the Judeo-Christian tradition, the origin of bad conscience in the repression of instincts and in the development of the State. He despises democracy, socialism, and feminism. He hates the English, and is ambivalent towards the French, Poles, and Italians. He abhors Christianity, German nationalism, and the notion of a pure Germanic-Aryan race, and wants to create a new caste that will rule Europe, of which contemporary Jews will partake. It is in this historical and personal context that the *Antichrist* should be read.[110]

6

Antichrist: The Justice of Yahweh versus the Judgment of Christ

Dear friend, yesterday, your letter in hand, I took my customary afternoon walk in the outskirts of Turin. Purest October light everywhere. . . . Everything comes easy now, everything I do thrives. That the first volume of the *Revaluation of all Values* is finished, ready for printing—I tell you this with a feeling I can't put into words. There'll be four books, appearing separately. This time, old artilleryman that I am, I'm moving in my big guns. I fear I'll be blasting the history of mankind into two halves. . . . I'm moving against the Germans on all fronts; you'll have no cause to complain about "ambiguity." This irresponsible race, which has on its conscience all of our civilization's great disasters, and which at every decisive moment of history had 'something else in mind'— . . . today has in mind "The Reich" . . . there has never been a more crucial moment in history—*but who'd be expected to know that?* . . . Toward me there is still no animosity at all. They simply don't hear anything I say, so they're neither "for" nor "against" me.[1]

The year 1888 was the last of Nietzsche's intellectual life, and also the most productive. It began with *The Case of Wagner* and ended with *Nietzsche Contra Wagner*, a compilation of passages Nietzsche arranged from previous works only days before his mental collapse. Between these two works, Nietzsche quickly wrote *Twilight*, *The Antichrist*, and *Ecce Homo*. The latter, although perceptive in many respects, displays the rapid breakdown of inhibitions that characterize that year's writings: "For when truth enters into a fight with the lies of millennia, we shall have upheavals, a convulsion of earthquakes . . . the like of which have never yet been seen on earth. It is only beginning with me that the earth knows *great politics*."[2]

The *Antichrist* is the first essay of the four part *Revaluation* Nietzsche anticipated; it was the only essay of the series he completed before his mental collapse. The work was not published until 1895 because Elisabeth feared it would be confiscated for blasphemy.

The *Genealogy* and the *Antichrist* should be viewed as a continuum. After comparing the two works, I will then place the *Antichrist* in its nineteenth-century theological context, and in dialogue with Ernst Renan, Nietzsche's main theological opponent.

Viewed as a whole, the structure of the *Genealogy* is a treatise on the "genealogy of morals" in a somewhat literal sense. The first essay, from the original Aryan race to Napoleon, places the slave revolt and the Judeo-Christian tradition at the center. The second goes from the origin of bad conscience and its expression in the state to the atonement (Christianity) and ends with the announcement that the Antichrist and antinihilist must triumph over God and nothingness. And the third begins with a discussion of Nietzsche's former heroes Wagner and Schopenhauer, and ends with the claim that Christian morality and the ascetic ideal must be overcome: "And, to repeat in conclusion what I said at the beginning; man would rather will *nothingness* than *not* will."[3]

In the *Antichrist*, the problem posed at the outset is "not what shall *succeed* [emphasis mine] mankind in the sequence of living beings," but what type shall be bred and willed for being "higher in value, worthier of life, more certain of a future," in contrast to the Christian.[4]

The *Genealogy's* first essay is not only a critique of culture and an historical exposition in the literal sense; it seeks to create Nietzsche's "new caste which will rule Europe." Nietzsche strives to create a race which will resurrect the qualities of nobility that have been repressed by the slave morality. And he constructs his essay to accomplish this task.

If Nietzsche desired to create a noble race including his Old Testament heroes, the Greeks, the Romans, and European Jews, the opposition he draws in the *Genealogy* between Judaism and Greece would seem contradictory. But this opposition is based on his distinction between ancient noble heroes and conquered Judea that becomes the antithesis of Greece and Rome. Sections 7, 9, and 16 are decisive for Nietzsche's cultural agenda.

In section 7, in contrast to the Greek barbaric nobles, Nietzsche attributes the slave revolt in morality to the priestly caste that reaches its fruition within Christianity: "That with the Jews there begins *the slave revolt in morality*: that revolt which has a history of two thousand years behind it and which we no longer see because it—has been victorious."[5] The moral revolt which "has two thousand years behind it" is an allusion to the Christian religion; the "victorious" morality of modern-day Germany that Nietzsche abhors is the priestly morality of Judea that is continued in Christianity. The point here is simply that

Nietzsche is describing Christianity's inheritance of priestly Judea, as distinct from original Israel. And he expounds this point in section nine.

After describing the slave revolt (7) and stating that the Judeo-Christian morality of modern Germany has triumphed over the masters, "everything is becoming Judaized, Christianized, and mob-ized (what do the words matter!," sec. 9), Nietzsche does not use the term "Israel" or "Jews" again in the essay unless he is referring specifically to Christians. There is one exception to this (sec. 16), which I will address shortly. The language in the first essay borders on wrath, particularly when he uses the word Jew: "everywhere that man has become tame or desires to become tame: *three Jews*, as is known, and *one* Jewess (Jesus of Nazareth, the fisherman Peter, the rug weaver Paul . . . Mary)."[6] However, he adopts the rhetoric not to fuel secular or Christian anti-semites, who were his enemies. He is attempting to annoy Christians who denied their Jewishness, as well as create conflict between anarchists and Christians over the sole ingredient which separated them: Christianity's relation-ship to Judaism. By attacking priestly-prophetic Judaism, Nietzsche is deni-grating that strand of Judea that Christian antisemites claimed as their ancestor, which allegedly professed the coming Messiah.

In section nine, Nietzsche continues to say that the mob has won and that if "this has happened through the Jews, very well!":

The masters have been disposed of; the morality of the common man has won. One may conceive of this victory as at the same time a blood-poisoning (it has mixed the races [Judaism and Christianity] together)—I shan't contradict; but this intoxication has undoubtedly been *successful*.

Nietzsche continues to describe how the "poison" has spread throughout the "entire body of mankind," particularly Europe. One can imagine Nietzsche's contention that Jewish and Christian blood was "mixed" would have enraged racial theorists, both those who desired the Christian elements (such as Elisa-beth and Förster), and those who did not, but nonetheless exalted the Ger-manic *Volk* as a chosen nation (such as Dühring).[7]

Nietzsche's final reference to the Jews as distinct from Judeo-Christianity occurs in section 16. After stating that the negative Jews were the priestly nation par excellence, in an obvious reference to modern Jews he adds: "one only has to compare similarly gifted nations—the Chinese or the Germans, for instance—with the Jews, to sense which is of the first and which of the fifth rank."[8] Thus, from section six onward, Nietzsche chronicles the slavish priestly morality, the birth of (Judeo)-Christianity out of the "spirit of revenge," and ele-vates the Jews over the Germans.

Nietzsche employs the symbol of the cross to transfer priestly Judea into the Christian religion, which marks the demise of the great age in the history of Israel.[9] This consequently frees original Israel from Judeo-Christianity, which makes it possible for the former to be praised as a natural and heroic culture, like the Homeric Greeks.

In section 8 the priestly caste attains the ultimate goal of its vengefulness through the bypath of the Redeemer, who is the "ostensible opponent and disintegrator of [original] Israel." Whereas originally the conflict of noble and slave morality is between Greece and priestly Judea (5,7); at the end of the essay the symbol of this struggle "inscribed in letters across all human history" is Rome and Judeo-Christianity (16): "How on the other hand, did the Jews feel about Rome? A thousand signs tell us; but it suffices to recall the Apocalypse of John, the most wanton of all literary outbursts that vengefulness has on its conscience." And at the conclusion of the *Antichrist*, the anarchists and Christians, who share the same origin (*ressentiment*), are viewed in opposition to Rome.[10] Nietzsche clearly disdains Christianity, but he has a dialectical view of the Greeks, Jews, Romans, and Germans. However, the bipolar opposites of slave and noble moralities that he constructs in the first essay of the *Genealogy* and continues in the *Antichrist* are as follows: Aryans/slaves, Greece/Judea, Rome/Christianity, Rome/Christians-anarchists. Nietzsche is constructing hierarchies of slave-revolts enroute to modern Germany. His admiration for the finest elements of ancient Aryan, Greek and Roman cultures, including its political structures, cultural goals, and character traits, are set in contrast to the slavish characteristics of decadent Hellenism, priestly Judea, and Christianity. Anarchists and Christians, whom Nietzsche explicitly associates with modern-day antisemitism and *ressentiment*, are viewed as major obstacles to the new European aristocracy he seeks to create. The fourth paradigm should read: Nietzsche's European aristocracy/Christians-anarchists. The slavish enemies of Rome and Nietzsche who have "won for the present" (Judeo-Christianity and antisemitism), must thus be overcome.

In the *Genealogy*, Nietzsche has separated the priestly strand of Judaism from original Israel through the Redeemer (Judeo-Christianity becomes the religion of *ressentiment*). In the *Antichrist*, Nietzsche presents Jesus who was free from "any feeling of *ressentiment*" and totally severs him from the Judeo-Christian tradition: "There was only *one* Christian, and he died on the cross."[11] In partial agreement with liberal Christians that practice, not dogma, was the measure of Christian faith, and against the traditional view that belief in Jesus Christ was the only way to salvation as foretold by the Hebrew prophets, Nietzsche argues: "To reduce being a Christian to a matter of considering something true, to a mere phenomenon of consciousness, is to negate Christianism."[12] He then clinches his argument against both conservatives and liberals by asserting that even if judged by the standards of praxis, Jesus nonetheless stands alone as the *only* Christian: "*In fact, there have been no Christians at all. The 'Christian,' that which for the last two thousand years has been called a Christian, is merely a psychological self-misunderstanding.*"[13] With that declaration, the severance between the Redeemer and the entire Christian tradition is consummated.

Within Nietzsche's scheme, Jesus stands in contrast to both poles of the Rome/Judea paradigm. In the *Genealogy* Jesus appears in a negative role as the continuation of negative Judea. In the *Antichrist*, Jesus is the ultimate denouement of the slave revolt who dissolves the whole system of sin and judgment. Because Christianity rejects Jesus and his message against *ressentiment*, it reverts to the slavish type: "This 'bringer of glad tidings' died as he had lived, as he had taught—*not* to 'redeem men' but to show how one must live. . . . He does not resist . . . he suffers, he loves *with* those, *in* those, who do him evil. *Not* to resist, *not* to be angry, *not* to hold responsible—but to resist not even the evil one—to *love* him."[14] According to Nietzsche, the early community did not understand the "exemplary character of this kind of death, the freedom, the superiority over any feeling of *ressentiment*: a token of how little they understood him altogether!"[15] Elsewhere, Nietzsche claims only "we spirits who have *become free* have the presuppositions for understanding something that nineteen centuries have misunderstood":[16]

> *God on the cross*—are the horrible secret thoughts behind this symbol not understood yet? All that suffers, all that is nailed to the cross, is *divine*. All of us are nailed to the cross, consequently *we* are divine. . . . Christianity was a victory, a nobler outlook perished of it— Christianity has been the greatest misfortune of mankind so far.[17]

Nietzsche's most often quoted phrase from the *Antichrist* that the only Christian "died on the cross" was not merely a rhetorical embellishment; it was a literal utterance that has a paradoxical relation to his view of nobles who were free from *ressentiment* and who did not first create evil enemies that they might affirm themselves.[18] Jesus fulfills the former requirement, but in his passive resistance does not represent heroic self-affirmation. It is Paul, "the greatest of all apostles of vengeance" who is "the first Christian" that takes resentment, the doctrine of the Last Judgment, and personal immortality into Christianity—not Jesus:[19] "In a formula: *deus, qualem Paulus creavit, dei negatio*" [God, as Paul created him, is the negation of God].[20] Paul is the means to "priestly tyranny and herd formation";[21] Jesus is a *Jew* who is free from *ressentiment* and the bad conscience:

In the whole psychology of the 'evangel' the concept of guilt and punishment is lacking. . . . 'Sin'—any distance separating God and man—is abolished: *precisely this is the 'glad tidings'*. . . .

It is not a 'faith' that distinguishes the Christian: the Christian *acts*, he is distinguished by acting *differently*: by not resisting, either in words or in his heart, those who treat him ill; by making no distinction between foreigner and native, between Jew and not-Jew. . . .

The life of the Redeemer was nothing other than *this* practice—nor was his death anything else. . . . This alone is the psychological reality of 'redemption.' A new way of life, *not* a new faith.[22]

Both the *Genealogy* and the *Antichrist* seek the origins of Christianity and both works give varying accounts. In the former, when chronicling the slave revolt of Judeo-Christianity, the Redeemer appears in a purely negative role, as the "seduction to Jewish values and new ideals" who serves as the bypath for slave morality which is characterized by vengeance, the Last Judgment, and the concept of election.[23] In the *Antichrist*, Nietzsche continues to condemn the church, personal immortality, and the Last Judgment as systems of torture, but attributes these teachings to Paul.[24] Jesus is a free spirit, the "bringer of glad tidings," an exemplar who was free from resentment and whose message was that the kingdom of God was a state of the heart and not a judgment over Christ's enemies: *ruling* Jewry.[25] Jesus also represents the continuation of the slavish Jewish instinct as a "holy anarchist" who summoned outcasts and sinners, the chandalas within Judaism, to oppose all law, hierarchy, and order, to oppose the "saints of Israel."[26] Jesus was a political criminal in an absurdly unpolitical community, and this is what brought him to the cross: "He died for *his* guilt. All evidence is lacking, however often it has been claimed, that he died for the guilt of others."[27] In short, Nietzsche is portraying Jesus as a counter-ideal to Judeo-Christianity, but also as a counter-ideal to all realism and nobility based on life-affirming power and self-affirmation, as represented by original Israel, Greece, and Rome.

For Nietzsche, although the cross symbolizes freedom from *ressentiment*, Dionysian suffering, not Jesus, represents a total affirmation of life through the negation of otherworldly ascetic ideals. In the *Nachlass*, Nietzsche writes:

Dionysus versus the 'Crucified'; there you have the anti-thesis. It is *not* a difference in regard to their martyrdom—it is a difference in the meaning of it. Life itself, its eternal fruitfulness and recurrence, creates torment, destruction, the will to annihilation. In the other case, suffering—the 'Crucified as the innocent one'—counts as an objection to this life, as a formula for its condemnation. One will see that the problem is that of the meaning of suffering; whether a Christian meaning or a tragic meaning.[28]

The *Genealogy* is concerned with the slave revolt which has 2,700 years behind it. The *Antichrist* elevates Jesus as a type against Judeo-Christian *ressentiment*, but who is also the antithesis of heroic nobility, which is characterized by strength and power, as exemplified by original Israel and the ancient Greeks. The *Genealogy* demeans the ostensible Redeemer for continuing the slave revolt, the *Antichrist* shows him as the leader of the rabble who continues the revolt, but also as one who opposes revenge. Paul is the path to the Last Judgment, which is vengeful, futuristic, and exclusive; Jesus symbolizes the Kingdom of God, which is spiritual, present, and universal: "The kingdom of God is nothing that one expects; it has no yesterday and no day after tomorrow, it will not come in 'a thousand years'—it is an experience of the heart; it is everywhere, it is nowhere."[29] Thus, although Jesus is distinct from decadent Judeo-Christianity, he by no means aspires to the status of Godhead as exemplified by the gods of Greece or ancient Yahweh.

Nietzsche states that Jesus taught that it was everyone's equal right to be a child of God. The disciples, or the "unhinged souls," could not endure this conception of universal equality; therefore, they elevated Jesus extravagantly "to sever him from themselves." This, Nietzsche says, was precisely the way the post-exilic Jews, out of revenge against their enemies—severed God from themselves and elevated Him. Nietzsche, who is making a counter-argument to the concept of chosenness, sighs, "the one God and the one Son of God—both products of *ressentiment*."[30] Nietzsche writes:

> As soon as the cleft between the Jews and the Jewish Christians opened, no choice whatever remained to the latter but to apply *against* the Jews themselves the same procedures of self-preservation that the Jewish instinct recommended, whereas hitherto the Jews had applied them only against everything *non*-Jewish. The Christian is merely a Jew of 'more liberal' persuasion.[31]

Although this rude passage might give the impression that Nietzsche was demeaning fellow Jews; a closer look reveals that it would have irritated Christian antisemites, such as Elisabeth, who regarded herself as one of God's chosen people. She claimed the priestly-prophetic strand of Judaism for professing the Christ whom she accepted, while degrading original Israel and contemporary Jews for rejecting him. Nietzsche observes: "Judge not, they say, but . . . consign to hell everything that stands in their way."[32]

Just as the *Genealogy's* first essay is continued in the *Antichrist*; the second essay, "Guilt, Bad Conscience, and the Like," is expounded theologically. Whereas the *Genealogy* describes the denaturing of natural human instincts in relation to the judicial system, the state, and the atonement; the *Antichrist* chronicles the denaturing of Yahweh in relation to justice, revenge, and modern day Christianity, in its political and moral aspects.

According to Nietzsche, the denaturing of Yahweh, who was originally a "God of justice" and power signifying the "self-affirmation" and "self-confidence" of a people, began with the Hebrew prophets, particularly Isaiah. Whereas Israel during the time of kings stood in a natural relationship to all things and Yahweh "was the expression of a consciousness of power, of joy in oneself, of hope for oneself," the prophets began interpreting natural causality in terms of reward and punishment.[33] With this transposition, morality was no longer connected to the instincts and conditions necessary for the preservation and enhancement of life, it became the antithesis of life itself. With the notions of punishment and reward ascribed onto a newly created God of Judgment, the simplistic psychological principle of obedience and disobedience to the will of God made revelation a necessity ("the will of God must be *known*"). The concept of sin became indispensable in the hands of vengeful priests, who used this as a tool of power, oppression, and control within society. All natural occurrences, such as birth, marriage, death, and sickness were "denatured" in order to make the priest indispensable. The severed natural realm, which was formerly intertwined with the conception of Yahweh, first had to be consecrated by the priest in order to be rendered holy.[34] It was out of this utterly *false* soil, Nietzsche writes, that Christianity grew up.[35]

Here, the *God of power* is associated with original Israel: "Yahweh is the God of Israel and therefore the god of justice; the logic of every people that is in power and has a good conscience."[36] The *God of Judgment* is associated with Judea and then Christianity (the "bad conscience"), beginning with Isaiah. And the *God of ressentiment* is regarded as the "good" God, represented by the sweet and sentimental Jesus, on the one hand, and the vengeful God of Isaiah-Paul, on the other. Fusing a god of bad conscience with a meek Savior results in—to borrow a metaphor—the notion of a "wrathful Lamb," which Nietzsche abhors (Rev. 5vv.). The concept of immortality, Nietzsche insists, has so far been the greatest, and most malignant attempt to assassinate *noble* humanity: "The *ressentiment* of the masses forged its chief weapon against *us*, against all that is noble, gay, high-minded on earth. . . . And let us not underestimate the calamity which crept out of Christianity into politics."[37]

Nietzsche incessantly explores how theological concepts, political societies, and ethics are connected to human instincts. The philosopher traces the genealogy of gods from the Yahweh of Power (original Israel) to God as Judge (historical Judaism) to the Christian God, who is "the *antinatural* castration of a god . . . a god of the good alone."[38] He then relates the Christian god to the political milieu of modern Europe, which he disdains.

Nietzsche writes that the Christian god is the "god of great numbers," the cosmopolitan god for private lives, the "democrat among the gods," the god of the weak, poor, and sick par excellence. In contrast to ancient Yahweh who represented the strength of a people, signifying wrath, revenge, envy, scorn, and power, the Christian god is pale, weak and decadent, a "sheet anchor for the drowning." God has become a declaration against life and against nature. Through ascetic ideals such as the beyond and redemption, God has become "a staff for the weary," the "deification of nothingness," the "deity of decadence," the will to nothingness pronounced holy: "Almost two thousand years—" Nietzsche exclaims, "and not a single new god!"[39]

Nietzsche's preference for Yahweh to the Christian God is a theological rendition of his political stance, which endorsed original Israel and contemporary Jewry over against that of the Christian nation. His historical account of the denaturing of Israel, as presented in the *Antichrist*, elevates the Justice of Yahweh over the Christ of both Judgment and 'love,' understood as the Savior who would punish the Jews and all non-Christians for their unbelief at the end times, and as a god of mercy who would forgive *Christians* for their sins.[40]

On the one hand, Christianity adopts the apocalyptic God of the prophets, and projects strength, power, and vengeance (repressed instincts) onto God. On the other hand, through selfless notions of salvation through Christ, love for neighbor, and peace of soul, they moralize God, stripping themselves of power and making him a god of the weak alone ("of course they do not *call* themselves the weak; they call themselves 'the good'").[41] Just as Nietzsche insists that the sublimation of evil instincts are necessary for virtues and the cultivation of exemplary human beings; he also insists that "the evil god is needed no less than the good god":[42]

How can anyone today still submit to the simplicity of Christian theologians to the point of insisting with them that the development of the conception of God from the "God of Israel," the god of a people, to the Christian God, the quintessence of everything good, represents *progress*? Yet even Renan does this. As if Renan had the right to be simple-minded! After all, the opposite stares you in the face. When the presuppositions of *ascending* life, when everything strong, brave, masterful, and proud is eliminated from the conception of God . . . and the attribute 'Savior' or 'Redeemer' remains in the end as the one essential attribute of divinity—just *what* does such a transformation signify? what, such a *reduction* of the divine?[43]

The above passage most likely refers to Renan's sentiments pertaining to the Christian and Jewish God(s) as recorded in his widely popular *The Life of Jesus*. After stating that Jesus' "great fact of originality" was that he had "nothing in common with his race," Renan writes: "Neither the Jew nor the Mussulman has understood this delightful theology of love. The God of Jesus is not that tyrannical master who kills us, damns us, or saves us, according to his pleasure. . . . The God of Jesus is not the partial despot who has chosen Israel for His people. . . . He is the God of humanity."[44] Although Renan claimed that his god was humanitarian, it will become more evident as Nietzsche "unmasks" this god, that it was not.

While the *Genealogy* is largely a political text opposed to a general decline of vitality throughout Europe, Nietzsche's foremost agenda in the *Antichrist* is to wage war against "theologians' blood"; the theological instinct that, among other things, was characterized by an incapacity for philology. His main target is the antisemitic French theologian Renan ("that 'simple-minded' 'buffoon in *psychologicis*'"),[45] and includes the "insidious theology" of the Tübingen Seminary.[46] The fact that Nietzsche read Julius Wellhausen just prior to writing the *Antichrist* strongly suggests that the Old Testament scholar largely influenced Nietzsche's work.[47] Both Wellhausen (1844-1918) and Renan (1823-92) have been singled out by historians as two of the most prominent Biblical scholars who contributed to the deprecation of Jews in the latter half of the nineteenth century. That Nietzsche was concerned with both of them is significant. Placing the *Antichrist* in the theological climate of Nietzsche's time, and then in dialogue with his opponent Renan, will conclude this chapter.

In regards to the Jews, just as Nietzsche stands politically against Christian and anti-Christian antisemitism, his theology is over against both Catholic and Protestant versions of contemporary Christianity. Conservative Protestants upheld the principle of the Christian state. They sought to exclude Jews and also non-Protestants (particularly Catholics) from holding public posts. However, the increased intervention of the Second Reich into the private lives of individuals, coupled with rising leftist movements, eventually brought conservatives, ultramontane Catholics, and to a certain extent, orthodox Jews together in an alliance. On the other end of the spectrum, liberal Protestants opposed the Christian state and its right to exclude non-Christians from governmental posts, drawing on the secular Enlightenment. They also thought Christian consciousness should be formed not through ecclesiastical and political institutions, but through a direct encounter with the historical Jesus.[48] The liberal's opposition to the state and to racial antisemitism, coupled with their Enlightenment approach to theology through the fields of Biblical criticism and philology, served to align them politically with liberal Jews, who constituted the visible leadership of European Jewry during the Second Reich.[49]

However, the Christians' turn to historical religion divided them not only from orthodox and liberal Judaism, but also from secular, humanistic Jews. The overarching goal of the liberal Christians was to achieve national and cultural unity based on historical and Christian principles, into which the Jews could then be assimilated. The fact that the Jews refused to convert to Christianity was a disappointment to liberal Protestants. Although the liberal Protestants tended to stand aloof from active engagement in political issues, did not seek power in politics, and in principle opposed antisemitism, by the end of the nineteenth century, their cultural influence contributed to the resurgent nationalism of the Second Reich.[50]

Liberal Protestantism during Nietzsche's time was divided into two dominant strands of thought; pragmatic and scientific, as expressed by the Ritschlian and Tübingen schools. The Ritschlian school descended from Kant, emphasized the prophetic and practical side of religion, particularly Biblical faith; and sought to separate faith from historical proofs in order to rescue Christianity from the historical-critical research common to the scientific school. The scientific movement, made possible by Strauss, led by Baur and then the Tübingen school after his death in 1860, abandoned a doctrinal attitude to scripture. They vigorously applied Hegelian ideas to the development of Christianity, especially primitive Christianity, and to the problems of Biblical criticism. Despite the differences between these two schools, the liberals were united in their pursuit to find a common ground between faith and knowledge, science and religion, that could withstand both the onslaught of modern science as well as strict modern anthropological interpretations of Lutheranism.[51]

In general, Nietzsche selectively uses but polemicizes against both these liberal schools. His concern with character, conduct, morality, and the creation of higher culture is similar to those issues central to the Ritschlians. However, he does not adhere to its fundamental ideology or democratic liberalism which sought, as stated in Ritschl's speech commemorating Luther's 400th birthday (1883), to elevate Christianity as the "spiritual domination of the world."[52]

Nietzsche adopts the essential Tübingen exegetical principle that rejected supernatural and miraculous interpretations of scripture. As a trained philologist Nietzsche's application of critical methods disheartened him from sharing the Biblical faith many Ritschlians held ("For as a philologist one sees *behind* the 'holy books'; as a physician, *behind* the physiological depravity of the typical Christian").[53] And though the Tübingen tradition claimed to reject supernaturalism, it still adhered to a traditional belief in the grace and providence of a God that Nietzsche no longer endorsed ("'Divine providence' of the kind in which approximately every third person in 'educated Germany' still believes would be an objection to God so strong that one simply could not imagine a stronger one").[54] Both schools tended to view Jesus, in one sense or another, as related to the Messianic fulfillment of Hebrew scripture, a tenet that especially irritated Nietzsche. In *Daybreak*'s aphorism, "The Philology of Christianity," he writes:

> How little Christianity educates the sense of honesty and justice can be gauged fairly well from the character of its scholars' writings: they present their conjectures as boldly as if they were dogmas and are rarely in any honest perplexity over the interpretation of a passage in the Bible. Again and again they say "I am right, for it is written—" and then follows an interpretation of such impudent arbitrariness that a philologist who hears it is caught between rage and laughter and asks himself: is it possible? Is this honourable? Is it even decent? . . . But after all, what can one expect from the effects of a religion which in the centuries of its foundation perpetrated that unheard of philological farce concerning the Old Testament: I mean the attempt to pull the Old Testament from under the feet of the Jews with the assertion it contained nothing but Christian teaching and *belonged* to the Christians as the *true* people of Israel, the Jews being only usurpers. And then there followed a fury of interpretation and construction that cannot possibly be associated with a good conscience: however much Jewish scholars protested, the Old Testament was supposed to speak of Christ and only of Christ, and especially of his Cross; wherever a piece of wood, a rod, a ladder, a twig, a tree, a willow, a staff is mentioned, it is supposed to be a prophetic allusion to the wood of the Cross. . . . Has anyone who asserted this ever *believed* it?[55]

Nietzsche's philosophy was designed to be a thorn in the side of both liberal and conservative Christians who sought, in various ways, to demonstrate Christian superiority over against Judaism and the Jews. He also typifies that which the liberals as a whole set out to avoid: the tendency to reinterpret Lutheranism in strict anthropological categories.

Theologically, although Nietzsche adopts some moral tenets of the Ritschlians, he does not adhere to its Biblical faith which was based on the New Testament he disdained ("There is nothing in it [NT] that is free, gracious, candid, honest. . . . Everything in it is cowardice").[56] Although he adopts critical methods, he rejects the conclusions reached by the Tübingen school, led by Wellhausen, which pinpointed the historical date of Judaism's moral and spiritual decay to the Mosaic law. "Our age is proud of its historical sense," Nietzsche quips in the *Antichrist*.[57] He then goes against the entire grain of the Ritschlian, Tübingen, and conservative traditions by imputing deterioration not to original Israel, but to prophetic Judea, and even more to Christianity. "The process of decay," Nietzsche announces, begins "with the death of the Redeemer."[58] In section 37 he reiterates:

> How could it [our age] ever make itself believe the nonsense that at the beginning of Christianity there stands the *crude fable of the miracle worker and Redeemer*—and that everything spiritual and symbolical represents only a later development? On the contrary: the history of Christianity, beginning with the death on the cross, is the history of the misunderstanding, growing cruder with every step, of an *original* symbolism.[59]

Nietzsche continues to say that Christianity diffused to broader and cruder masses of people, and that the church is that in which *diseased barbarism* itself gains power. The church, Nietzsche claims, is the embodiment of mortal hostility against all integrity, and against all frank and gracious humanity.

Nietzsche's two main concerns in the *Antichrist* are identical to those which generally preoccupied nineteenth-century liberal Protestantism as a whole: the relationship between Christianity and Judaism, and the historical quest of Jesus in relation to his Jewish roots. Consequently, the *Antichrist* marks Nietzsche's brief attempt at a biographical/historical portrait of Jesus as a psychological type, of which Strauss and Renan were pioneers in their respective works of the same title. Although Jesus' scattered appearances throughout Nietzsche's writings are significant and memorable, prior to the *Antichrist*, they can virtually be counted on one hand. The work also marks Nietzsche's concentrated effort to elaborate on how apocalyptic elements of Judaism were related to the Judeo-Christian tradition, which were also main issues addressed by Renan, whose antisemitic biography of Jesus was a bestseller throughout Europe.

Renan presents two opposing views of the kingdom of God that "existed in the mind of Jesus simultaneously": one is described as "spiritual deliverance" and includes "the children"; the other is "the literal accomplishment of the apocalyptic visions of Daniel and Enoch" and concerns heretics, Samaritans, Pharisees, and pagans.[60] Nietzsche's major problem is with the latter.

In chapter 10, "The Preachings on the Lake," Renan writes that Jesus' preaching, in his early ministry, "was gentle and pleasing, breathing Nature and the perfume of the fields."[61] After meeting with opposition from his "enemies," Jesus eventually comes to regard himself as the violent judge who would return to condemn the world and judge his opponents.[62] By chapter 20, Jesus is beset even more with bitterness, resentment, and reproach toward those who would not believe in him. Renan writes:

He was no longer the mild teacher who delivered the "Sermon on the Mount," who had met with neither resistance nor difficulty. . . . And yet many of the recommendations which he addressed to his disciples contain the germs of a true fanaticism. . . . Must we reproach him for this? No revolution is effected without some harshness. . . . The invincible obstacle to the ideas of Jesus came especially from orthodox Judaism, represented by the Pharisees. Jesus became more and more alienated from the ancient Law.[63]

In regards to this development of affairs, Nietzsche jests: "[T]here is a gaping contradiction between the sermonizer on the mount, lake and meadow . . . and that fanatic of aggression, that mortal enemy of theologians and priests whom Renan's malice has glorified as *le grand maître en ironie*."[64]

Renan writes that Jesus increasingly "came to think of himself" as "the destroyer of Judaism"; he "completely lost his Jewish faith," and that "far from continuing Judaism, Jesus represents the rupture with the Jewish spirit": "The general march of Christianity has been to remove itself more and more from Judaism. It will become perfect in returning to Jesus, but certainly not in returning to Judaism."[65] Renan concludes that the Old Jewish party, the Mosaic Law, was responsible for Jesus' death; therefore, nineteenth-century Jews are responsible for his: "Consequently, every Jew who suffers today for the murder of Jesus has the right to complain. . . . But nations, like individuals have their responsibilities, and if ever crime was the crime of a nation, it was the death of Jesus."[66]

Renan's book, released in 1864, was not only popular within the academy; it sold like a "Waverly novel" among the populace from the first hour of its publication. Five months after its release, eleven editions (100,000) had been exhausted and it was already translated into German, Italian, and Dutch, to be rapidly followed by additional translations. In 1927, the book, which is now regarded as one of the two antisemitic bestsellers throughout Europe in the nineteenth century, was still read more widely than any other biography on Jesus.[67]

In the *Genealogy*, Nietzsche refers to Renan in connection with Dühring and the Aryan myth; in the *Nachlass* (1884) he regards him as a weak-willed representative of "herd animal" democratic Europe; and in *Twilight*, he names him as one among the family of Rousseau, and derogatorily calls him a democrat:[68]

With no little ambition, he wishes to represent an aristocracy of the spirit: yet at the same time he is on his knees before its very counter-doctrine, the *évangile des humbles*—and not only on his knees. To what avail is all free-spiritedness . . . if in one's guts one is still a Christian, a Catholic—in fact, a priest! . . . This spirit of Renan's, a spirit which is enervated, is one more calamity for poor, sick, will-sick France.[69]

In the *Antichrist*, Nietzsche addresses Renan's notion of the Last Judgment. He connects what he regards as the "propaganda" of the early Christian community which "created its god according to its needs and put words into its Master's mouth," to "those wholly unevangelical concepts it now cannot do without: the return, the 'Last Judgment,' every kind of temporal expectation and promise."[70] Nietzsche traces antisemitism from the early Christian community to Rousseau to contemporaries such as Renan and Dühring, whom Nietzsche regards as those needing to be reckoned with.[71]

Nietzsche not only opposes Renan's preference for the Christian God to that of the powerful Yahweh, he opposes Renan's notion of Jesus as a genius and a hero. When Renan regards Jesus as a genius, it is in reference to Jesus' initial coming to self-consciousness that he would be a violent judge ushering in the apocalyptic kingdom, which would consist of a "sudden renovation of the world."[72] According to Renan, Jesus applied to himself the title "Son of Man" and affirmed the "coming catastrophe" in which he was to figure as judge, clothed with full powers which had been delegated to him from the Ancient of Days. Renan writes: "Beset by an idea [the Kingdom of God], gradually becoming more and more imperious [impérieux] and exclusive, Jesus proceeds henceforth with a kind of fatal impassability in the path marked out by his astonishing genius."[73] In the *Antichrist*, Nietzsche is responding to that passage:

> To repeat, I am against any attempt to introduce the fanatic into the Redeemer type; the word *impérieux*, which Renan uses, is alone enough to annul the type. The 'glad tidings' are precisely that there are no longer any opposites; the kingdom of heaven belongs to the *children*. . . . Such a faith is not angry, does not reproach, does not resist; it does not bring 'the sword'——.[74]

Renan located the origin of Christianity with the prophet Isaiah, discarded original Israel, and held nineteenth-century Jews, Israel's remnants, responsible for the death of Jesus.[75] Nietzsche's position is the exact reverse. Although Nietzsche concurs with Renan that Christianity originated with the prophet Isaiah, he disagrees that this represents spiritual *progress*, but rather, the origin of Israel's demise which has culminated in the Christianity of *ressentiment*. The slave morality of *ressentiment* Nietzsche insists, began with the death on the cross; it reached its most profound form of vengefulness when the disciples totally misunderstood Jesus' message concerning the Kingdom of God, and instead opted for the apocalyptic Last Judgment. "What are the glad tidings?," Nietzsche repeatedly asks. The glad tidings Jesus brings are that the concepts of guilt, sin, and punishment are abolished. Sin, that which separates humans from God, is destroyed. The Kingdom of God is nothing that one expects; it has no yesterday or today; it will not come in the future or in a thousand years: "The kingdom of God is *in you*."[76] Situating the origin of Christianity with the prophet Isaiah was crucial for Christian antisemites. They used the raging words of Isaiah ("Hear and hear, but do not understand; see and see, but do not perceive. Make the heart of this people calloused," . . . Isa. 6:9-10) against German-Jewry for rejecting salvation and the Savior. Isaiah is repeated and used against the Jews in the New Testament (Mk 4:12; Acts 28:25). According to the Gospels, because Israel rejected salvation in Christ, it forfeited its election to the "new Israel," the Gentiles: "This salvation of God has been sent to the Gentiles," says Paul, "they will listen" (Acts 28:28).

Nietzsche and Renan's portraits of Jesus are similar inasmuch as they both tend to present Jesus as a blissed-out flowerchild, in the Dostoevskian sense, who is far removed from reality. However, Renan elevates Jesus as a hero who represents "the summit of human greatness" and as the founder of the "final and absolute religion," whereas Nietzsche assigns neither Jesus nor Christianity that triumphalist status.[77] Nietzsche qualifies his remark that Jesus *could* be regarded as a free spirit, using the word somewhat *tolerantly* (emphasis mine). By ironically picturing Jesus as an amoral type of holy anarchist, while endorsing a God of power and Justice, Nietzsche, as Poliakov notes when addressing a passage from *Daybreak*, refrains from going back to the "safety net" of his previous religious beliefs: "By evoking ancient Jehovah and not Christ, Nietzsche abstained from taking the last step, that is, of becoming a Christian once more facing the Jews. . . . But he would not have been Nietzsche if in this matter, too, he had not inverted the signs."[78]

Overall, Nietzsche's *Antichrist*, which he describes as his entrance into the "queer and sick world of the Gospels," is not especially innovative for what it does say, but for what it does not say.[79] Unlike many nineteenth-century biographies of Jesus, particularly Renan's, there is no mention of Jesus' Messianic consciousness as that of a wrathful Judge who would return to slay his enemies; no mention of the bickering and conflict between Jesus and the Pharisees, especially just prior to his crucifixion; there is no contempt on the part of Jesus toward his alleged Jewish opponents—contempt for Jews is ascribed to the New Testament authors: "But," Nietzsche smirks, "even the Pharisees and scribes derive an advantage from such opposition; they must have been worth something to have been hated in so indecent a manner"; nor is there contempt for the Roman governor who allegedly ordered Jesus to death. According to

Nietzsche, Pilate is the only single figure in the whole New Testament who commands respect, for he called the concept of truth into question.[80] Numerous New Testament passages that Nietzsche views as vengeful are attributed to the apostles "who put words of vengeance into Jesus' mouth";[81] the New Testament is demeaned and not Hebrew scripture, and so on. In this fashion, Nietzsche not only performs a revaluation by taking the side of the Roman and Jewish authorities against early Christianity and the Jesus movement, but also by taking an opposing stance to contemporary biographies, written by Christians, which sought vengeance against Jews and Romans. And while Renan staked his claim as the pioneer who discovered that Semites were a lesser race: "I am the first to recognize that the Semitic race . . . represents . . . an inferior composition of human nature;"[82] Nietzsche took pride in exposing the humanitarian God of Renan and other antisemites as a travesty: "What defines me, what sets me apart from all the rest of mankind, is that I have *unmasked* Christian morality."[83]

Overall, the revaluation was designed to promote the Yahweh of power against a renewed God of Judgment and the God of "love"; the Kingdom of God over the Last Judgment. Nietzsche's revaluation of values ultimately promoted the skeptical truth of strong spirits, versus the fanatical lies of the "sick" and the "weak":

> By a lie I mean: wishing *not* to see something that one does see; wishing not to see something *as* one sees it. . . .
> . . . Of necessity the party man becomes a liar. German historiography, for example, is convinced that Rome represented despotism and that the Germanic tribes brought the spirit of freedom into the world. What is the difference between this conviction and a lie? May one still be surprised when all parties, as well as the German historians, instinctively employ the big words of morality, that morality almost continues to exist because the party man of every description needs it at every moment?
> "This is *our* conviction; we confess it before all the world, we live and die for it. Respect for all who have convictions?" I have heard that sort of thing even out of the mouths of anti-Semites. On the contrary, gentlemen! An anti-Semite certainly is not any more decent because he lies as a matter of principle.[84]

Nietzsche's reckless, disjointed, unscholarly style in the *Antichrist*, coupled with his portrait of Jesus, has earned the work its contemporary reputation as an endlessly entertaining and witty essay, but insignificant as both a theological text and as an original or profound biographical portrait of Jesus. However, viewed in the context of his time, the work is theologically perceptive and politically bold—which Elisabeth clearly saw as evidenced by her fear that the book would be confiscated. Because most contemporary readers consult the *Antichrist* to discern Nietzsche's view of Jesus, and tend to regard Nietzsche's view as favorable, what would have been regarded as heretical in Nietzsche's day is typically overlooked. The controversial elements, however, initially had little to do with Nietzsche's full-fledged assault on institutional religion, his emphasis on the non-divinity of Jesus; his opposition to trinitarian formulas; his rejection of the miraculous and supernatural elements of the gospels, including the resurrection; his insistence on viewing God's kingdom as an individual-spiritual realm, as opposed to a metaphysical one; and/or his reference to Jesus as an idiot. Many of these views—excepting the last—were, in fact, held by Renan, Strauss, Ritschl, and most other liberals for decades. What primarily made Nietzsche's work sacrilegious was the prominence he afforded to the Jewish God, which was unprecedented in its defiant repudiation of the dominant culture's religious and political ideology.

In summary, my hypothesis as stated in this and the previous chapter is threefold. First, the *Genealogy* as a whole is a polemic against Nietzsche's major enemies for the purpose of ushering in his ideal master race, particularly Christianity and antisemitism as embodied in the Lutheran state-church and in anarchists such as Eugen Dühring. Overall, Nietzsche opposes democracy, socialism, and feminism, any political party that represents homogenization. Opposed to religiopolitical theories grounded in Rousseauian notions of altruistic human nature and on a general will of the *Volk*, Nietzsche argues that morality has a base which is rooted in the history of human tyranny and then Judeo-Christian resentment. This view of human nature is not only in keeping with his philosophy and psychology of sublimation. He utilizes his stance politically to refute Christian and anarchist theories that first *required* an innocent humanity, and then, as in the case of Dühring and conservative Christianity, sought historical redemption for fallen humanity through the economy and/or through Christ, both of which excluded the Jewish people. The need for redemption, Nietzsche argues, was rooted in human suffering; the response to this condition (creation or vengeance) ultimately served to distinguish nobles from slaves. Those driven by repressed instincts, and thus resentment, first created evil enemies (Jews and philosophers), which was a notion totally foreign to nobles, who distinguished "good" and "bad" on the basis of sociological and self-affirmative personality traits. Nietzsche presents his psychological critique of Judeo-Christianity and its condemnation of egoism in the first essay of the *Genealogy*; his sociopolitical position is primarily stated throughout the second and third.

Secondly, the first essay of the *Genealogy* separates Judeo-Christianity from original Israel, marking the origin of Nietzsche's creation of a new caste that would rule Europe. This caste, with its Aryan, not exclusively Germanic foundation, was in contrast to theories put forth by Christian racists who elevated German-Christians over the Jews by transferring God's election from Judaism to Christianity through the Redeemer. Nietzsche does not identify the Aryan race with the Germans, separates original Israel from Judeo-Christianity, and then (in the *AC*) severs Jesus totally from the Christian tradition. He seeks a master race built on a revival of nobility and the imperial spirit. Nietzsche begins this process in the *Genealogy* and continues it in the *Antichrist*. He also continues the second essay of the *Genealogy* in the *Antichrist*, linking "guilt, bad conscience and the like" (the state-church) to Judeo-Christianity and its god, as distinct from Yahweh and original Israel. Ironically, his adoption of an essay style was perhaps intended to expound his views, but the nature of his mind is such that he confused matters in doing so. The *Genealogy* is rarely seen as a whole; the *Antichrist* is not connected to it.

The *Genealogy* begins with Aryan humanity; the *Antichrist* ends with Nietzsche's proclamation of a revaluation of all values: "Wherefore Greeks, whence Romans," Nietzsche cries in the concluding sections.[85] He then reiterates his position that German-Christianity has "cheated us out of the harvest of ancient culture"; that the Reformation defeated the noble Renaissance, and that the French Revolution defeated the classical ideal (*GM* I, 16; *AC* 61). Addressing his major enemies, Christians and anarchists (antisemites), Nietzsche writes:

> Indeed, it makes a difference to what end one lies; whether one preserves or *destroys*. . . . The Christian and the anarchist: both decadents, both incapable of having any effect other than disintegrating, poisoning, withering, bloodsucking; both the instinct of mortal hatred against everything that stands, that stands in greatness . . . that promises life a future. Christianity was the vampire of the *imperium Romanum*. . . .
>
> The sneakiness of prigs, the conventicle secrecy, gloomy concepts like hell, like sacrifice of the guiltless . . . above all, the slowly fanned fire of revenge, of chandala revenge—all that is what became master over Rome.[86]

Finally, the *Antichrist* is largely a polemic against liberal Christianity, as represented by Renan and Wellhausen. Through its historical-critical methods, as well as its propaganda concerning the Last Judgment expressed in terms of Messianic consciousness, Nietzsche clearly sees how conservative theological concepts inform liberals and perpetuate antisemitism, either unconsciously, or consciously as in the case of Renan. Nietzsche attempts to refute such theories through his fundamental conviction that Jesus was not the Messiah or the Savior in any sense of the word. In what was perhaps an appeal to liberals, Nietzsche says:

> We know, today our *conscience* knows, what these uncanny inventions of the priests and the church are really worth, *what ends they served* in reducing mankind to such a state of self-violation that its sight can arouse nausea: the concepts 'beyond,' 'Last Judgment,' 'immortality of the soul,' and 'soul' itself are instruments of torture, systems of cruelties by virtue of which the priest became master. . . . Everybody knows this, *and yet everything continues as before.*[87]

He also opposes the Christian god on the basis of an empirical skepticism: "A humanitarian God cannot be *demonstrated* from the world we know: today you can be compelled to admit this much. But what conclusions do you draw? You are all *afraid* of the conclusion . . . and, in short, you hold fast to your God and devise from him a world we do *not* know."[88]

At its core, Nietzsche's lifelong evaluation of Christianity was a means to enlightenment and yet burdened with a sense of the tragic, as manically expressed in *Ecce Homo*: "Have I been understood? The uncovering of Christian morality is an event without parallel, a real catastrophe. He that is enlightened about that, is a *force majeure*, a destiny—he breaks the history of mankind in two. One lives before him, or one lives after him."[89]

Historically, although Nietzsche attempted to abolish Christianity and antisemitism, he simultaneously criticized its ancestry—and thus Judaism—in the process. In this sense, he stood in a precarious position: his approach was partially based on his thesis that traditionally, elements of Judaism merged with Christianity, constituted a vengeful religion. His opinion was formed and further confirmed through empirical observation, manifested by the Christian antisemitism of his time. Regardless, Nietzsche's writings, if grossly misquoted could—and indeed were—eventually misused to support racial antisemitism. Even so, during his time, he firmly believed the "problem of the Jews" was spread through Christianity and that the former led to the latter, as exemplified by Dühring. Essentially, while many laid the axe to Jewish roots, Nietzsche sought to cut the fruit off the tree. Nietzsche did not seek to cut off the Jews, but rather to value their ancient roots and integrate their modern descendants into a new society. He vehemently opposed both Christian and anti-Christian antisemitism, although his antisemitic enemies, led by Elisabeth, eventually used his words against him and the Jewish people. Nietzsche concludes:

> With this I am at the end and I pronounce my judgment. I *condemn* Christianity. It is to me the highest of all conceivable corrup-

tions . . . it has turned every value into an un-value, every truth into a lie, every integrity into a vileness of the soul. Let anyone dare to speak to me of its 'humanitarian' blessings! . . . This eternal indictment of Christianity I will write on all walls, wherever there are walls—I have letters to make even the blind see. . . .

And time is reckoned from the *dies nefastus* with which this calamity began—after the *first* day of Christianity! *Why not rather after its last day*? *After today*? Revaluation of all values![90]

Conclusion:
The Nazis' Mythologizing
of Nietzsche

Dear friend,

  I pluck up the courage also to tell you that in Paraguay
things are as bad as they could be. The Germans . . . are in
rebellion, demanding their money back—there is none.
Acts of violence have already occurred; I fear the
worst. . . . This does *not* prevent my sister from writing to
me for October 15, with the utmost scorn, that she sup-
poses I want to become "famous" too—that would be a
nice state of affairs, to be sure! And what scum I had
sought for company—Jews, who have been around licking
all the plates, like Georg Brandes. . . . And she calls me
"sweet Fritz"? . . . This has been going on for seven years.

  My mother still has no notion of this—that is *my* mas-
terpiece. For Christmas she sent me a game: "Fritz und
Lieschen."[1]

This book has attempted to interconnect Nietzsche's life and writings in relation
to Christianity, Judaism, antisemitism, and nineteenth-century Germany.
Although it is by no means exhaustive, the work points to an interpretative
framework which includes historical contextualization and also a chronological
approach to Nietzsche's writings. Nietzsche remarked several times that readers who were unfamiliar with previous works would confront enormous interpretive problems, even to the point where the text at hand would prove "incomprehensible."[2] This especially appears to be the case regarding the *Genealogy*
and the *Antichrist*. These two works display continuity of thought that is central
for discerning Nietzsche's political and religious viewpoints.

  Nietzsche's views on Christianity are multifaceted. But it is evident that
antisemitism in relation to Christian theology and the Lutheran state-church was
of primary concern to Nietzsche throughout much of his life. Jewish-Christian relations in nineteenth-century Germany have been neglected in Nietzsche
studies and are central to his thought.

That antisemitism played such a major role in Nietzsche's break with Wagner, his sister, and even his publisher; that he urged those closest to him to renounce antisemitism and suffered personal sacrifice for doing so; that his later writings show increased preoccupation with contemporary Jews, Christianity, and German nationalism; and that he raved against antisemites during the hours of his transition to insanity, make clear that the issue of antisemitism—and Nietzsche's almost pathological response to it—was not a passing phase nor peripheral to his existence. However, the question as to why Nietzsche identified with the Jews, who only composed one percent of the population, remains unclear.

Most all commentators assert that Nietzsche had a strong empathy with the Jews because he viewed them as a suffering and creative people; thus, in his own painful and unique existence, personally identified with them.[3] Others, such as Alfred Low, stress cultural and political elements. Low states that Nietzsche saw the Jews as political allies because the Jews, in Nietzsche's own words, were "the most conservative power in an insecure and threatened Europe," who had no use for "revolutions of socialism or militarism."[4] Low states that Nietzsche's vehement aversion to antisemitism was not a private affair driven by a liking for individual Jews or the Jewish people as a whole; rather, Nietzsche saw antisemitism as a form of socialism, and thus viewed it as a slave revolt "against European culture, a movement destined to become the antipode of his own philosophy and the archenemy."[5] Arnold Coutinho holds that Nietzsche's affinity with the Jews was not only in conformity with Nietzsche's "cherished Nordic principles of chivalry," but also with "his supernational tendencies as an 'independent spirit' transcending all boundaries."[6] And Arnold Eisen employs the "Freudian analysis of ambivalence" in his hypotheses that remorse was a prime factor underlying Nietzsche's positive affinity with contemporary Jews.

According to Eisen, Nietzsche's lavish praise of contemporary Jewry was compensation for his excessive condemnations of ancient Judaism: "I do not think one need engage in psychobiography . . . to discern the guilt underlying Nietzsche's outbursts of fury at Judaism, its moral code and its God."[7] Eisen's suggestion, though original, is untenable, for Nietzsche's opposition to antisemitism precedes his systematic attacks against ancient Judaism. Moreover, Nietzsche does not attack the Jewish God (ancient Yahweh), but the God of Judeo-Christianity.[8] A brief biographical summary of Nietzsche's life and his stance toward Judaism, Christianity, and antisemitism, will illustrate the course his views underwent, offering suggestions as to why he allied himself with the Jewish minority of his culture.

It is clear that there was nothing in Nietzsche's upbringing that steered him away from antisemitism; if anything, the reverse is true. In his youth, although antisemitism was commonplace throughout Germany, the Jews were simply not an important issue in Nietzsche's family; his exposure to anti-semitism, and his own casual antisemitic tendencies, began in college and were strengthened during his association with Wagner (1869-76).[9]

As Duffy and Mittelman show, the first "glimmering of a positive atti-tude" toward contemporary Jews occurs in a personal letter written in 1872.[10] Although this predates his encounter with Rée, whom Nietzsche met in 1873, Nietzsche's friendship with Rée was instrumental in changing his stance. The Nietzsche-Rée friendship corresponds with Nietzsche's growing discontent with Wagner's prejudices; and, as shown in chapter 1, the Wagners' disap-proval of Rée and Nietzsche's disregard for their opinions, was central in his decision to sever his ties with them. After the break, and with the appearance of *Human, all-too Human* (1878-80), Nietzsche's attitude toward the Jews abruptly changes. It is here that Nietzsche begins to express a concern for the dangerous national hostilities that scapegoated Jews for Germany's misfor-tunes.[11]

From this point on (including *Daybreak* and the *Gay Science*, 1881-82), although Nietzsche is not wholly uncritical of contemporary Jews, he consis-tently displays an enthusiastic and positive attitude toward modern Jews; his views toward ancient Judaism are both positive and negative, the features he condemns are almost always connected to his criticisms of Christianity.[12] Although *Zarathustra* (1883-85) contains sparse references to Jews, and does not mention the term "Christianity" once, the work abounds in Judeo-Christian themes, and was written in the throes of turmoil surrounding the loss of the holy trinity (Nietzsche, Rée, and Salomé), Wagner's death, and also Elisabeth's newfound relationship with the antisemitic Förster.[13]

Nietzsche's exit from the Wagner circle and Elisabeth's continuing asso-ciation with Wagnerites, had caused tension between them for years. How-ever, her marriage to Förster in 1885 was the major incident that Nietzsche regarded as a personal betrayal: "You have gone over to my antipodes. . . . I will not conceal that I consider this engagement an insult—or a stupidity— which will harm you as much as me."[14] Nietzsche's aversion to antisemitism had been established long before the marriage. Hence, the point is that Nietzsche felt double-crossed not because Elisabeth was—or remained—Chris-tian (or Wagnerian), but because she allied herself in matrimony with a leading antisemite. Nietzsche's opposition to antisemitism was thus not only devised as a weapon he could use against the Christian religion or his family, it was a phe-nomenon he despised on its own terms. Because of Elisabeth (who was a Chris-tian embracing antisemitism), and Wagner (who was an antisemite who became Christian), Nietzsche increasingly came to associate antisemitism with Chris-tianity, the latter of which he already began to disrespect in his youth.

Elisabeth's marriage marks the beginning of Nietzsche's political involvement, perhaps because he realized that he had to come to grips with a cultural phenomenon that had deeply affected his own life. A few weeks after the wedding, Nietzsche began writing *Beyond Good and Evil* (1886), in which he announced that he "never met a German who liked the Jews," regarding the Jews as the "purest race." Nietzsche elects the Jews to partake in his "new caste that would rule Europe" and bring about the much needed revaluation.[15]

In light of the fact that Nietzsche emerges as an advocate for contemporary Jews, his ambivalent views toward priestly-prophetic Judaism, especially the bitter and shrill tone in the *Genealogy* (1887), have been described by modern scholars as unequivocal, careless, unguarded, and irresponsible.[16] Essentially, they are neither. Nietzsche's views were formed by, and should be interpreted within, the theological and political categories that preexisted in Germany. It must be remembered that antisemitism in nineteenth-century Germany was the rule; Nietzsche, an exception. As a minority who was an obscure author, Nietzsche was essentially a powerless voice opposing very prominent leaders. That antisemites themselves regarded Nietzsche as an "insolent" enemy and attacked his later works, is evidence that they did not view his texts to be as ambivalent as do modern-day readers.

Whereas Christian theology tended to demean ancient Hebrews and modern Jews, claiming the prophets as their ancestors, Nietzsche took the opposing stance (*AC* 1888). Nietzsche's ambivalence toward the prophetic-priestly strand was not driven by any profound contempt for historical Judaism per se, nor was it solely designed to attack its offspring. Rather, Nietzsche's position was a logical consequence arising from his opposition to both Christianity and antisemitism. The Hebrew prophets were necessary to the Christian tradition; both liberal and conservative Christians cut off the Jews precisely on the basis that they had rejected Jesus the Messiah, whom the prophets had foretold. Hence, if Nietzsche were to completely affirm priestly-prophetic Judaism, he would basically be affirming Christian antisemitism. This is why the *Übermensch* is central: he represents the Messiah who has yet to come. In the *Genealogy*, when describing Christianity's inheritance of Judaism, Nietzsche temporarily diverts from ambivalence to a purely negative stance toward post-eighth-century Judaism; in the *Antichrist*, he resumes his positive/negative struggle with Christianity's self-proclaimed ancestor, all the while severing Jesus from the Christian tradition. In short, Christianity, not Nietzsche, created the terms; he was simply reversing its dominant theology. As a result, the threefold distinction of Jews is a necessary weapon as Nietzsche becomes more politically involved. Affirming ancient Hebrews and contemporary Jews, while deriding Judeo-Christianity as that tradition rooted in *ressentiment*, serves two primary functions. First, it flips antisemitic Christian theology on its head (in

Nietzsche's scheme, Christians are "not the *true* people of Israel"; Jesus is a Jew but not a Christian).[17] Second, it opposes anti-Christian antisemitism which derided original Israel (and the entire Judeo-Christian tradition as well). In a word, one could say that if one were to oppose antisemitism in nineteenth-century Germany in both its Christian and anti-Christian forms, one would end up with the exact position that Nietzsche has. Nietzsche's language is indeed violent and *excessive*, but not uncalculated, careless, or irresponsible:[18] "Now a comic fact . . . I have an 'influence,' very subterranean, to be sure. . . . I can even abuse my outspokenness . . . perhaps they 'implore' me, but they cannot escape me. In the *Anti-Semitic Correspondence* . . . my name appears in almost every issue."[19]

It is widely recognized that Nietzsche admired the prophets for possessing a love of life, creativity, and as the first people who were capable of reversing traditional values. To this extent, Nietzsche, a creator of values himself, felt an affinity to them.[20] However, Nietzsche clearly opposes those values in his attempt to liberate European culture from the Judeo-Christian ethical system, which he believed was rooted in power driven by impotence and a thirst for revenge.

From a political standpoint, Nietzsche's antidemocratic and antisocialist stance unquestionably corresponded with his contempt for Christianity, which he regarded as egalitarian and as the driving force behind these political move-ments. However, Nietzsche also linked democracy and socialism with anti-semitism. Nietzsche's tendency to regard socialism (particularly Dühring's socialism) as the secular form of Christianity, coupled with the fact that he regarded Renan as a democrat, further supports this view. The argument as to whether Nietzsche despised democracy and socialism *because* they were egal-itarian or *because* they were antisemitic easily becomes circular, and misses the point entirely. It is not coincidental that Nietzsche identifies the leading Chris-tian and anti-Christian antisemites of his time (Renan, Dühring, Stöcker/Förster), nor insignificant that he accurately associates these individu-als with democracy, socialism, and Christianity. That is, Nietzsche indeed opposes these groups and individuals because they are egalitarian; however, in simultaneously opposing their strong antisemitic streaks, he exposes the hypocrisy of the "preachers of equality" who, in fact, did not seek to offer equal rights for all its citizens. Dühring even went so far as to advocate exter-mination of Jewish citizens themselves: "You preachers of *equality*. To me you are . . . secretly vengeful. But I shall bring your secrets to light . . . that your rage may lure you out of your lie-holes and your revenge may leap out from behind your word justice."[21]

Nietzsche's elevation of "genuine philosophers" and contemporary Jews as those harbingers of the new aristocratic culture he sought to bring about, as well as his desire to resurrect the heroic qualities of ancient pre-Christian cultures, was not formed in an historical vacuum. In large measure, his aristocratic radicalism was also a logical consequence which arose from opposing the dominant political ideologies of his time which, in their socialist, democratic, and Lutheran forms, were predominantly nationalistic; opposed to the assimilation and emancipation of Jews; and/or based on the masses' Christian spiritual elitism. Regardless of one's opinions toward Nietzsche's alternative position as to who the spiritual elites really were, or to his alternative political visions, it is relevant to point out that Nietzsche did not win.

That the Jews were becoming affluent citizens in German society obviously did not provoke Nietzsche's growing concern; the expanding national resentment did: "The anti-Semites do not forgive the Jews for possessing 'spirit'—and money. Anti-Semites—another name for the 'underprivileged.'"[22] It is out of this national conflict, which is now regarded as the incubation period of antisemitism, that Nietzsche's critique of culture arose. During the eighties, the mounting racist propaganda prompted Nietzsche to rebut Aryan mythologies, as evidenced in the *Genealogy* and in personal notes written during that time. Nietzsche was well acquainted with the works of Renan, Gobineau, and Paul de Lagarde; his language reflects the political climate created by theorists who advocated racial supremacy: "*Aryan influence*," Nietzsche wrote, "has corrupted all the world."[23] *Zarathustra* is primarily concerned with the psychology of Christianity in relation to revenge and eschatology; the *Genealogy*, with Germany's political climate and Aryan mythologies; and the *Antichrist*, with antisemitic Christian theology. Although most commentators regard the *Antichrist* as key to understanding Nietzsche's stance toward the Judeo-Christian tradition, it is the least profound of the three texts.

In short, Nietzsche's connection with Jews, including his early relationship with Rée; his encounter with the Austrian Jew, Paneth, in which they discussed the possibility of regenerating the Jewish masses (in the early eighties); and his association with Brandes, who was responsible for Nietzsche's initial popularity, illustrates that Nietzsche's affinity with the Jews was not an indifferent or abstract argument constructed to scorn the Christian tradition and/or Wagnerites; it arose from a genuine concern for the future of European Jews, a concern Nietzsche expresses early on in *Daybreak*: "Among the spectacles to which the coming century invites us is the decision as to the destiny of the Jews of Europe. That their die is cast, that they have crossed their Rubicon, is now palpably obvious: all that is left for them is either to become the masters of Europe or lose Europe as they once a long time ago lost Egypt, where they had placed themselves before a similar either-or."[24]

Nietzsche's identification with his Jewish contemporaries thus includes personal, religious, political, cultural, and not least of all, prophetic elements.

The question as to why Nietzsche strongly aligned himself with the Jewish people is almost impossible to discern—it is difficult to establish anyone's motives for anything—let alone Nietzsche's. However, it is accurate to say that his concerns were ethically grounded, and unfortunately, justified. The question itself is at least a tremendous advance from the Nazi myth perpetuated by Brinton and others, who sought to portray Nietzsche as one who derided the Jews of his time as "parasites and decadents"; the Antichrist who was the true forerunner of Hitler's ideology.[25]

The personal and psychological dimensions of Nietzsche's life are central to the inner dynamics underlying his political and religious viewpoints. I have tried to demonstrate the chaotic, tormented nature of Nietzsche's existence not to discredit his perceptions, but to emphasize the intense struggle which made those perceptions possible. Nietzsche's immense capacity for introspection, as recognized by Freud, coupled with his genius for acute cultural analysis, served as a dialectical base from which his "hermeneutics of suspicion" on Western culture arose. As Heller notes: "Nietzsche's is the eye that now sees through everything until all that is left to see through is blank nothingness; and even then this eye would turn around, fairy-tale-like, and see through the seer."[26] Conversely, Nietzsche's warped intolerance—as manifest in his misogyny—largely informed his critique of *ressentiment* in relation to Christianity, via his contempt for his mother and Elisabeth. These defects, his failed relationships with Wagner and Rée, and also his chronic physical pain, resulted in his inability to form or sustain intimate human relationships later in life, with the exception of Overbeck. As a recluse, Nietzsche chose to be an outcast of German society. Perhaps this is another reason he sided with the Jews, who were branded as such without having a choice. As Golo Mann observes:

> Gloomy predictions about the future of man must take the form of warnings because nothing is ever predetermined. Even Nietzsche, an arrogant genius, did not presume to predict the development of the future as something inevitable. He only felt the crisis like a seismograph registers as earthquake and suffered from it without knowing what its form would be; the cries of joy [*sic*] which he uttered over it were like the noises which a frightened child makes in the dark to reassure itself. As a critic of imperial Germany he was unjust and immoderate, as in almost everything he wrote. Yet he hit the heart of the matter and at the time he was the only one to do so. This explains the solitude which suffocated him.[27]

This study has proved its two main assumptions, while also going beyond them. First, I have shown that Nietzsche was, above all else, a philosopher of life. Therefore, his writings should be connected to his concrete personal history. Second, through biography and a careful analysis of Nietzsche's texts, I have shown that Nietzsche's critique of Christianity and culture was composed of psychological and ethical factors. On the one hand, Nietzsche's assault on the Christian tradition was steeped in his own resentment against Wagner and his extended family, both of whom he loved yet deeply abhorred. On the other hand, Nietzsche's attack was compelled by an empathy for the Jewish people, as manifest in his courageous fight against the rampant antisemitism of his time. The fusion of these primary forces resulted in Nietzsche's unique contribution to the history of Western thought, as the first to mercilessly question the foundation and validity of Christian morality: "[T]o demand that all should become 'good human beings,' herd animals, blue-eyed, benevolent, 'beautiful souls' . . . would deprive existence of its *great* character. . . . —And this has been attempted!— Precisely this has been called morality."[28]

In regards to ancient Judaism, analyzing Nietzsche's later writings demonstrates that Nietzsche's views are coherent when placed in their proper historical and political context. I have shown that Nietzsche protects original Israel, and that paradoxically, Nietzsche's wrath against priestly-prophetic Judaism was actually directed at Christian antisemitism. Even so, this is not to suggest that Nietzsche was wholly uncritical of historical Judaism, for he particularly abhorred the concepts of election and the Last Judgment, which, he believed, originated with Judaism and were developed in (antisemitic) Christianity and the modern Germanic notion of the *Volk*. In the *Antichrist*, Nietzsche makes a final attempt to salvage Jesus from these conceptions, with his alternative notion of the universal kingdom of God. In regards to modern Jewry, placing Nietzsche's texts in dialogue with the religious and political ideas of his major opponents, has proven that Nietzsche was fighting against the social persecution that was being launched against the Jews in the latter third of the nineteenth-century.

The original Bayreuth circle that Nietzsche fled as a thirty-one-year-old has a fascinating history which led to the rise of National Socialism. That the Nazis heralded Nietzsche as an antisemitic intellectual forebear should arouse suspicion, for, as ideological followers of Wagner, Renan, and Dühring, they were undoubtedly aware that Nietzsche was an enemy and apostate of their tradition. Although it is beyond the scope of this project to fully investigate why the Nazis used Nietzsche as a mouthpiece, it was a convenient way of silencing him.[29] Moreover, whereas many writing after the Nazi era have been quick to point out Nietzsche's negative critique of ancient Judea, works addressing Nietzsche's evaluation of Christian antisemitism, are virtually non-existent. Although Nietzsche detractors and some well-meaning humanists have traditionally discredited Nietzsche by stressing his abhorrence of socialism, democracy, and Christianity, this book has shown that these evaluations are inadequate when viewed apart from the complex political and religious milieu in Germany, and from Nietzsche's resistance to the antisemitic movement.

Although it is perhaps impossible to discern why Nietzsche was concerned about the Jews, Elisabeth's role in suppressing Nietzsche's works after his breakdown will shed light on the centrality of antisemitism in her life. After sketching Elisabeth's relationship to National Socialism, I will provide a concluding hypothesis as to why Elisabeth and the Nazis mythologized Nietzsche as an antisemite. Although there is an abundance of literature on Nietzsche available in the English-speaking world, only two biographies have been written on Elisabeth. This is mainly because her documents were kept under lock and key under the reign of the Third Reich, and were extremely difficult to access throughout the duration of the Cold War. Now that the Nietzsche Archive in Weimar is open to the public, scholars will be in a better position to assess Elisabeth's role in relationship to Nazi Germany. A recent book by Ben MacIntyre, *Beyond the Fatherland: The Search for Elisabeth Nietzsche* (1992), helps to reconstruct the events that took place after Nietzsche's insanity in 1889, and are succinctly stated in a review by Robert Olen Butler:

> When Elisabeth returned to Germany [from Paraguay] in 1892, Friedrich was already mad and partly paralyzed from syphilis. But his great works . . . were already written, and she seized control of his person, his writings and the very interpretation of his philosophy.
>
> She wrote a detailed and self-aggrandizing biography of her brother; tricked her mother into signing over his care and works to her; carefully controlled and even censored the publication of his past books; forged and altered his documents; and patched together scraps of idle and ultimately rejected thoughts of the philosopher as an authentic, indeed finally synthesizing, work, "The Will to Power." As a focus for all of this, she established another mansion for herself, the Villa Silberblick in Weimar, where she gathered all of Friedrich's papers in the Nietzsche Archive and stashed the mad philosopher himself in an upstairs room. Ironically, Nietzsche, who struggled for recognition when sane, struck the world's romantic fancy as a madman, and with his sister's gifts for promotion he became internationally famous and influential. But with Elisabeth's distortions prevailing, Nietzsche, the great anti-dogmatist, was turned into a philosophic godfather of the most heinous dogma of all time, Nazism. And Elisabeth was directly involved in that outcome. At the end of her life she openly and actively embraced, encouraged, and provided phony philosophical credentials for Adolf Hitler.[30]

Although MacIntyre's work is helpful for reconstructing the events which led to Nazi Germany, and the political propaganda that Elisabeth emanated from the Nietzsche-Archive in Weimar, he does not expound on *why* Elisabeth mythologized her brother, save for the fact that she simply wanted to use his philosophy for her own political purposes; to claim her stake as the rightful heir and sole interpreter of Nietzsche's thought. A concise chronological reconstruction of events, in regards to Elisabeth and Nietzsche's association with the Wagner circle, and then to the history of controversy over Nietzsche's relationship to National Socialism, will thus conclude this book, offering the theory that Nazi leaders harbored a personal vendetta against Nietzsche and that they sought to discredit and silence him by steering readers *away* from his publications.

Nietzsche had access to an inner Wagner circle that is now regarded as the root of National Socialism. Upon leaving the circle in 1876, he wrote that Wagnerites were leading "the Jews to the slaughterhouse" as scapegoats for Germany's misfortunes.[31] Utterances, images, and metaphors concerning Jews and their extermination are recorded on several occasions throughout Nietzsche's works. These include a passage in *Daybreak* where—immediately prior to expressing concern for the destiny of European Jewry—Nietzsche writes of the "inhumaneness" of former times in which "Jews, heretics and the extermination of higher cultures" was done out of a lust for power and with a good conscience: "The means employed by the lust for power have changed, but the same volcano continues to glow . . . what one formerly did for the 'sake of God' one now does for the sake of money. . . ."[32] Passages also occur in the *Genealogy*, wherein Nietzsche writes of Dühring's attempt to "assassinate the future of man";[33] in *Zarathustra*, "The good are *unable* to create . . . they sacrifice the future to *themselves*—they crucify all man's future. The good have always been the beginning of the end;"[34] and in the *Antichrist*, wherein Nietzsche, battling his enemies, writes that the concept of immortality has been the greatest, and "most malignant attempt to assassinate *noble* humanity. . . . The *ressentiment* of the masses forged its chief weapon against *us*, against all that is noble, gay, high-minded on earth. . . . And let us not underestimate the calamity which crept out of Christianity into politics."[35] In a passage from *Zarathustra* which addresses Dühring—the first proto-Nazi who preached Jewish extermination—the "foaming fool" (Dühring) speaks of "smelling the slaughterhouses and ovens of the spirit" and warns Zarathustra to go away from the town.[36] Speaking in parables, Zarathustra expresses fear that his enemies will misuse his words. The following year, his antisemitic enemies, including Elisabeth, *do* retaliate by using the emotionally abusive tactic of regarding Nietzsche as an antisemite which Nietzsche revolts against—as recorded in several letters of 1887 (including those which were later suppressed by Elisabeth): "It is a manner of honor to me to be absolutely clean and unequivocal regarding anti-Semitism, namely *opposed*, as I am in my writings."[37]

After the threefold distinction of Jews emerged in *BGE*, Nietzsche composed the *Genealogy*, a polemic against Judeo-Christianity and the Germanic-Aryan race (which the Nazis would later exploit). In 1887, fearing that his works would be confiscated by the Second Reich, he sent many works to Brandes who promoted his philosophy at the University of Copenhagen. In his last productive year, Nietzsche wrote *Twilight*, compiled two polemical works against Wagner and wrote *Ecce Homo*. He also penned the *Antichrist*, which was a polemic against Renan and antisemitic Christian theology. Throughout his writings, desperate utterances and pleas to be "heard" continually recur and become more excessive over time. These include the famous passage from the *Gay Science* in which the madman announces that "we" have killed God; excerpts from his notebooks (published by Kaufmann): "For a long time now our whole civilization has been driving . . . towards a catastrophe. . . . Where we live, soon nobody will be able to exist;"[38] *BGE*, which marks his political involvement: "only listen:! . . . I have not met a German yet who was well disposed toward the Jews . . . ;"[39] up until his mental collapse, in which frantic utterances burst forth: "There has never been a more crucial moment in history. . . . They simply don't hear anything I say. . . ." And again, "Have I been understood? The uncovering of Christian morality is an event without parallel, a real catastrophe. He that is enlightened about that, is a . . . destiny—he breaks the history of mankind in two. One lives before him, or one lives after him."[40] In an excerpt from the *Nachlass* that reechoes his cry from *Ecce Homo*, "we shall have upheavals, a convulsion of earthquakes, the like of which have never yet been seen on earth," Nietzsche writes: "Externally: age of tremendous wars, upheavals, explosions. . . . *Consequences*: (1) *barbarians* (at first, of course, below the form of culture so far [e.g. Dühring]." The term "E.g., Dühring" is found only in 1911 (p. 500). In early January 1889, Nietzsche, ranting against antisemites, goes insane.

After Nietzsche's breakdown, Elisabeth seized his works, withholding from the public those writings that Nietzsche himself did not get a chance to publish; namely, the fourth part of *Zarathustra*, the *Antichrist*, *Nietzsche Contra Wagner*, and *Ecce Homo*. Elisabeth heavily censored the latter work which contained many remarks that were directed against her. She also censored *Zarathustra* IV which, as has been shown by Roger Hollinrake, closely corresponds with Wagner's operas, especially *Parsifal*. The extent to which she doctored these works and many of Nietzsche's personal documents is impossible to calculate. She destroyed many of Nietzsche's documents, and Wagner destroyed Nietzsche's Bayreuth letters at the time of their break.[41] As Elisabeth gained control of Nietzsche's literary estate, Franz Overbeck refused to relinquish to Elisabeth his personal letters from Nietzsche which, interestingly enough, are the primary personal documents that remain which contain many of Nietzsche's negative remarks against antisemitism, Wagner, and Elisabeth. On 25 August 1900, on what would have been the thirtieth wedding anniversary of Cosima and Richard Wagner, Nietzsche, solely under Elisabeth's care after her mother's death several years earlier, dies.

In Elisabeth's skewed two-volume biography of her brother, *The Life of Nietzsche* (the first two parts written between 1895-1904), to be followed by popular adaptations, *The Young Nietzsche* and *The Lonely Nietzsche* (1912-15), she addresses the issue of antisemitism in the latter volume. She correctly states that Nietzsche was not an antisemite, but also lies outright that she was not an antisemite either and, like her brother, disliked it. Elisabeth is clearly annoyed that she has to address the issue of her and Förster's antisemitism, which leads one to believe that she was under political pressure to do so.[42] Overall, in her biography and when forging or altering Nietzsche's personal documents, she continually attempts to cover up the bitter conflict over antisemitism among Nietzsche, herself, Förster, and Wagner. For instance, in *The Lonely Nietzsche* she regards "art"—not antisemitism—as the reason for the Wagner-Nietzsche break, and claims that the reason Nietzsche did not attend her and Förster's wedding was because he couldn't bear to say goodbye. The fact that Overbeck retained—and published Nietzsche's letters in 1907—made it difficult for her to cover up the conflict between herself and her brother, and perhaps is why she was forced to raise the issue of antisemitism in the preface to her updated 1914 biography.[43] A legal battle and feud between Overbeck and Elisabeth over Nietzsche's documents ensued for years; the feud "between the house of Overbeck and the Nietzsche Archive" is discussed in detail by Elisabeth in the preface to volume 2. Elisabeth did not get the letters.

Elisabeth patched together scraps of Nietzsche's notes on "race" and "breeding" (that the Nazis eventually used and which most likely initially referred to Elisabeth's Aryan breeding colony), and continued to create Nietzsche's image in a distorting manner. Well before the 1920s, Elisabeth's Nietzsche was a militarist, German nationalist, and somewhat of a Christian. By misquoting him out of context, she heavily implied antisemitism in his writings. In the 1930s, she aligned herself with Hitler and her Nazi friends who decided to utilize her brother. By the time of Elisabeth's death in 1935, Nietzsche's conversion to Nazism was complete and he emerged as one of the most famous "antisemites" of all time. The Nazis used "Nietzsche's" notes, compiled by Elisabeth years earlier, and were aided by Elisabeth in creating pamphlets of "essential Nazi Nietzsche sayings" that deceived people into thinking that he advocated positions of National Socialism. In regards to his published works, they exploited terms such as the "blond beast" to create the illusion that Nietzsche was an Aryan racial supremacist. They misquoted (or invented) remarks on Judaism and the Jews while committing their monstrosities in his name. In this fashion, the Nazis completely overturned Nietzsche's life and writings, which opposed antisemitism and the Aryan mythology of the Germans, all the while retorting, when challenged by Nietzsche defenders, that the "true Nietzsche" was not to be found in his publications.

The Nazi's use of Nietzsche caused (and continues to cause) an upheaval from the moment National Socialism arose. In the 40s, persons such as Kaufmann, Bataille, Jaspers, Camus, and the Mann brothers, fought to protect Nietzsche's writings from Nazi perversions, while others such as McGovern, Lukacs, and Brinton held that the Nazis were justified in using certain elements of Nietzsche's philosophy. Generally speaking, the former stated that Nietzsche foretold the coming of the Nazi era, the latter held that Nietzsche served to cause it. It became commonplace to take a middle position. Over time, many gradually came to recognize that Nietzsche was not an antisemite but then quickly went on to discuss "other elements" of Nietzsche's philosophy that the Nazis were allegedly "attracted" to. This position, though fashionable, is weak because it tosses aside the central issue that the Nazis *had* to, and in fact *did* claim Nietzsche was a ferocious antisemite. That is, even *they* did not think people would be foolish enough to believe Nietzsche could possibly be linked with their party unless he was first turned into a Jew hater.

The entire Nazi-Nietzsche myth was *built* on the premise of his antisemitism. Regardless, the issue of Nietzsche's politics and/or of his Nazi affiliation strayed—and continues to stray—further and further away from its core: the issue of the Jews. Today, elements of Nietzsche's philosophy, such as vague notions of his anti-Christianity and his antidemocracy (elements which the Nazis could not have cared less about) are cited as vital links between Nietzsche and National Socialism. (As if Nazism were *clearly* anti-Christian and its antisemitism were of secondary importance!)

The powerful psychological image of the Nazis decimating the Jews in Nietzsche's name has made it virtually impossible to even think about Nietzsche or his politics *before* that era—or to regard his political views with any respectability. This gives testimony to the Nazis as master propagandists. During and after the Nazi era, the natural defense erected by Kaufmann and others was thus to "depoliticize" Nietzsche, or conversely, to assert that the Nazis were justified in using select philosophical elements. Either way, Nietzsche's writings and his politics were put on the defense. Generally, since the 40s, Nietzsche has been an antisemite or a "Nazi" until proven otherwise (if one is in the least bit surprised that Nietzsche was a passionate advocate for the Jews, it is because they were deceived by Hitler's myth to begin with). To compound confusion even more, many writers automatically (and erroneously) assumed that because the Nazis used Nietzsche they saw something "appealing" in his writings; thus, often without proper knowledge of *how* they misappropriated his texts or *how* they compiled or used unpublished notes, they proceeded to search Nietzsche's publications to discern "appealing" elements. Not surprisingly, many came up with snippets and excerpts that the Nazis probably never even heard of.

On the whole, taking into consideration the cultural myths that surround Nietzsche and the history of lies, forgeries, and numerous interpretive positions that people have taken when addressing this thinker, it still remains a crucial fact that Nietzsche was a staunch opponent of antisemitism and that his extremely rare position during his time did not win for him many popularity contests. As one Jewish commentator in Germany wrote in 1934: "Today one must hammer into the brain that it was Jews who almost alone took a stand for Nietzsche and against trite materialism: Georg Brandes in the north, Henri Bergson in the west, Berdyczewski in the east."[44]

Even if we were to assume, with the most radical anti-Nietzsche interpreters today, that Nietzsche *caused* Hitler's Germany, it is still the case that Nietzsche's writings are historically invaluable for gaining insight into the Wagner circle, the phenomenon of antisemitism in both its religious and political forms, German nationalism, and Aryan racial supremacy, all of which he opposed. It is precisely those elements of his philosophy that Elisabeth and the Nazis sought to suppress and that this work has tried to highlight. The point here is not to elevate Nietzsche as a hero, a saint, or a savior—that was one of his greatest fears—but only to stress that his writings are important to the study of antisemitism and to the history of the European Holocaust.[45]

In short, my position is contrary to those positions which assume that the Nazis "liked" Nietzsche, that they learned from him, and/or that they "misunderstood" him. I rather hold that the Nazis understood Nietzsche all too well and *that* is precisely why they attempted to destroy him—and sever a vital part of Jewish history. The Nazis were not attracted to Nietzsche, they were repulsed and enraged by him precisely *because* he upheld the Jews and dared to defy many precursors of the Third Reich: namely, Richard and Cosima Wagner, Renan, Wellhausen, Dühring, Lagarde, Chamberlain, Gobineau, Stöcker, Förster, and Elisabeth Förster-Nietzsche.[46] The Nazis use of Nietzsche was not based on any "misinterpretation" or "selective appropriation," it was based on a twisted sense of spite and was an act of retaliation. Alfred Rosenberg's odd inscription on a wreath that he placed on

Nietzsche's grave, "To the Great Fighter," gives testimony to this, for it makes little sense when viewed apart from its sinister context. The Nazi appropriation of Nietzsche, however, was not solely rooted in revenge, it was also a means of silencing him, a technique that began with Elisabeth. If, for a moment, one imagines that in Nietzsche's time, Wagnerites had strong intentions to annihilate all or part of European Jewry—and to cover their traces in the process—Nietzsche's writings, initially made popular by a Jew, would be an obstacle. As Nietzsche started to become popular, Elisabeth clearly saw this, as evidenced by her immediate panic to suppress or destroy Nietzsche's documents, writings, and ideas—especially in regards to antisemitism. Later, as master propagandists, the Nazis continued Elisabeth's quest to confuse matters and to suppress his views in precisely the manner in which they did. On the one hand, they heralded Nietzsche as an antisemitic ally to cover their tracks and to discredit his opposition to antisemitism. On the other hand, they realized that if their crimes were discovered, Nietzsche would *still* serve as a scapegoat, which he indeed has. The fact that Nietzsche, among other things, wrote about and against Jewish extermination, coupled with the fact that Elisabeth immediately set out to mythologize her brother and to destroy or alter his documents, leads one to strongly suspect that the intent to destroy the Jews was already formulated during Nietzsche's time. I concede that Nietzsche, as a former member of an inner Wagner circle who had access to their "secret" correspondence sheet, knew of that design, was frightened to death, and that Elisabeth and then later the Nazis sought to silence, discredit, and destroy him. One does not forge documents, destroy letters, censor publications, create 'books' out of scribbled notes, and cover up bitter strife regarding antisemitism for *no reason* at all, and mere bigotry does not appear to be a sufficient enough motive. The process of manipulating Nietzsche, which began with Elisabeth and culminated with Hitler, was no "selective appropriation" or "misinterpretation"; it was based on the plain fact that they sought to silence an obnoxious foe, which they indeed did. The Nazis may have fooled the world, but they did not fool the Jews. According to Steven Aschheim, German-Jewish leaders looked to Nietzsche and Nietzschean folk wisdom for consolation while suffering under the Nazi regime, often quoting Nietzsche's famous phrase: "What does not destroy me makes me stronger."[47]

Here we must pause and reflect. When it was gradually discovered that Nietzsche was not an antisemite, as the Nazis claimed, a lesson should have been learned that Hitler was someone who simply could not be trusted. However, instead of enquiring as to why the Nazis targeted Nietzsche, the scapegoating process continued for three main reasons. The first is that many genuinely feared Nietzsche and believed that his thoughts influenced, and indeed caused Nazism. The second is that Nietzsche's anti-Judaic position had not been clarified and has continued to "haunt" him (as Elisabeth and Hitler knew it would). And the third is that many did not—and still do not—want to hear what Nietzsche actually said. This was precisely the political genius behind Elisabeth and Hitler's strategy of "squeezing" Nietzsche between religion and politics: even after Nietzsche's opposition to antisemitism were discovered, they perhaps rested content knowing that much of Western culture would not think highly of his anti-Christianity—regardless of its position toward National Socialism. It is in the interest of many to cleanly separate the moral Christian religion from the barbarisms of "pagan Nazism," and to portray the former as antithetical to the latter. However, Hitler died a Roman Catholic and Goering, a Lutheran; the Nazis employed Christian symbols to arouse the existing anti-semitism of the Christian masses, drawing especially upon the vehement anti-Jewish works of Luther; and, as has been repeatedly shown by numerous Holocaust studies, the destruction of the Jews in Europe was not carried out by a few political pagans, but was made possible by the compliance or indifference of the German nation, which was predominantly Christian. This is not to say that Christianity and Nazism are identical, or even that Nazism was especially well disposed toward Christianity. Perhaps in some aspects it was not. However, the chasm between Nazism and Christian Germany is not nearly as wide as many like to imagine—and the growing tendency to portray Nazism as an "anti-Christian" movement is itself becoming a myth; a myth that serves to relieve the Christian religion, once again, of any responsibility whatsoever for creating the distorted image of the Jew in Western civilization and for fertilizing the ground for Nazi Germany. In *Mein Kampf*, Hitler writes that the "great founder of Christianity" [Jesus] was nailed to the cross *because* he drove the wretched Jews from the Lord's temple.[48] Regardless of whether he actually believed this or not, or was merely vulgarizing Jesus as yet another propaganda tool, he would never have spoken highly of Moses, nor would he have regarded him as the "great founder" of Judaism as a political maneuver against Christianity. Nazism was clearly *anti-Jewish*: its relationship to Christianity was, at best, ambiguous. Hitler himself remarked that he was only putting into practice what Christianity had preached for two thousand years; and one need only look at Wagner and Elisabeth to recognize that the relationship between Christendom and Nazism is more akin to a merge than a chasm. The fight between Nietzsche and Elisabeth over the Jews cannot simply be viewed as a sibling rivalry between a brother and a sister; it should be seen in the larger context of the religious and political powers that these two figures represent. The Jew—even as victim—was seen by many as the enemy, as was Nietzsche. And the postwar controversy surrounding Nietzsche is precisely *that* he threatens the ingenious propagandic illusion that Nazism was "anti-Christian" in its "atheism" or worship of Wotan, and that if one opposes

Christianity, as Nietzsche did, moral chaos, romantic paganism, and social anarchy (such as Nazism) will ultimately ensue. But the fact of the matter is that social anarchy, moral chaos, "negative paganism," and proto-Nazism were already taking place in Nietzsche's time—indeed, even within the confines of his immediate family—and Nietzsche clearly named Christian and anti-Christian antisemitism as the major ingredients which served as the core for a polluted cultural decay. The god(s) that these antisemites adopted—or did not adopt—did not positively inform their moralities, but were super-added to their anti-Jewish racism and mattered little in providing a moral corrective. Indeed, as Nietzsche acutely diagnosed, the fact that the Jew was disgraced and humiliated by Christendom since the first century as the demonic murderer of God was the *root* of the problem to begin with, and provided a divine *sanction* for unparalleled religious bigotry and resentment in Western civilization. And that is precisely one of the hard truths Nietzsche uttered that many simply do not want to hear.[49]

If any future discussion concerning Nietzsche's relationship to Nazism is to occur, it must be made clear as to what psychological motivations and ideological concerns are driving the participants, now that new information has been made readily available by reputable postwar historians and scholars. And these discussions, it seems to me, must no longer take place in the realm of myth, World War II propaganda, anachronisms, uninformed opinions, and miscitations or narrow selections of Nietzsche's texts, but in the realm of scholastic integrity and a comprehensive sense of historicity. The damage done to Nietzsche and his work is irrevocable; but perhaps the saving grace is that serious thinkers, scholars, and historians can learn a great deal from this man about antisemitism and nineteenth-century German culture. This is especially timely in our age, considering that outrageous myths and lies that the Holocaust never took place are growing in alarming numbers.

Overall, exploring Nietzsche's life and thought in relation to Judeo-Christianity has not only served as an entry point into a complex personality and thinker, it has also provided a passage to history which, as evidenced, can be written from many different perspectives. I have attempted—as accurately as possible—to present Christianity and culture through the voice and story of one individual. In my view, this person tragically exemplifies the turbulent transition to modernity in a variety of ways, including the struggle for God in the midst of atheism. Nietzsche symbolically stands as the incarnation of a deep-seated religious crisis between Judaism and Christianity that had simmered for two thousand years, leading to the Holocaust only decades after he wrote. Nietzsche not only embodies and suffers this crisis, but brilliantly critiques it.

Nietzsche's overall quest was for a new faith and revolutionary change— beginning with the individual. Though ignored or scorned by his contemporaries, and then exploited, glorified, or trivialized by others, his writings continue to bear validity by the sheer force of their spirit and their insistence to be heard. As long as Nietzsche continues to disturb and create conflict, inciting critical responses to the issues that he raised, his philosophical task will not have been in vain.

NOTES

INTRODUCTION

1. Letter to Elisabeth, Bonn, 11 June 1865, no. 2, p. 7, *Selected Letters of Friedrich Nietzsche*, ed. and trans. Christopher Middleton (Chicago: University of Chicago Press, 1969). Hereafter cited as *L*.

2. This is by no means to suggest that the views of political scholars are similar to Brinton's, it is only to say that their primary concerns are the same. Cf. ch. 8 in Crane Brinton, *Nietzsche* (1941; New York: Harper, 1965) and "The National Socialists' Use of Nietzsche," *Journal of the History of Ideas* 1 (1940): 131-50.

3. Walter Kaufmann, *Nietzsche: Philosopher, Psychologist, Antichrist*, 4th ed. (1950; Princeton: Princeton University Press, 1974), 418.

4. David Allison, ed., *The New Nietzsche* (Cambridge, Mass.: MIT Press, 1985), xxiv.

5. Tracy Strong, *Nietzsche and the Politics of Transfiguration* (Berkeley: University of California Press, 1975), 202.

6. Ernst Benz's *Nietzsches ideen zur Geschichte des Christentums and der Kirche* (Leiden: E.J. Brill, 1956), largely deals with Nietzsche's relation to individual thinkers, such as Schopenhauer, Tolstoy, and Dostoevsky. For essay collections see *Nietzsche and Christianity*, *Concilium* 145 (May 1981), ed. Claude Geffré and Jean-Pierre Jossua, and *Studies in Nietzsche and the Judaeo-Christian Tradition*, ed. James C. O'Flaherty, Timothy F. Sellner, and Robert M. Helm (Chapel Hill: University of North Carolina Press, 1985). Virtually all Nietzsche commentators—at some point—make reference to Nietzsche's relationship to Christianity; however, comprehensive treatments of his views are seldom found. Nietzsche's disdain for the Christian tradition is simply assumed, and thus deemed unworthy of further consideration. Consequently, the depth and complexity of Nietzsche's religious and political critique of the Judeo-Christian tradition as a whole, is usually overlooked.

7. In the preface to *Nietzsche and Christianity*, trans. E. B. Ashton (Gateway, 1961), Jaspers, a Christian philosopher, states that he wants to show how much of a Christian the `Anti-Christ' Nietzsche is in order to "invite reflection upon the core of truth" inherent in Nietzsche's attacks, which were driven by `Christian motives.' When briefly addressing Nietzsche's thoughts on Judaism, in defense of Nietzsche, Jaspers writes: "Christianity strikes Nietzsche as an altogether Jewish phenomenon. . . . To

Nietzsche, Christianity—not Jesus—is merely the final consequence of Judaism" (pp. 32-34). The implication is that Nietzsche views Judaism as decadent, has a positive disposition toward Jesus, and is thus 'acceptable' in a Christian framework. Elsewhere Jaspers reiterates: "Nietzsche made distinctions, separating Jesus himself from the other, all-distorting roots of late Antiquity and Judaism, and finally from the secular transformation of Christian values into socialism, liberalism, and democracy" (p. 48). Jaspers is correct that Nietzsche respects Jesus, but he also has contempt for him. Most all Nietzsche scholars and Germanic historians correctly assert that Nietzsche's negative evaluation of Judaism was rooted in his contempt for Christianity, not that Nietzsche opposed Christianity *because* it had Jewish roots, as Jaspers implies.

Jaspers writes that the proper way to study Nietzsche, and to gain insight into his anti-Christianity, is twofold. First, "we must always be aware that we are not reading a finished achievement" and are dealing with fragments of his thought. And second, because Nietzsche's work lies under "the cloud of his illness . . . the extravagances, affects, and situations which arose from his illness . . . have nothing to do with the meaning of his work" and should be separated from his writings to enable us to grasp the "real truth more purely" (p. 100). I strongly disagree with Jasper's second contention. The consummating nature of chronic pain was central to Nietzsche's existence and thus cannot be separated from his writings. As will be shown, Nietzsche's experience of suffering profoundly shaped his philosophy, his positive affinity with ancient Hebrews and contemporary Jews, and also his skeptical critique of Judeo-Christianity. Jasper's major work on Nietzsche is *Nietzsche: An Introduction to the Understanding of his Philosophical Activity*, trans. Charles F. Wallraff and Frederick J. Schmitz (South Bend: Gateway, 1965).

8. Cf. Frederick Copleston, *Friedrich Nietzsche: Philosopher of Culture* (London, 1942), 181-95; A. C. Coutinho, "Nietzsche's Critique of Judaism," *Review of Religion* 3 (1939): 161-66; Arnold M. Eisen, "Nietzsche and the Jews Reconsidered," *Jewish Social Studies* 48.1 (1986): 1-14; Jacob Golomb, "Nietzsche's Judaism of Power," *Revue des Études juives* 146-47 (July-December, 1988): 353-85; Alfred D. Low, *Jews in the Eyes of the Germans: From the Enlightenment to Imperial Germany* (Philadelphia, 1979), 377-88; and Nathan Rotenstreich, *Jews and German Philosophy: The Polemics of Emancipation*, (New York, 1984).

9. Both Kaufmann (pp. 290-92) and Golomb (p. 353) point to Crane Brinton as the culprit in the English-speaking world largely responsible for perpetuating distortions of Nietzsche's treatment of the Jews. Kaufmann exposes Brinton's unfamiliarity with Nietzsche—and his incompetent scholarship—when critiquing Brinton's *Nietzsche*. Brinton claims that "most of the stock of professional anti-Semitism is represented in Nietzsche," and that Nietzsche "held the Jews responsible for Christianity, Democracy, Marxism" (p. 215). Brinton then cites six references to substantiate this claim. Kaufmann discovers that out of the six references two of Nietzsche's quotes do not even mention the Jews; two speak against antisemitism; one is a reference that does not even exist; and none mention the 'triad' of Christianity, Democracy, and Marxism. Kaufmann also discovers that the 'triad' comes from the Nazi scholar, Heinrich Härtle, as do all six ref-

erences, and that Brinton copied the references from Härtle's work without checking them himself. The results are embarrassing; however, even after reading Kaufmann's findings Brinton refused to correct the bogus references in the new edition published in 1965. Brinton's book includes a picture of Hitler staring at a Nietzsche bust at the Nietzsche-Archive in Weimar (interestingly, only half of Nietzsche's face is shown and Hitler is frowning); throughout the entire work, the widely respected historian erroneously attributes sections from *Beyond Good and Evil* to the *Genealogy of Morals.*

10. Michael Duffy and Willard Mittelman, "Nietzsche's Attitudes Toward the Jews," *Journal of the History of Ideas* 49 (1988): 301-17. Golomb (1988) also recognizes these distinctions, but his primary focus is not chronological, but designed to situate Nietzsche's views toward Jews and Judaism within the framework of Nietzsche's overall psychology and philosophy.

11. Duffy and Mittelman, 315.

12. See ch. 7 "The Feminist Movement and Nietzsche," in R. Hinton Thomas, *Nietzsche in German Politics and Society 1890-1918* (La Salle: Open Court, 1983). For a discussion of feminism and the assimilation of Nietzsche by German-Jewry, see ch. 4 in Steven Aschheim's superb cultural history, *The Nietzsche Legacy in Germany, 1890-1990* (Berkeley: University of California Press, 1992).

13. For further discussion of the problems surrounding the *Nachlass*, see Kaufmann's appendix "Nietzsche's `Suppressed' Manuscripts," in *Nietzsche*. The issues are complicated and center around Elisabeth's tampering and suppression of her brother's notebooks and letters at the Nietzsche-Archive in Weimar. Elisabeth suppressed some remarks directed against herself, her husband, Wagner, antisemitism, the Germans, Jesus, and Christianity, as well as others. Although the suppressed remarks indirectly bear on the primary concerns of this work, I regard the notes and letters as secondary to Nietzsche's texts, wherein his ideas are sufficiently presented.

1. NIETZSCHE'S EARLY YEARS

1. Letter to Franz Overbeck, Sils-Maria, Engadine, 23 June 1881. *Nietzsche: A Self-Portrait from His Letters*, trans. and ed. by Peter Fuss and Henry Shapiro (Cambridge, Mass.: Harvard University Press, 1971), no. 65, p. 55. Hereafter cited as *SP*.

2. Letter to Malwida von Meysenbug, Venice, late April 1884, *SP*, no. 96, p. 78.

3. Elisabeth Förster-Nietzsche, *The Life of Nietzsche*, trans. A. M. Ludovici, 3 vols. (New York: Sturgis and Walton Company, 1912), 1:12.

4. It has been suggested that Nietzsche's father died insane from syphilis and that Nietzsche inherited the disease from him. However, not only is his father's alleged insanity a conjecture, it is highly improbable that Nietzsche contacted the disease from him, considering the time that elapsed before Nietzsche's mental breakdown at age

forty-four. Nietzsche wrote at the age of fourteen in "Aus meinem Leben" that his "beloved father suddenly became *gemütskrank*" (an imprecise term meaning 'mentally disordered' or 'melancholy'). Förster-Nietzsche, whose biographies are notoriously dishonest and unreliable, changes Nietzsche's quote to read: "my beloved father suddenly became seriously ill as a result of a fall," thus causing further speculation. See R. J. Hollingdale's *Nietzsche: The Man and his Philosophy* (1965; London: Routledge and Kegan Paul, 1985), 11ff., for a succinct discussion of the issues surrounding the ambiguity of his father's death and Nietzsche's relation to it.

5. For a detailed discussion of Nietzsche's childhood years, see Ronald Hayman *Nietzsche: A Critical Life* (1980; New York: Penguin, 1984), ch. 1 et seq.

6. "Aus meinem Leben," quoted in Hayman's *Nietzsche*, 26.

7. "Fate and History," quoted in Hayman's *Nietzsche*, 44-45.

8. Friedrich Nietzsche, *Thus Spoke Zarathustra*, trans. Walter Kaufmann (New York: Viking Press, 1966), pt. I, "On the Thousand and One Goals." See also *Daybreak* 108.

9. *The Poetry of Friedrich Nietzsche*, trans. and ed. Philip Grundlehner (New York: Oxford University Press, 1986), 25-26.

10. Hollingdale, *Nietzsche*, 27.

11. Hayman, 66.

12. Letter to Elisabeth, Bonn, 11 June 1865, *L*, no. 2, p. 6.

13. *Zarathustra*, III, "On Apostates."

14. Autobiographical Writings from 1856-69. Quoted in Ivo Frenzel, *Friedrich Nietzsche: An Illustrated Biography*, trans. Joachim Neugroschel (1966; New York: Pegasus, 1967), 18.

15. Friedrich Nietzsche, "Schopenhauer as Educator," *Untimely Meditations*, trans. R. J. Hollingdale, intro. J. P. Stern (Cambridge: Cambridge University Press, 1983), sec. 2, p. 133.

16. "Arthur Schopenhauer," *The Encyclopedia of Unbelief*, v. 1, 1985.

17. Cf. M. S. Silk and J. P. Stern, *Nietzsche on Tragedy* (1981; Cambridge: Cambridge University Press, 1984), 46ff.

18. Letter to his mother, Sulz, 28 August 1870. *Selected Letters of Friedrich Nietzsche*, trans. A. N. Ludovici, ed. Oscar Levy (London: Soho Book Company, 1985), p. 64. Hereafter cited as *SL*.

19. Letter to his mother and sister, Basle, 12 December 1870, *SL*, p. 72. Cf. letter to Carl von Gersdorff, Basle, 12 December 1870, *SP*, no. 15, p. 13. That Nietzsche became

disillusioned by the wars he himself was involved in is not to suggest that he was a pacifist. For further discussion on Nietzsche's experience of war, see Peter Bergmann, *Nietzsche, "The Last Antipolitical German"* (Bloomington: Indiana University Press, 1987), 78-83. Nietzsche's letters to his family and his stress over war are antithetical to the "uniform" loving, militaristic image of Nietzsche that Elisabeth created for decades after her brother's insanity.

20. Cf. "An Attempt at a Self-Criticism" in *The Birth of Tragedy*, trans. Walter Kaufmann (New York: Vintage, 1967), which Nietzsche added in 1886, fourteen years after initially writing the book.

21. Wagner to Nietzsche, beginning of January 1872, *The Nietzsche-Wagner Correspondence*, trans. Caroline V. Kerr, ed. Elisabeth Förster-Nietzsche (1921; New York: Liveright, 1949), p. 94, hereafter cited as *NWC*; Hayman, 146.

22. See the introduction by J. P. Stern in Nietzsche's *Untimely Meditations*, trans. Hollingdale, xii-xiii.

23. David Strauss, *The Old Faith and the New*, trans. Mathilde Blind (London: Asher & Co., 1874), 90.

24. Friedrich Nietzsche, "David Strauss: The Confessor and the Writer," *Untimely Meditations*, sec. 7, p. 29.

25. "David Strauss, the Confessor and the Writer," sec. 7, p. 31.

26. Ibid., sec. 6, p. 28.

27. Friedrich Nietzsche, *The Antichrist*, *The Portable Nietzsche*, trans. Walter Kaufmann (New York: Penguin Books, 1982), 28. See also the preface to *Human*, II (added in 1886) for Nietzsche's commentary on Strauss.

28. Friedrich Nietzsche, "On the Uses and Disadvantages of History for Life," *Untimely Meditations*, sec. 9, pp. 112-13.

29. "On the Uses and Disadvantages of History for Life," sec. 9, pp. 113-14.

30. Ibid., p. 113.

31. "Schopenhauer as Educator," sec. 5, p. 159. In Nietzsche's early philosophy, saints are regarded as exemplars. Later however, although he agrees that these three types have tried to rise above the masses, the saint is pictured as one who has extirpated passions and has thus destroyed the chances of living nobly. See Kaufmann's *Nietzsche*, pp. 280-81.

32. "On the Uses and Disadvantages of History for Life," sec. 9, p. 111.

33. Nietzsche was Burckhardt's younger professorial colleague at the University of Basle. For a discussion of their relationship, see Erich Heller's "Burckhardt and Nietzsche," in *The Importance of Nietzsche* (Chicago: University of Chicago Press, 1988).

34. Friedrich Nietzsche, *The Gay Science*, trans. Walter Kaufmann (New York: Random House, 1974), 55.

35. *The Gay Science*, 297.

36. *Antichrist*, preface.

37. *The Gay Science*, 55.

38. *Antichrist*, preface.

39. *Human, All-too-Human*, trans. Marion Faber (Lincoln: University of Nebraska Press, 1984), 291.

40. *The Gay Science*, 290.

41. *Antichrist*, preface.

42. *The Gay Science*, 335.

43. *Human, All-too-Human*, 230.

44. *Zarathustra*, II, "Upon the Blessed Isles," trans. Hollingdale.

45. *Zarathustra*, II, "On Self Overcoming"; *GS* 349; *TW* "Skirmishes," 14.

46. Friedrich Nietzsche, "Richard Wagner in Bayreuth," *Untimely Meditations*, sec. 8, pp. 231-32.

47. *Cosima Wagner's Diaries*, ed. Martin Gregor-Dellin and Dietrich Mack, trans. Geoffrey Skelton, 2 vols. (London: William Collins Sons & Co. Ltd, 1976), 29 May 1872, 1:491.

48. *Cosima Wagner's Diaries*, 25 September 1873, 1:680.

49. Ernest Newman, *The Life of Richard Wagner*, 4 vols. (New York: Alfred A. Knopf, Inc., 1933-1946), 4:326.

50. Newman, 326.

51. Wagner to Nietzsche, Tribschen, 14 January 1870, *NWC*, pp. 30-31.

52. Nietzsche to Wagner, Basle, 10 November 1870, *NWC*, p. 71.

53. Nietzsche's notebook entries are quoted in Stern's introduction to *UM*, xxviii.

54. *UM*, introduction, xxvii.

55. *UM*, introduction, xxviii.

56. Förster-Nietzsche, 1:393 (1912 translation).

57. Newman, 517, 689.

58. Cf. Newman, 589-91.

59. Newman, 522ff.

60. Newman, 297, 598; Kaufmann, 39.

61. Kaufmann, 38.

62. Kaufmann, 37.

63. Förster-Nietzsche, 1:368; Wagner to Nietzsche, Wahnfried, 9 June 1874, *NWC*, p. 213.

64. Newman, 533. Cf. *EH*, "Human."

65. *Cosima Wagner's Diaries*, 1 November 1876, 1:931.

66. Förster-Nietzsche, *The Lonely Nietzsche*, 2:11-13. For a discussion of Wagner's obsessive hatred of the Jews, see Jacob Katz *The Darker Side of Genius: Richard Wagner's Antisemitism* (Hanover and London: University Press of New England, 1986) and Margaret Brearley "Hitler and Wagner: The Leader, the Master and the Jews," *Patterns of Prejudice* 22.2 (1988): 3-22. Katz's book provides a comprehensive survey of Wagner's antisemitism, tracing it through his diaries and letters. Brearley's essay provides fascinating insights into the antisemitism prevalent in Wagner's prose writings and operas, including *Parsifal*, which Nietzsche regarded as an "outrage on morality."

67. Förster-Nietzsche writes that both von Meysenbug and Rée were mistaken to hold that "Wagner's judgment was warped by his excessive prejudice against Jews." She insists that *they* did not know her brother's amiable feelings toward Wagner during that time. Elisabeth claims that Wagner "generally refused to admit the presence of Dr. Rée" because he thought that her brother would come to grief through Rée and that Nietzsche "ruefully remembered" Wagner's words years later, "when they proved true." She continues to say that her brother's disappointment with Wagner's art did not kill his affection or loyalty for Wagner; rather, the incident that "finally touched her brother very closely" was Wagner's conversion to Christianity, thus deceitfully implying that Wagner's new religious affiliation—not antisemitism—was the main cause of the break; cf. vol. 2, 10ff. Cosima writes in her diary that Nietzsche and von Meysenbug visited on the 2nd; although she records von Meysenbug's visit on the 6th, she does not mention Nietzsche. It could be that Wagner refused to admit Rée on the 2nd (after discovering he was 'an Israelite'), that Nietzsche and Wagner had words, and that Nietzsche refused to return on the 6th, the night before the Wagners left for Rome, wherein Richard met his soon to be friend and Aryan racial theorist, Count Gobineau (*Inequality of Human Races*, 1854), for the first time. Regardless, the final meeting between Nietzsche and Wagner took place somewhere between the 2nd and 6th of November, shortly after Cosima recorded her derogatory remarks about Rée. Unfortunately, Wagner destroyed Nietzsche's Bayreuth letters and Cosima's diary entries are curiously uninformative. Cosima's diaries were not made available to the public until 1976.

68. *Cosima Wagner's Diaries*, 24 December 1876, 1:938. See letters no. 425 (1874), p. 831, and no. 455 (1877), p. 874, in *The Selected Letters of Richard Wagner*, trans and ed. Steward Spencer and Barry Millington (New York: Norton, 1987), hereafter cited as *SLRW*. Nietzsche was further outraged when Wagner took the liberty of writing to Nietzsche's doctor, urging him to accept his diagnosis that Nietzsche's peculiar behavior and physical ailments were caused by habitual masturbation. Wagner, who had advised Nietzsche years earlier to "get married, or else write an opera," suggested to Nietzsche's doctor a water cure! After suggesting that Nietzsche marry or write an opera, Wagner, who mocked Nietzsche's aspirations as a musician, adds: "The one would do you just as much good and harm as the other. But, of the two, I prefer marriage—," no. 425.

69. Quoted in Dietrich Fischer-Dieskau, *Wagner and Nietzsche* (New York: Seabury, 1976), 162. At the Easter fair in 1879, *Human* sold 150 copies, as opposed to the hoped-for thousand copies.

70. In a letter to Salomé in 1882 and in *Ecce Homo* (1888), Nietzsche romanticizes the sequence of events. He says that Wagner's *Parsifal* and *Human, All-too-Human* "crossed like swords" in the mail, and that he received Wagner's opera at the same time Wagner received his book. However, Nietzsche received Parsifal at the beginning of January; *Human* was not yet published and was sent out to his 'friends' in the spring, cf. *L*, pp. 166 and 188. Nietzsche, however, did send off *Human*'s manuscript to the printer at the time Wagner sent *Parsifal*; he may have simply confused the two.

71. Friedrich Nietzsche, *The Case of Wagner*, trans. Walter Kaufmann (New York: Vintage, 1967), epilogue; *WP* 87. The Hungarian pianist and composer Franz Liszt (1811-86) was Cosima's father. He retired to Rome in 1861, joined the Franciscan order four years later, and eventually joined the Wagners in Bayreuth, where he died in 1886.

72. *Nietzsche Contra Wagner, The Portable Nietzsche*, "How I broke away from Wagner," sec. 1. The original passage appears in the preface to *Assorted Opinions and Maxims*, trans. R. J. Hollingdale, intro. Erich Heller (Cambridge: Cambridge University Press, 1986).

73. *Zarathustra*, III, "On Apostates," sec. 1. See also *Z* IV, "The Magician," for Nietzsche's account of his break with Wagner, and *Z* II, "Upon the Blessed Isles," for an account of Tribschen, which he regarded as the isle of the blessed.

74. *Human*, 475. Nietzsche's apparently negative remark in this long aphorism that "perhaps the youthful Jew of the stock exchange is the most repugnant invention of the whole human race" is often quoted out of context by commentators to demonstrate Nietzsche's overall attitude toward Jews. As Golomb notes, this is a "gross distortion" of Nietzsche's views that are driven by strong emotions and the personal, political, and ideological commitments of such scholars, 353. Duffy and Mittelman view the few negative remarks as vestiges of Nietzsche's early antisemitism, which do not obscure his general praise for the creative gifts of the ancient Jews nor his "overwhelmingly positive

attitude toward modern Jewry," 307. It seems even more appropriate, however, to emphasize the term *perhaps*, and view this passage in the context of Nietzsche's break from the Wagner circle. Nietzsche was attempting to offend Wagnerites—and succeeded in doing so.

75. Quoted in Heller's Intro. to *Human*, p. xi. Cf. Robert Gutman, *Richard Wagner* (1968; San Diego: Harvest, 1990), 360; and Nietzsche's letter to Peter Gast, Basle, 31 May 1878, *L*, no. 80, p. 166. Although Wagner wrote to Overbeck that "out of friendship" he had decided *not to read* Nietzsche's book, Cosima's diary reveals that Wagner devoted most of May and June to studying it. For an exceptional commentary on Newman's "odd interpretation" of the break, see the widely acclaimed Wagner biography by Gutman, 352ff. Gutman writes that Newman resents and "stacks the cards" against Nietzsche because he "dared to challenge" the master's music. But, says Gutman, Nietzsche's challenge was essentially ethical, not musical: "For Nietzsche, Bayreuth had turned out to be a 'contemptible little German affair.' . . . And Wahnfried's paranoiac antisemitism frightened him. It became one of the major issues over which he broke with Bayreuth," 358.

76. H. F. Peters, *Zarathustra's Sister: The Case of Elisabeth and Friedrich Nietzsche* (1977; Markus Wiener, 1985), 46ff. See also Wagner's letters to Overbeck, no. 474, p. 897, and no. 466, p. 884, in *SLRW*. The following year Wagner continues to insist that Nietzsche was "forcefully driven" from him and also that Nietzsche's life was ruled by psychic spasms: "It saddens me, however, to be so completely excluded from any part in Nietzsche's life and difficulties," no. 474.

77. Nietzsche ends his passage by stating that the symbol of the cross appears in an age which no longer knows the meaning and shame of the Cross: "Can one believe that things of this sort are still believed in?"

78. For a discussion of Wagner's views on Christianity and Jesus, see ch. 4 in Leon Stein, *The Racial Thinking of Richard Wagner* (New York: Philosophical Library, 1950) and ch. 7 in Alan David Aberbach, *The Ideas of Richard Wagner* (University Press of America: Lanham, 1988). Wagner sought the Jesus of a pre-Christian era, a "universal man of God" who transcended his Judaic background. He thus linked Jesus with Adam, not David. See also *GS* 99: "Wagner is Schopenhauerian in his hatred of the Jews to whom he is not able to do justice even when it comes to their greatest deed; after all, the Jews are the inventors of Christianity."

79. Friedrich Nietzsche, *Ecce Homo*, trans. R. J. Hollingdale (New York: Penguin, 1988), "Why I am so Clever," sec. 5.

80. Letter to Elisabeth, Genoa, 3 February 1882, *SL*, p. 145.

81. Friedrich Nietzsche, *Beyond Good and Evil*, trans. Walter Kaufmann (New York: Random House, 1966), 41: "One has to test oneself to see that one is destined for independence and command—and do it at the right time. Not to remain stuck to a person—not even the most loved—every person is a prison, also a nook."

82. Letter to von Meysenbug, Naumburg, 14 January 1880, *SP*, no. 59, p. 51. According to Peters, although Nietzsche realized he would offend Wagner he was still hoping to get at least some positive response from Wagner after sending him *Human*, and was disappointed at his silence, p. 48ff. Although Nietzsche does state that his "excommunication from Bayreuth" revealed Wagner's failure to display "greatness of character," he knew Wagner well enough to foresee that his book would provoke irreconcilable outrage from Wagner, cf. *L*, no. 80, pp. 166-67. And lest there be any ambiguity, Nietzsche assured the break with his sarcastic salutation on one of the Wagners' two copies.

83. *Zarathustra*, I, "On the Way of the Creator."

84. *Zarathustra*, I, "On the Friend."

85. *Zarathustra*, prologue, sec. 4; *BGE* 216.

86. Letter to Franz Overbeck, received 2 May 1884, *L*, no. 123, p. 224.

87. Cf. "Discussion of Nietzsche's *Ecce Homo*," Scientific meeting on 28 October 1908 in *Minutes of the Vienna Psychoanalytic Society*, vol. 2: 1908-1910, ed. Herbert Nunberg and Ernst Federn, trans. M. Nunberg (New York: International Universities Press, 1967), pp. 25-33. Freud's analysis of Nietzsche was informed by deep respect: "In my youth Nietzsche signified a nobility which I could not attain," as well as by professional friction, Ernest Jones, *The Life and Work of Sigmund Freud*, 3 vols. (New York: Basic Books, 1953), vol. 3, p. 460. Colleagues often pointed out to Freud that Nietzsche was the first to discover many of Freud's psychological insights: the significance of repression, of flight into illness, and the normal sexual and sadistic instincts. Freud's response was to credit Nietzsche with anticipatory ideas, while insisting that he came to his own theories independently of the philosopher, Sigmund Freud, *On the History of the Psycho-Analytic Movement*, trans. Joan Riviere (New York: Norton, 1966), 15. According to Freud, in later years he denied himself "the very great pleasure of reading the works of Nietzsche, with the deliberate object of not being hampered . . . by anticipatory ideas." See also the discussion of "Nietzsche 'On the Ascetic Ideal' (Section 3 of *Genealogy of Morality*)," Scientific Meeting on 1 April 1908 in *Minutes of the Vienna Psychoanalytic Society*, vol. 1: 1906-8, ed. Herman Nunberg and Ernst Federn, trans. M. Nunberg (New York: International Universities Press, 1963), pp. 355-61.

88. Quoted in Hollingdale's *Nietzsche*, 28. The quote is from Nietzsche's essay "On the Childhood of the Peoples."

89. Letter to Gustav Krug, Pilatus, 4 August 1869; *L*, no. 17, p. 56.

90. *Human*, 25.

91. Cf. especially the preface to *Human* (added in 1886) wherein Nietzsche writes of the "great liberation" that comes for those who are fettered suddenly, "like the shock of an earthquake" (sec. 3).

92. *Twilight of the Idols*, "The Four Great Errors," sec. 8.

2. ZARATHUSTRA'S WORLD

1. Letter to Dr. Otto Eiser, Naumburg, January 1880, *SP*, no. 60, p. 51.

2. Letter to Franz Overbeck, Rapallo, 22 February 1883, *SP*, no. 87, p. 72.

3. Cf. *The Gay Science*, 357.

4. Letter to Peter Gast, Marienbad, 20 August 1880, *SP*, no. 63, p. 53.

5. Cosima Wagner's Diaries, 6 July 1880, v. 2, p. 505.

6. It is generally agreed that Nietzsche's insanity was due to syphilis. However, because Nietzsche was a sexual ascetic for most—if not all of his life—there is speculation as to whether Nietzsche inherited the illness from his father, from visiting a brothel in his college days, or from dirty needles while a nurse in the Franco-Prussian war. It is often assumed that Nietzsche contacted syphilis when he was at Bonn because he admitted that he *had* visited a brothel. However, he also insisted that he came out touching nothing but a piano. According to Nietzsche's friend, Paul Deussen (1845-1919), Nietzsche was taken to a brothel in Cologne by his fraternity brothers. He was so taken aback that he proceeded directly to the piano until it was time to leave, cf. Paul Deussen, *Erinnerungen and Friedrich Nietzsche* (Leipzig: F. A. Brockhaus, 1901), 22ff., and Carl Pletsch, *The Young Nietzsche* (New York: Free Press, 1991), 66-67.

7. Letter to Franz Overbeck, Genoa, November 1880, *SP*, no. 64, p. 54.

8. Overbeck (1837-1905) was a professor of New Testament studies and Church History at Basle. He and his wife Ida, who were married in '76, became Nietzsche's confidantes and most trusted friends in his mature years. Overbeck served as Nietzsche's unofficial business manager from the time Nietzsche left Basle until 1897, nine years after Nietzsche's insanity. Erwin Rohde (1845-98) was a classical philologist who, along with Nietzsche, followed Ritschl from the University of Bonn to Leipzig. He married in 1877 and started becoming estranged from Nietzsche a year later with the appearance of *Human*, which he found alien to Nietzsche's "true nature." The friendship eventually disintegrated after an attempted reunion in Leipzig in 1886. Peter Gast (1854-1918) was a student of Overbeck and Nietzsche's who also served as the editor and proofreader of Nietzsche's manuscripts; a warm relationship developed between the two. After Gast moved to Venice as a musician in 1878, their relationship was maintained through correspondence and occasional visits. Gast and Overbeck supervised Nietzsche's literary estate after his insanity in 1888, until his sister Elisabeth began taking control in 1893. For a concise discussion of Nietzsche's correspondents, see *SP*, 155ff.

9. According to Salomé, Nietzsche himself proposed to her once, and had Rée propose to Salomé on his behalf the second time. Kaufmann sees this occurrence as highly unlikely. Based on additional evidence concerning Salomé's falsified documents, as presented by Rudolph Binion's *Frau Lou* (1968), Kaufmann concludes that

Salomé's claim that Nietzsche proposed marriage to her was a tale "although she was apparently waiting for him to do so" (pp. 48-51). For further discussion see chapter two in William Beatty Warner's *Chance and the Text of Experience* (Ithaca, 1986). Warner argues that Kaufmann and other Nietzsche interpreters find pleasure in marginalizing Salomé's emotional influence on Nietzsche in order to present the philosopher as a genius immuned to any encounter with an 'other.' These side debates on minor details concerning Nietzsche's life illustrate the difficulties involved with obtaining accurate and reliable biographical information, as layers upon layers of lies and forgeries have surfaced from decade to decade. The Nietzsche scholar's nightmare is not so much to obtain the minutest details about Nietzsche's life; but rather, to discern what the few people closest to him were trying to hide.

10. Lou Salomé, *Nietzsche*, trans. and ed. Siegfried Mandel (1894; Redding Ridge: Black Swan Books, 1988), 54.

11. Hollingdale, *Nietzsche*, 151-55; Peter Pulzer, *The Rise of Political Anti-Semitism in Germany and Austria* (Cambridge, Mass.: Harvard University Press, 1988), 91. Förster and Elisabeth, who were both Wagnerians, met in 1877. But it was not until the early eighties that their relationship became more involved, as Elisabeth expressed an increased desire to join Förster's cause against the Jews and also to marry him.

12. *The Times*, 1 February 1883. Bernhard and his brother Paul, who was also a prominent antisemitic politician, were the sons of a widow who was a close friend of Nietzsche's mother. Bernhard was removed from his teaching post by the Berlin City Council for assaulting a Jew on a Berlin street car.

13. Unpublished letter, Naumburg, 7 January 1883. Quoted in Peters' *Zarathustra's Sister*, 71.

14. Letter to Franz Overbeck, Leipzig, early September 1882, *SP*, no. 80, p. 67.

15. *Zarathustra*, prologue, 9.

16. Quoted in Peters' *Zarathustra's Sister*, 69.

17. Letter to Paul Rée, Santa Margherita, end of November, 1882, *SP*, no. 81, p. 68.

18. Letter to Lou Salomé and Paul Rée, Santa Margherita, mid-December, 1882, *SP*, no. 82, pp. 68-69.

19. Friedrich Nietzsche, *Ecce Homo* and *On the Genealogy of Morals*, trans. Walter Kaufmann (New York: Random House, 1967), "Why I am so Wise," sec. 8. Kaufmann's translation of *EH* will be used hereafter unless otherwise specified.

20. Quoted in Kaufmann's preface to *Thus Spoke Zarathustra*, xiv.

21. Letter to Peter Gast, Rapallo, 19 February 1883, *SP*, no. 86, p. 71.

22. Letter to Franz Overbeck, Rapallo, received 11 February 1883, *SP*, no. 85, pp. 70-71.

23. *Zarathustra*, II, "The Stillest Hour."

24. *Zarathustra*, prologue, 5.

25. Letter to Franz Overbeck, received 11 February 1883, *L*, no. 110, p. 207. Cf. C. G. Jung, *Nietzsche's Zarathustra*, 2 vols., ed. James Jarrett, Bollingen Series 99 (Princeton: Princeton University Press, 1988).

26. *Zarathustra*, prologue, 3.

27. Ibid.

28. Ibid., prologue, 4.

29. *Zarathustra*, I, "On the New Idol."

30. Cf. *EH*, "Human," 2: "I think I know the Wagnerians. . . . Not a single abortion is missing among them, not even the antisemites. —Poor Wagner! Where had he landed! —If he had at least entered into swine! But to descend among Germans!"

31. *Zarathustra*, I, "On the Friend."

32. Ibid., "On Little Old and Young Women." Here Nietzsche is writing about how women should love men; not how men should love women.

33. *Zarathustra*, II, "On the Pitying."

34. *Zarathustra*, I, "On the Adders Bite."

35. Letter to Elisabeth, Sils-Maria, end of August 1883, *SL*, 165ff.

36. *Zarathustra*, I, "On Little Old and Young Women." Interestingly, Nietzsche does not put these words in Zarathustra's mouth, but has them spoken by a woman. There is no evidence to suggest that Hitler ever read a word of Nietzsche; however, as will become evident, he most certainly was aware of Nietzsche's opposition to antisemitism. Hitler apparently had a penchant for whips. In *Mein Kampf*, when alluding to the gospels, Hitler writes that Christ's attitude to the Jewish people was clearly expressed when he "took to the whip to drive from the temple of the Lord this adversary [the Jew] of all humanity" (p. 307).

37. In the passage from *Zarathustra*, the iron (the man) asks the magnet (the woman): "'Whom does woman hate most?' The woman responds: 'I hate you most because you attract, but are not strong enough to pull me to you.'"

38. This is not to suggest that Nietzsche does not speak negatively of women prior to *Zarathustra*. I only stress the positive elements in his pre-*Zarathustra* writings in order to demonstrate the drastic change which took place from *Zarathustra* onward. In *Human*, a section entitled "Women and Child" contains sixty aphorisms. Not one of the sixty aphorisms, which were published in 1878, would be classified as misogynist—by modern standards. See especially *Daybreak*, "Misogynists," 346; and *GS* 68, which perhaps reveals his own inner struggle with misogyny.

39. Cf. *L*, p. 220.

40. Letter to Malwida von Meysenbug, Venice, late April 1884, *SP*, no. 96, p. 79.

41. *Human,* 380.

42. *Ecce Homo*, "Why I Write Such Good Books," sec. 5.

43. Letter to Peter Gast, Rapallo, 19 February 1883, *SP*, no. 86, p. 71.

44. *Ecce Homo*, "The Case of Wagner," sec. 1.

45. *Cosima Wagner's Diaries*, 4 February 1883. The following day, Cosima writes that Nietzsche's breach of faith again crossed Wagner's mind.

46. Letter to Peter Gast, Sils-Maria, 1 July 1883, *SL*, p. 155ff.

47. Letter to Overbeck, 2 April 1884. Quoted in Bergmann's *Nietzsche*, 157. Nietzsche's meeting with Josef Paneth 'opened Nietzsche's eyes' to the fact that his reputation was being damaged.

48. Letter to Franz Overbeck, Genoa, rec. 24 March 1883, *L*, no. 113, p. 210.

49. Letter to Peter Gast, Sils-Maria, 26 August 1883, *SL*, p. 162ff.

50. Cf. *L*, p. 220.

51. Letter to von Meysenbug, Genoa, end of March, 1883, *L*, no. 114, p. 211.

52. Unpublished letter, Rome, 4 April 1883. Quoted in Peters, 72.

53. Letter to his mother, Sils-Maria, August 1883, *SL*, p. 159. Cf. *L*, no. 122, p. 222: "I have no news about [the proceedings against] Schmeitzner. The question is most awkward for me, for I thought I would have a good opportunity to do a real service to my *mother* and so improve things between us somewhat, and then this anti-Semitism gets under my feet again!"

54. Only days before his mental collapse, Nietzsche devised his seventh and last work, *Nietzsche Contra Wagner*, which was a compilation of passages on Wagner (some slightly revised) taken from Nietzsche's previous writings.

55. Letter to Peter Gast, Turin, 4 January 1889, *SP*, no. 164, p. 141.

56. Letter to Cosima Wagner, Turin, c. 4 January 1889, *SP*, no. 167, p. 142; Martin van Amerongen, *Wagner, a Case History*, trans. Stewart Spencer and Dominic Cakebread (George Braziller, 1983), 53.

57. Letter to Jacob Burckhardt, Turin, 5 January 1889, *SP*, no. 168, p. 144.

58. The note was to Fraulein von Salis-Marschlins (1855-1929), an acquaintance of Nietzsche's family whom he had met in Zurich in 1884. She had a doctorate of philosophy and wrote on feminist issues. After 1889, she became a friend and supporter of Elisabeth's. Quoted in Kaufmann's *Nietzsche*, 46, n. 27.

59. Letter to Franz Overbeck, rec. 7 January 1889, *L*, no. 205, p. 346.

60. For the legal battles and related issues surrounding Nietzsche's literary estate and the Nietzsche-Archive, see Peters, chapter 22 et seq., and Ben MacIntyre, *Beyond the Fatherland: The Search for Elisabeth Nietzsche* (New York: Farrar Straus Giroux, 1992), ch. 7. To date, these are the only English-speaking biographies available on Elisabeth, tracing her activities from her Paraguay experiment to the turn of the century to the time of Nazi Germany. For Elisabeth's rendition of "the feud between the house of Nietzsche and the house of Overbeck," see the preface to vol. 2 in *The Lonely Nietzsche* (1913).

61. For a concise and excellent discussion on the Nazis' distortion of Nietzsche's writings, see Rudolf E. Kuenzli, "The Nazi Appropriation of Nietzsche," *Nietzsche Studien* 12 (1983): 428-35. Nazi writings include Alfred Bäumler, *Nietzsche der Philosoph und Politiker* (Leipzig, 1931); Heinrich Härtle, *Nietzsche und der National-sozialismus* (Munich, 1939); and Alfred Rosenberg, *Friedrich Nietzsche* (Munich, 1944). The Nazis also printed small anthologies of "essential Nazi sayings" of Nietzsche. These were published under the name of Nietzsche without any indication of an editor; it served to deceive people into thinking that they were actually reading Nietzsche's works. One of these anthologies is entitled *Judentum\Christentum\Deutschtum* (Berlin, c. 1936) which contains bits and pieces taken from Nietzsche's unpublished and discarded notes, arranged in a manner that would convince people that he was advocating positions of National Socialism.

62. MacIntyre, 164.

63. See ch. 10 in Kaufmann, especially p. 289.

64. Historically, anti-Nazi commentators who defended Nietzsche against the Nazis include Georges Bataille, *Sur Nietzsche* (Paris, 1945), Thomas Mann, "Nietzsche's Philosophy in the Light of Contemporary Events" (Washington, Library of Congress, 1948), and Albert Camus, *The Rebel* (1956; New York, 1958), 65ff. Mann writes that Nietzsche did not create fascism, but that fascism created him. Nietzsche was "remote from politics and innocently spiritual"; he functioned as an instrument who registered and presaged the dawning imperialism "like a quivering floatstick," and who "indicated the fascist era of the West in which we are living and shall continue to live for a long time . . . despite the military victory over fascism" (pp. 27-28). Camus emphatically insists that we must become Nietzsche's advocates: "In the history of the intelligence, with the exception of Marx, Nietzsche's adventure has no equivalent; we shall never finish making reparation for the injustice done to him" (p. 75).

The most extreme radical members who 'nazified Nietzsche' are George Lichtheim, who states that if not for Nietzsche, Hitler's troops "would have lacked inspiration to carry out their programme of mass murder in Eastern Europe," *Europe in the Twentieth Century* (New York, 1972) 152; Georg Lukács, who writes from a Marxist perspective, *The Destruction of Reason*, trans. Peter Palmer (1962; London, 1980); and William McGovern, *From Luther to Hitler* (New York, 1941). McGovern regards

Nietzsche's irrationalism and his will to power Darwinistically, interpreting Nietzsche's master (aristocratic) and slave (democratic) morality in accordance with evolutionary principles (p. 410ff.). Similarly, Lukács accepts politicized notions of the will to power, the superman, and the eternal recurrence as mythical functions expressing a "barbaric and tyrannical social order." He states that although Nazi scholars misappropriated Nietzsche, he was actually more of a Nazi than the Nazis were aware: "Therefore one cannot dismiss the closeness of Nietzsche's thinking to Hitler's by disproving false assertions, misrepresentations, etc., by Bäumler or Rosenberg," p. 380. (Nietzsche writes in *Ecce Homo* that only "scholarly oxen" could have conceived the overman Darwinistically, "Books," I.) See also Werner Dannhauser, "Friedrich Nietzsche," *History of Political Philosophy* (Chicago, 1972), and Walter H. Sokel, "Political Uses and Abuses of Nietzsche in Walter Kaufmann's Image of Nietzsche," *Nietzsche-Studien* 12 (1983): 436-42. The most fruitful discussions of Nietzsche's relationship to National Socialism occurred among authors writing in English-speaking journals in the 40s and early 50s. Cf. Herbert Marcuse "Was Nietzsche a Nazi?," *American Mercury* 59 (1944): 737-40, and F. C. Copleston, "Nietzsche and National Socialism," *Dublin Review* 208 (April 1941): 225-43, for representations of the first and second groups, respectively.

Nietzsche's Nazi affiliation is not discussed in great detail after Kaufmann; however, as Bruce Detwiler recently noted in his *Nietzsche and the Politics of Aristocratic Radicalism* (University of Chicago Press, 1990), whenever a political exposition is made of Nietzsche's writings, it is immediately looked upon with suspicion; hence, "the question of Nietzsche's politics lingers on" (p. 3). Cf. Allan Bloom, "The Nietzscheanization of the Left or Vice Versa," in *The Closing of the American Mind* (New York, 1987). Bloom is concerned with the "political consequences" that could arise from Nietzsche's value relativism which America currently revolves. The Nazi appropriation of Nietzsche clearly has not gone unchallenged or undiscussed; yet it is firmly embedded within much of the world's consciousness—and always will be. That does not mean, however, that it will always reflect a negative judgment upon Nietzsche; the reverse could actually be the case.

65. Friedrich Nietzsche, *Daybreak*, trans. R. J. Hollingdale (New York: Cambridge University Press, 1982), 204.

66. Letter to his mother and his sister, Nice, 21 March 1885, *Unpublished Letters of Friedrich Nietzsche*, trans. and ed. Kurt F. Leidecker (New York: Philosophical Library, 1959), no. 50, p. 112.

67. Cf. the review of *Hitler's Table Talk* (conversations with his generals during WW II) in *Times Literary Supplement* (London, 4 January 1952), p. 2. The article concludes: "There is nothing here to sustain the view that Hitler was a close student of Nietzsche; it would be nearer the truth to say that he translated Wagner into political terms." These sentiments were expressed by several postwar historians despite the popular consensus which was largely shaped by political propaganda. See page xxiii in Peter Viereck, *Metapolitics: The Roots of the Nazi Mind* (1941; New York, 1961) for further discussion.

68. Quoted in Donald L. Niewyk, *The Holocaust* (Lexington: D.C. Heath and Company, 1992), 15. As Niewyk reports: "Like Hitler, Wagner looked forward to a time when there would be 'no more Jews.' Like Hitler, he yearned for 'the emancipation from the yoke of Judaism' and spoke urgently of 'this war of liberation.' Whether Wagner would have assented to the nucleus of Hitler's *Weltanschauung*—to the 'elimination,' 'ridding,' 'evacuation,' 'reduction,' (read: 'extermination') of the Jews—is another question. Feeling himself to be misunderstood and thwarted by his surroundings, the young Hitler lost himself in Wagner's world. There he could find consolation, understanding, and the welcome affirmation of his personal prejudices—an affirmation he later repeatedly sought and would later also admit had provided the major impetus for his reading."

69. *Ecce Homo*, "Human," sec. 2. Nazi scholar Alfred Bäumler went to great lengths arguing that Nietzsche's disdain toward Germany was really directed toward the non-Germanic elements of the Germanic character (i.e., Christian and Roman), and that his ultimate goal was a return "to the Germanic depth of the German being." Nietzsche had to oppose the Germanic Wagner, claims Bäumler, because of envy; cf. Kuenzli, 431.

70. For further reading on the intellectual origins of fascism, see Hans Kohn, *The Mind of Germany* (New York, 1960); George Mosse, *The Crisis of German Ideology* (New York, 1981); Fritz Stern, *The Politics of Cultural Despair* (Berkeley, 1973); Peter Viereck, *Metapolitics*; and David Weiss, *The Fascist Tradition* (New York, 1967). Kohn insists that Nietzsche was no intellectual forerunner of National Socialism, but does note (what he views as) the "dangerous implications" of his violent language and his praise of heroic greatness during his last productive years (p. 207ff.); Mosse describes how Nietzsche, in spite of Bäumler's misinterpretation and Nietzsche's ridicule of Lagarde's works, was nonetheless appropriated as a Nordic prophet (p. 204ff.); Stern insists that Nietzsche "had nothing to do with the birth of Germanic ideology," that he had nothing but contempt for its intellectual forebears (e.g., Wagner, Dühring, and Lagarde), and that he would have continued his battle against the collective tyranny of the Germanic community (p. 283ff.); Viereck, acknowledging an intellectual debt to Nietzsche, writes how "uncannily Nietzsche had predicted the Nazi future" through experiencing Wagner and his "proto-Nazi" sister: "It is in no way Nietzsche's fault that *The Will to Power* . . . fell into German nationalist hands" (p. xx ff.). And Weiss flatly refuses to entertain Nietzsche's alleged affinity to Fascism, stating that intellectual historians who do so have confused the issue by an outmoded method that regards a handful of theorists as major carriers of the intellectual tradition: "Such esoteric and brilliant thinkers as Fichte and Nietzsche have no real influence on large groups or classes of men, and thus no direct influence on that great abstraction we call history. They are altogether too complicated and subtle to be heard beyond a few" (p. 3).

71. Kuenzli, 429; Brinton, "National Socialists," 134.

72. *The Gay Science*, 377. The notes that Elisabeth arranged under the title *Zucht and Züchtung* (Discipline and Breeding) better suited her own ideas, not her brother's.

They were derived from thousands of random scribblings, jottings, and notes that Nietzsche had written down over an extended period of time. In the passages on breeding, it is unclear as to whether the term has cultural or biological connotations. In other words, one can speak of well-bred children (in a cultural or biological sense). Tracy Strong observes that after leaving Basle Nietzsche stops using the word *erziehen* (which has cultural connotations, such as "bring up" and/or "educate") in favor of the more biological term *züchten*, which means to breed, raise and cultivate, and is normally used in connection with animals or plants (p. 274). In note 397, biological categories are used in reference to the taming of the beasts and the breeding of a particular species. In note 862 cultural terms are used in reference to a powerful *doctrine* that is "powerful enough to work as a breeding agent: strengthening the strong, paralyzing and destructive for the world weary" (see also 462 and 1053).

Considering that the notes on breeding were meager in proportion to Nietzsche's many other concerns and that he specifically condemned the 'morality of breeding' and the morality of taming in *Twilight* as "immoral," it was preposterous for Elisabeth and the Nazis to lift the drafts out of context; cf. "Improvers." Elisabeth's Paraguay experiment to breed German families was explicitly condemned by Nietzsche; it appears that she and the Nazis tried to create the illusion that "Nietzsche's" thoughts on breeding informed their racism. It should be stressed, once again, that preoccupation with the notes serves to divert readers *from* Nietzsche's texts in which his alternative view on an ideal "future race" is formulated (see chs. 5 and 6). Overall, the *Nachlass* is invaluable for supplementing Nietzsche's publications, but the notes should not be read in isolation from his texts, which was precisely Elisabeth's, and then Bäumler's strategy. For further discussion of the *Nachlass* and posthumous material, see Kaufmann's prologue and ch. 2, especially 76ff.

73. Salomé, 28-30.

74. Newman, 522.

75. Cf. Jacques Derrida, *Spurs: Nietzsche's Styles* (Chicago, 1979).

76. *Beyond Good and Evil*, 139. Cf. 145, 231-39.

77. Cf. *Beyond Good and Evil*, translators preface, sec. 3.

78. Friedrich Nietzsche, *The Will to Power*, trans. Walter Kaufmann and R. J. Hollingdale (New York: Random House, 1967), 864; *DB* 346.

3. CHRISTIANITY, CULTURE, AND THE *VOLK*

1. Letter to Malwida von Meysenbug, Sils-Maria, 24 September 1886, *SP*, no. 111, p. 91.

2. *Ecce Homo*, trans. Hollingdale, "Why I am so Clever," sec. 1.

3. *Ecce Homo*, trans. Hollingdale, "Why I am so Clever," sec. 10.

4. *The Gay Science*, 141. Quotation is from Goethe's discussion of Spinoza's dictum in his *Ethics*, "Whoever loves God must not expect God to love him in return." See also *GS* 135: "The Christian presupposes a powerful, overpowering being who enjoys revenge."

5. Cf. *Twilight*, "'Reason' in Philosophy," and "How the 'True World' Finally Became a Fable."

6. *Antichrist*, 43; *D* 90.

7. *Will to Power*, 191.

8. Stöcker's speech, "Our Demands on Modern Jewry," is found in Richard S. Levy, *Antisemitism in the Modern World* (Lexington: D. C. Heath and Company, 1991). More will be said about Stöcker in chapter 5. See *AC* 57, "Whom do I hate most among the rabble of today? The socialist rabble, the chandala apostles, who undermine the instinct, the pleasure, the worker's sense of satisfaction with his small existence—who make him envious, who teach him revenge. The source of wrong is never unequal rights but the claim of 'equal' rights'"; and *Z* II, "On the Rabble": "The bite on which I gagged the most is not the knowledge that life itself requires hostility and death and torture-crosses— . . . but the rabble? . . . And I turned my back on those who rule when I saw what they now call ruling: higgling and haggling for power—with the rabble."

9. Quoted in Low, 386; *Kroners Taschenausgabe*, v. 77, p. 266; v. 78, p. 239; and v. 73, p. 405.

10. *Daybreak*, 205. See also *GS* 136; *BGE* 248; *EH*, "Clever," 4; *WP* 832.

11. *Daybreak*, 207.

12. *Daybreak*, 92.

13. *Beyond Good and Evil*, 58.

14. *Daybreak*, 22.

15. *Daybreak*, 22.

16. Friedrich Nietzsche, *On the Genealogy of Morals* and *Ecce Homo*, trans. Walter Kaufmann and R. J. Hollingdale (New York: Random House, 1967), I, 9. See also *Daybreak*, 9.

17. *Zarathustra*, I, "On the Way of the Creator."

18. *Zarathustra*, I, "On the Way of the Creator."

19. *Daybreak*, 20.

20. *The Gay Science*, 1.

21. *Zarathustra*, III, "Upon the Mount of Olives."

22. *Zarathustra*, III, "On Passing By." In *Ecce Homo* Nietzsche reiterates: "To *suffer* from solitude is likewise an objection—I have always suffered only from the multitude."

23. *Human*, 226.

24. *Daybreak*, 63.

25. *Daybreak*, 101.

26. *Twilight of the Idols*, "What the German's Lack," sec. 4.

27. *Beyond Good and Evil*, 62.

28. *Mixed Opinions and Maxims*, 359. Nietzsche does not mention Christianity in this aphorism, but it well represents his viewpoint towards all types of dogmatism.

29. *HU* 129; *BGE* 67: "Love of one is a barbarism; for it is exercised at the expense of all others. The love of God, too."

30. *Twilight of the Idols*, "Skirmishes of an Untimely Man," sec. 37. On the whole, Nietzsche's polemic against neighbor love was based on his disdain for what he viewed as an oppressive religious community's attempt to extinguish one's freedom and one's intellect for the good of the whole. In *Zarathustra's* "On Love of the Neighbor," Nietzsche observes: "Your love of the neighbor is your bad love of yourselves . . . but I see through your 'selflessness.' . . . The *you* is older than the *I*; the *you* has been pronounced holy but not yet the *I*." In contrast to Christianity, Zarathustra commands: "I teach you not the neighbor, but the friend," Z, I, "On Love of the Neighbor."

31. *Human*, 49.

32. *Human*, 133.

33. "Is it really *necessary* that there should actually *be* a God, and a deputizing Lamb of God, if *belief* in the *existence* of these beings suffices to produce the same effects?" (*Mixed Opinions and Maxims*, 225). "That someone *feels* 'guilty' or sinful is no proof that he is right, any more than a man is healthy merely because he feels healthy" (*GM* III, 16).

34. *Twilight of the Idols*, "Improvers," sec. 2.

35. *Twilight of the Idols*, "Improvers," sec. 5. *GM* III, 21ff.

36. Friedrich Nietzsche, *The Wanderer and his Shadow. Human, All-too-Human*, trans. R. J. Hollingdale (Cambridge: Cambridge University Press, 1986), 42.

37. *Antichrist*, 44.

38. *Will to Power*, 222.

39. *The Gay Science*, 359.

40. *BGE* 250. In this sense, Nietzsche reasons that Europe owes to Judea both the 'best (contemporary Jewry) and the worst' (contemporary Christianity) in terms of providing the impetus for traditional ethical values.

41. *Daybreak*, 61.

42. *Mixed Opinions and Maxims*, 97.

43. *Mixed Opinions and Maxims*, 96.

44. *Antichrist*, 21.

45. "They have called 'God' what was contrary to them and gave them pain. . . . And they did not know how to love their god except by crucifying man" (*Zarathustra*, II, "On Priests").

46. *Daybreak*, 89.

47. *Will to Power*, 212.

48. *Human*, 116.

49. "A god who died for our sins: redemption through faith; resurrection after death—all these are counterfeits of true Christianity for which that disastrous wrongheaded fellow [Paul] must be held responsible" (*Will to Power*, 169).

50. *Human*, 475.

51. *Beyond Good and Evil*, 251.

52. *Will to Power*, 213.

53. *Will to Power*, 89.

54. *Antichrist*, 39.

55. *Will to Power*, 166.

56. *Antichrist*, 35.

57. *Beyond Good and Evil*, 164.

58. *Antichrist*, 33.

59. *Will to Power*, 169.

60. *The Gay Science*, 358.

61. *The Wanderer and his Shadow*, 80. See also *D* 262, "The Demon of Power;" *GS* 358; *BGE* 46.

62. *Antichrist*, 45.

63. *Antichrist*, 61.

64. *Ecce Homo*, "Clever," sec. 5. For primary texts concerning Jews, see especially the book of Romans 9:1vv. for Paul's discussion of the relationship between Jews and Gentiles; Luther's vehement invective "On the Jews and their Lies," and Wagner's "On the Spirit of Judaism in Music."

65. *The Case of Wagner*, 11. "Long legs" most likely refers to a marching style.

66. *Zarathustra*, I, "On the New Idol."

67. *Twilight of the Idols*, "Skirmishes," sec. 37.

68. *Zarathustra*, I, "On the New Idol."

69. *Will to Power*, 211.

70. *Twilight of the Idols*, "Germans," sec. 4.

71. *Beyond Good and Evil*, 242.

72. *Beyond Good and Evil*, 212: "[E]quality of rights could all too easily be changed into equality in violating rights—I mean, into a common war on all that is rare, strange, privileged, the higher man, the higher soul, the higher duty, the higher responsibility, and the abundance of creative power and masterfulness."

73. *Beyond Good and Evil*, 242.

74. *Zarathustra*, III, "On Old and New Tablets," sec. 21.

75. *Ecce Homo*, "Why I am so Clever," sec. 9. Cf. "Schopenhauer as Educator," sec. 3, p. 142; *Mixed Opinions and Maxims*, 310 and 317, "Possessions possess"; and *Zarathustra*, I, "On the New Idol," in which the prophet Zarathustra, speaking against the New Idol, praises "a little poverty," stating that "whoever possesses little is possessed that much less."

76. *Beyond Good and Evil*, 260.

77. See especially *HU* 451, *AC* 57, as well as the entire section "What is Noble," in *BGE*.

78. Cf. *BGE* 264, *GM* II, 8; *Z* III, "On Old and New Tablets," sec. 4-5. Thus I am in complete agreement with Jacob Golomb in *Nietzsche's Enticing Psychology of Power*, that Nietzsche's emphasis on egoism and selfhood does not disrupt or contradict the moral and social order, but creates the ideal conditions for its proper functioning (pp. 309-10).

79. *Antichrist*, 57.

80. Nietzsche's scorn for underclasses frequently surfaces when referring to the historical origins of the Christian religion, as opposed to deriding underclasses in con-

temporary German society. *WP* 198: "The founder of Christianity had to pay for having directed himself to the lowest class of Jewish society and intelligence: They conceived him in the spirit they understood. It is a real disgrace to have concocted a salvation story, a personal God, a personal redeemer, a personal immortality and to have retained all the meanness of the 'person' and 'history' in a doctrine that contests the reality of all that is personal and historical." Cf. *AC* 27; *GM* I, 7ff.

81. *EH* "Books," sec. 2 (note).

82. *Beyond Good and Evil*, 260: "There are master morality and slave morality— . . . in all the higher and mixed cultures there also appear attempts at mediation between these two moralities—, and at times they occur directly alongside each other—even in the same human being, within a single soul." Apolitical scholars are quick to point out that Nietzsche's terms of masters and slaves, aristocracy and democracy, do not necessarily correspond to the social, economic, or political strata; the weak and the sick vis-à-vis the powerful and the strong do not designate physical traits, but spiritual characteristics in relation to one's power for creating values. But this is a dubious distinction, for external divisions nevertheless appear (especially in the *GM*) when Nietzsche "describes" the history of morality.

83. *Beyond Good and Evil*, 287.

84. *Zarathustra*, II, "On Priests."

85. *Beyond Good and Evil*, appendix, 4 (a).

86. Cf. *Minutes of the Vienna Psychoanalytic Society*, 28 October 1908, p. 32.

87. Albert Camus, *The Rebel*, trans. Anthony Bower (New York: Vintage, 1958), 68.

88. Robert G. Olson, "Nihilism," *Encyclopedia of Philosophy*, vols. 5-6.

89. *The Gay Science*, 125. Compare with Mt. which has traditionally been interpreted as the Christian charge directed against the Jews for Christ's murder.

90. Quoted in Kaufmann, 361-62.

91. Letter to Malwida von Meysenbug, Venice, May 1884, *SP*, no. 98, p. 81.

92. C. G. Jung, *Psychology and Religion* (New Haven: Yale University Press, 1938), 103-5.

93. Jung, 104.

94. Friedrich Nietzsche, *Gesammelte Werke*, Musarion-Ausgabe, 23 vols. (Munich, 1922-1929), 3, 52. *The Will to Power*, 2, 57. The translation is taken from Erich Heller's essay, "The Importance of Nietzsche," p. 5, which is more fluent than Kaufmann's.

95. *The Gay Science*, 343.

96. *Ecce Homo*, "Clever," sec. 5.

97. *Brief, Kritische Gesamtausgabe* 3:1, 18 August 1880, 35, hereafter cited as KGB; Bergmann, 143.

98. See Christopher Middleton's introduction to *L*.

99. Letter to Rohde, Nice, 22 February 1884, *L*, no. 121, p. 219.

4. *THUS SPOKE ZARATHUSTRA*

1. Letter to Carl von Gersdorff, Sils-Maria, 28 June 1883, *SL*, 153ff.

2. Letter to Erwin Rohde, Nice, 22 February 1884, *SP*, no. 95, p. 77.

3. For further contemporary readings and various interpretations of the text, see Kathleen Marie Higgins, *Nietzsche's Zarathustra* (Philadelphia: Temple University Press, 1987); Roger Hollinrake, *Nietzsche, Wagner, and the Philosophy of Pessimism* (London: George Allen & Unwin, 1982), which is a fascinating study of part four of *Zarathustra* in relation to Wagner's influence; Ernest Joós, *Poetic Truth and Transvaluation in Nietzsche's Zarathustra* (New York: Peter Lang, 1987); Laurence Lampert, *Nietzsche's Teaching: An Interpretation of Thus Spoke Zarathustra* (New Haven: Yale University Press, 1986); and W. Wiley Richards, *The Bible and Christian Traditions: Keys to Understanding the Allegorical Subplot of Nietzsche's Zarathustra* (New York: Peter Lang, 1991). Richards' work is not a commentary on the 'meaning' of the text; rather, he essentially compares the plot of *Zarathustra* with that of various New Testament texts. His work is a useful analytical tool; however, his main thesis that the plots of *Zarathustra* were intentionally patterned after gospel texts is dubious.

4. *Zarathustra*, prologue, sec. 1. Cf. *GS* 381; *AC*, foreword; *Z* I, "On Reading and Writing"; *EH* "Why I Write Such Good Books," sections 1 and 3, and *GM*, preface, 8, for Nietzsche's insistence that good readers need similar 'experiences.'

5. *Ecce Homo*, preface, sec. 4.

6. *Ecce Homo*, "Why I am so Clever," sec. 4.

7. *Zarathustra*, prologue, sec. 2. Cf. *BGE* 289 and 60, "To love man *for God's sake*. . . ."

8. Compare with *Daybreak*, 108.

9. *Zarathustra*, prologue, sec. 5.

10. Eugen Dühring (1833-1921) was a professor of philosophy and economics at the University of Berlin who was dismissed from his academic post in 1877 for personal attacks on his colleagues. His impact on German Social Democracy was short-lived but for a time powerful. Engel's polemic against his economic stance in his *Anti-*

Dühring initially kept him from fading into obscurity—although he is now cited frequently in Holocaust histories as the most radical racial antisemite of his time. Dühring was a violent antisemite, which, as will be shown in chapter 5, was Nietzsche's main concern. For a summary of Dühring's socialism, see Peter Gay's, *The Dilemma of Democratic Socialism* (New York, 1952), 94-104. Bergmann, 136; *WP* 130, 792.

11. *WP* 792.

12. *Daybreak*, 425.

13. *Zarathustra*, prologue, sec. 3.

14. *Zarathustra*, III, "On Old and New Tablets," sec. 26.

15. *Zarathustra*, I, "On the Afterworldly."

16. Ibid.

17. *Zarathustra*, prologue, sec. 7. Cf. Mt. 4:19, Mk. 1:17: "Come, follow me," Jesus said, "and I will make you fishers of men."

18. *Zarathustra*, III, "On Old and New Tablets," sec. 15; *EH*, "Destiny," sec. 4. See also *Daybreak*, 77, "On the torments of the soul": "Indeed, what a dreadful place Christianity had already made of the earth when it everywhere erected the crucifix and thereby designated the earth as the place 'where the just man is *tortured* to death'! . . . Imagine a harmless human being who cannot get over once having heard such words as these: 'Oh eternity! Oh that I had no soul! Oh that I had never been born! I am damned, damned, lost for ever. A week ago you could have helped me. But now it is all over. Now I belong to the Devil. I go with him to Hell. Break, break, poor hearts of stone! Will you not break? What more can be done for hearts of stone? I am damned that you may be saved! There he is! Yes, there he is! Come, kind Devil! Come!'"

19. *Ecce Homo*, "Destiny," sec. 4. Herbert Spencer (1820-1903) was an English philosopher who, in 1850, propounded the theory of constant struggle between humans, in which the (physically) strongest would win. Social Darwinism was a contributing factor to modern antisemitism, especially the view of Spencer and his disciples that among nations, too, the strongest was the best and therefore had a right to rule. For a discussion of antisemitism in the Second Reich, including the influence of Spencer, Dühring, and Wagner in promoting antisemitism, see ch. 2 in Yehuda Bauer, *A History of the Holocaust* (New York: Franklin Watts, 1982), and ch. 1, "The Jewish Problem in the Second Reich," in *The Twisted Road to Auschwitz*, Karl A. Schleunes (1970; Chicago: University of Illinois Press, 1990).

20. *Zarathustra*, II, "On the Virtuous"; *BGE* 53. See Mt. 23:12: "For whoever exalts himself will be humbled, and whoever humbles himself will be exalted."

21. *Zarathustra*, II, "On Immaculate Perception."

22. Michel Foucault, "Nietzsche, Genealogy, and History," *The Foucault Reader*, ed. Paul Rabinow (New York: Pantheon Books, 1984), 83. See also Eric Blondel's

Nietzsche: The Body and Culture: Philosophy as a Philological Genealogy, trans. Sean Hand (Stanford: Stanford University Press, 1991).

23. *Zarathustra*, I, "On the Despisers of the Body."

24. Ibid.

25. *Zarathustra*, prologue, sec. 6.

26. Hollinrake, 12; Richard Wagner, *My Life* (1911; New York: Tudor, 1936).

27. *Zarathustra*, prologue, sec. 8.

28. *Zarathustra*, III, "On the Spirit of Gravity," sec. 2.

29. *Beyond Good and Evil*, 1.

30. *Genealogy of Morals*, III, 24, the last section is a direct quote from *GS* 344.

31. *Zarathustra*, III, "On Apostates," sec. 2.

32. *Zarathustra*, prologue, sec. 8.

33. *Zarathustra*, III, "The Convalescent," sec. 2; *BGE* 229.

34. *Zarathustra*, I, "On the Afterworldly."

35. *Zarathustra*, I, "On the Afterworldly." Cf. *GMI*, 14ff.

36. *Ecce Homo*, trans. Hollingdale, "Why I am so Wise," sec. 2.

37. *Zarathustra*, II, "Upon the Blessed Isles."

38. "Your love of life shall be love of your highest hope; and your highest hope shall be the highest thought of your life" (*Zarathustra*, I, "On War and Warriors").

39. *Zarathustra*, II, "On the Tarantulas." See also *AC* 43 for the relations among the "great lie of personal immortality," equal rights "for equal souls," and modern politics, all of which Nietzsche regards as the "*ressentiment* of the masses . . . the greatest, most malignant attempt to assassinate *noble* humanity." In the very last section of the *AC* (62), he speaks again of "the equality of souls before God," claiming that Christianity is not humanitarian. Rather, it *created* distress to eternalize *itself*.

40. *Daybreak*, 67. In *BGE* 269, Nietzsche writes that Jesus invented hell in order to send those who did not love him, there.

41. *Zarathustra*, I, "On Free Death."

42. Ibid.

43. *The Will to Power*, 166.

44. *Zarathustra*, I, "On the Preachers of Death."

45. Rosemary R. Ruether, *Sexism and God Talk* (Boston: Beacon Press, 1983), 257.

46. *Antichrist*, 14.

47. See Walter Kaufmann's *Nietzsche*, pp. 200-205 and also chapters 6-9 for a detailed discussion; Paul Tillich's *A History of Christian Thought*, ch. IV, section F, "Nietzsche's idea of the will to power"; and Karl Jasper's *Nietzsche*, ch. 5, "Nietzsche's new exegesis (The will to power)," 293ff.

48. *Ecce Homo*, "Why I Write Such Good Books," sec. 1. For a discussion on "mastering one's virtues," see *BGE* 212.

49. *Zarathustra*, I, "On the Teachers of Virtue."

50. *Zarathustra*, II, "On the Tarantulas"; *AC* 57.

51. "For the game of creation . . . a sacred 'Yes' is needed; the spirit now wills his own will, and he who had been lost to the world now conquers his own world" (*Zarathustra*, I, "On the Three Metamorphoses").

52. *Zarathustra*, II, "On Self-Overcoming"; *Z* III, "On Involuntary Bliss": "And once I overcome myself . . . then I also want to overcome myself in what is still greater; and a victory shall seal my perfection." For more complete discussions on commanding and obeying 'wills,' cf. *Z* III, "On Old and New Tablets," sec. 4, and *BGE* 19, 199, and 211.

53. *Beyond Good and Evil*, 211, 16.

54. *Zarathustra*, prologue, sec. 5.

55. Paradoxically, although Nietzsche holds that Schopenhauer and these religions desire death, he also observes that they are deceived, for they are actually driven by the will to exist. Buddhism and Schopenhauer strive for self-preservation (which Nietzsche disdains as a virtue). Christianity goes even farther in its struggle against physical and bodily death by clinging to the doctrine of personal immortality. It thus does not know how to die at the right time.

According to Nietzsche, Buddhism is "a hundred times more realistic" than the latter, for Buddhism does not preach that one should struggle against sin, but against suffering. Consequently, the self-deception of moral concepts does not arise: "Buddhism is no longer confronted with the need to make suffering and the susceptibility to pain *respectable* by interpreting them in terms of sin—it simply says what it thinks: 'I suffer.' To the barbarian, however, suffering as such is not respectable: he requires an exegesis before he will admit to himself that he is suffering" (*Antichrist*, 23).

56. *Antichrist*, 21; *EH* "Wise," sec. 6. See also *AC* 42. Nietzsche claims that the fundamental difference between Buddhism and Christianity is that the former does not promise but fulfills; the latter promises everything but fulfills nothing.

57. *Zarathustra*, II, "On Redemption;" *Ecce Homo*, "Thus Spoke Zarathustra,"

sec. 8. Cf. Thomas J. J. Altizer's essay "Eternal Recurrence and Kingdom of God" in *The New Nietzsche* for a more detailed discussion on creation and redemption in relation to Nietzsche's eternal recurrence.

58. *Zarathustra*, II, "On Redemption."

59. See Robin Small, "Nietzsche, Dühring, and Time," *Journal of the History of Philosophy* 28.2 (1990): 229-50.

60. For a more literalistic interpretation of the eternal recurrence, see Erich Heller's fine essay: "Nietzsche's Terrors: Time and the Inarticulate" in *The Importance of Nietzsche*, and chapter 11 in Kaufmann's *Nietzsche*. Heller writes that "*without* the memory of having lived this same life before, this would not make any difference, and *with* that memory it would not be the same. Nonetheless, it is the hoped-for prophetic effect of the Eternal Recurrence and certainly not its 'scientific' validity that caused Nietzsche to love this 'impossible' idea so much" (p. 183). Kaufmann, quoting from Nietzsche's notebooks in which Nietzsche speaks of the doctrine scientifically, stresses that Nietzsche indeed believed in the scientific validity of his doctrine. Even so, Kaufmann concludes that the "eternal recurrence was to Nietzsche less an idea than an experience—the supreme experience of a life unusually rich in suffering, pain, and agony" (p. 323).

61. The *Gay Science*, 341; *BGE* 56.

62. *Antichrist*, 21.

63. *Zarathustra*, IV, "The Drunken Song," sec. 11.

64. For main passages on the eternal recurrence in *Zarathustra*, see *Zarathustra*, III, "On the Vision and the Riddle," and "The Convalescent; and *Zarathustra*, IV, "The Drunken Song."

65. *Twilight of the Idols*, "Skirmishes," sec. 49.

66. *Zarathustra*, II, "Upon the Blessed Isles."

67. Kaufmann, ch. 11.

68. *Zarathustra*, II, "On Priests." Kaufmann's point that Zarathustra's first public speech to the people begins with the words: "Behold, I teach you the *Übermenschen*," is well taken (Z, prologue 3; Kaufmann, 309).

69. Kaufmann, 310.

70. The passage occurs in part II, "On Priests." Nietzsche states at the beginning of the passage that someone should "redeem them from their redeemer." Hence, the message at the end of the passage that there has never yet been an overman, and that the greatest was all-too-human, seems quite clear. Even so, scholars from as many different disciplines have as many different interpretations—many of which have nothing to do with

Jesus. For instance even Richards (who seeks to understand the text Biblically in the context of the Christian tradition), writes that the passage should be taken as a double entendre: "Zarathustra at this stage has not yet overcome his humanity in spite of his avowal that he had gone through many births. The words *all-too-human* are taken from the title of one of Nietzsche's books." Richards concludes: "This reference thus subtly identified *him* with Zarathustra. The mystique of the Superman-Nietzsche unfolds" (p. 116).

This brief illustration concerning the 'problem of interpretation' is not to suggest that there is only one 'true' meaning; the beauty of Nietzsche's texts are that they are multilayered and contain many different levels of meaning. Even so, some interpretations are more accurate than others, and better resonate with the spirit of the author who wrote the words. A secondary interpretation of the passage is that Nietzsche is (also) referring to Wagner. At Wagner's funeral, a wreath was placed on his grave with the inscription: "Redemption for the redeemer!" which is the final sentence in *Parsifal*. Nietzsche writes in the first postscript of *The Case of Wagner*, trans. Walter Kaufmann (New York: Vintage, 1967), that everybody admired the "lofty inspiration" that had dictated this inscription as well as the "taste that distinguished Wagner's admirers": "But many (strangely enough!) made the same small correction: 'Redemption *from* the redeemer!'— One heaved a sigh of relief.—"

71. The review by the Christian antisemite, to my knowledge, has not been found.

72. For further reading on the Crusades in the Middle Ages see Bauer, 18ff., and Paul Johnson, *A History of the Jews* (New York, 1987), part three: Cathedocracy.

73. Stuart E. Rosenberg, *The Christian Problem: A Jewish View* (New York: Hippocrene Books, 1986), 10ff.

74. *Antichrist*, 32.

75. Nietzsche was undoubtedly aware that the literal view of Christian doctrines was not held by the sophisticated theological teaching of his day (as developed by the Ritschlian school in the eighties), and that Christian symbols were seen as subjective, existential 'truths,' true primarily for their power of motivation and commitment, but not provable scientifically (which is similar to Nietzsche's view). Even so, according to Nietzsche, theologians still interpreted reality and scripture in terms of Divine providence, grace, and faith. In the *Antichrist*, Nietzsche refutes the notion that one's existential commitment to a faith or doctrine proves its 'truth,' quoting a line from *Zarathustra* to demonstrate his point: "And if a man goes through fire for his doctrine, what does that prove? Verily, it is more if your own doctrine comes out of your own fire." Nietzsche is opposed to the idea that one's existential commitment should be viewed as a means to an end (to demonstrate a proposed truth or doctrine); existence should be an end in itself (*AC* 52-53).

76. *Beyond Good and Evil*, 4: "The falseness of a judgment is for us not necessarily an objection to a judgment; in this respect our new language may sound strangest. The question is to what extent it is life-promoting, life-preserving, species-preserving, perhaps even species-cultivating."

77. *Will to Power*, 55 and 1061ff.

78. "On the Uses and Disadvantages of History for Life," sec. 9, p. 111.

79. "Schopenhauer as Educator," sec. 6, p. 163.

80. See especially Nietzsche's early essay, "Philosophy in the Tragic Age of the Greeks," trans. Marianne Cowan (Washington, D.C: Gateway, 1987).

81. *Beyond Good and Evil*, 268.

82. *Beyond Good and Evil*, 276.

83. *Zarathustra*, I, "On the Flies of the Marketplace."

84. Even so, Barth (who sought to sever God further from nature and whose theology was christocentric—and inevitably demeaned women and Jews), failed to recognize that Nietzsche was, in contrast, an ecumenicist at heart.

Barth's most famous response to Nietzsche is recorded in his *Church Dogmatics*, v. III, pt. 2, sec. 45 (1961). In a six-page-long footnote, Barth's main thesis is that Nietzsche served as an outstanding example of how a human being should *not* live, and asserted that the philosopher was mentally deranged. Barth acknowledges that Nietzsche's alleged association to National Socialism was, for the most part, unwarranted ("It must not be forgotten that Nietzsche directed his most scathing terms against the German nationalism of his age"); that Nietzsche believed that the greatest witness against Christianity was the pitiable figure of the everyday Christian and the nineteenth-century state-church ("which is the very thing against which Jesus preached and taught His disciples to fight"); and also that Nietzsche critiqued Christianity primarily as an ethicist ("for he himself is finally concerned about a definite practice"), not as a metaphysician making truth claims about the existence of God. With the exception of those few observations, Barth has virtually nothing positive to say. Barth continually alludes to Nietzsche's attack on Christian morality; however, he basically assesses Nietzsche's personality traits. Focusing on Nietzsche's autobiographical work *Ecce Homo*, written only months before Nietzsche's mental collapse, Barth argues that Nietzsche's flight into solitude was in direct opposition to Christian anthropology, and must thus be rejected as a model for humanity. After portraying the philosopher as a madman, Barth then dismisses Nietzsche's analysis of Christian morality without ever really addressing it.

For Barth's commentary on Jews and Judaism, see the English translation of *Church Dogmatics* (Edinburgh: T. and T. Clark, 1957, 1961, and 1962), II 2, 195-305; II 3, 176-83, 210-27; IV, 3, second half, 876-78. According to Barth, although Israel remains in covenant with God, it has nonetheless denied its true election and calling. Therefore, "the synagogue became and was and still is the organization . . . which hastens toward a future that is empty. . . . Necessarily, therefore, the Jew . . . is dreadfully empty of grace and blessing" (cf. IV, 3, p. 877). Although Barth claimed to oppose antisemitism, his theology that Jews drew upon themselves the negative judgment of God and Christians is quite callous, especially when taking into consideration that he wrote during and after the Nazi regime. And that he places himself in a position to judge *Nietzsche's* relation to Nazism borders on the absurd, for he fails to take the log out of his own eye. Barth's theology provided yet another divine sanction for the distorted image of the Jew in Western culture that Nietzsche, in fact, spent much of his life attempting to refute.

85. *Zarathustra*, I, "On the Gift Giving Virtue," sec. 2.

86. *Zarathustra*, III, "On Old and New Tablets," sec. 12.

87. *Zarathustra*, II, "On Redemption."

88. Letter to Jacob Burckhardt, Sils-Maria, 22 September 1886, *SL*, p. 286ff. Burckhardt was always one of the first to receive a copy of Nietzsche's works; he usually replied, but in a reserved and distant manner. According to one source, as Nietzsche's isolation grew in the eighties, Nietzsche made demands on Burckhardt for critical and personal response that his older colleague was unwilling and perhaps unable to meet (*SP* 160). However, according to Heller, Nietzsche, in begging for Burckhardt's understanding and sympathy, was fundamentally mistaken in believing that Burckhardt knew "the desperate truth" Nietzsche believed he himself had discovered concerning the spiritual condition of the age. Heller writes that Burckhardt, like Nietzsche, was concerned with the "barbarous mob" and the spiritual stagnation of Germany, and that he too, had lost his religious faith. Even so, unlike Nietzsche, Burckhardt registered the loss in his intelligence alone. Heller reasons that Nietzsche's "burdening himself with the obsession of nihilism" must have been offensive to Burckhardt, setting in motion elements of despair with which the historian was uncomfortable. Heller writes of Burckhardt: "The all but inhuman coldness with which he responded—or rather did not respond—to Nietzsche's entreaties for a word of encouragement can hardly be accounted for in any other way." Cf. Heller, "Burckhardt and Nietzsche," 49 in *The Importance*.

89. *Zarathustra*, III, "On Passing By." For further passages on the 'language of silence,' see the preface to *Human* ("one *remains* a philosopher only by—keeping silent"), and an interesting passage which occurs after Nietzsche attacks the state-church (*GM* I, 9): "For at this point I have much to be silent about."

90. *Zarathustra*, prologue, sec. 8.

91. *Zarathustra*, prologue, sec. 9.

92. *Zarathustra*, III, "The Convalescent," sec. 2.

5. TOWARD THE GENEALOGY OF MORALS

1. Letter to Peter Gast, Nice, 24 November 1887, *SL*, p. 206.

2. Letter to Peter Gast, Nice, 20 December 1887, *SL*, pp. 208-9.

3. *Ecce Homo*, "Genealogy of Morals."

4. *Zur Genealogie der Moral* can be translated "On the" or *Toward the Genealogy of Morals*. Although Kaufmann chooses the former, other commentators view the latter as more accurate to the contents of Nietzsche's book. I prefer "Toward" not only because it denotes Nietzsche's work as a polemic, but also because it conveys that Nietzsche is heading toward a revaluation of all values.

5. *Beyond Good and Evil*, 251.

6. *Beyond Good and Evil*, 208.

7. William Beatty Warner, *Chance and the Text of Experience: Freud, Nietzsche, and Shakespeare's Hamlet* (Ithaca: Cornell University Press, 1986), 116.

8. "There is now a historiography that is *reichdeutsch*; there is even, I fear, an anti-Semitic one—there is a *court* historiography, and Herr von Treitschke is not ashamed—" (*Ecce Homo*, "Wagner," sec. 2). Sybel and Treitschke were both liberal nationalist historians. Antisemitism became a political force in Germany with Treitschke's series of articles published in the influential *Preussische Jahrbucher* in 1879. He is to be credited with the notorious phrase, "the Jews are our misfortune," which Hitler and the Nazis would later employ extensively.

9. *Beyond Good and Evil*, 251.

10. Peters, 91-92.

11. *BGE* 195, 251. More will be said about the relevance of the priestly-prophetic strand as claimed by Christian antisemites later in the work.
As stated in the introduction, Duffy and Mittelman are to be credited with making these distinctions. Time does not permit a detailed discussion. The threefold distinctions are presumed here and can briefly be stated as follows. First, the unthinking anti-semitism of Nietzsche's early years (1869-76) were heavily influenced by Nietzsche's association with Wagner. Second, at the time of the break (which corresponds with the beginning of Nietzsche's literary career) there is an abrupt change in Nietzsche's attitude toward the Jews. Finally, the authors' mark *Beyond Good and Evil* (1886) as distinctive because Nietzsche propounds that ancient Judaism's contribution to the 'slave rebellion' in morality originated with the priestly-prophetic strand. These views are continuous with Nietzsche's previous works, what makes this work unique is that Nietzsche's views are developed and clarified in relation to slave morality and resentment. *Beyond Good and Evil* is continuous with previous works in two other aspects: the preprophetic age is untouched by Nietzsche's criticism of the slave revolt in morality, and most importantly, Nietzsche continues his praise of modern Jewry. See especially p. 308ff. in Duffy and Mittelman for further discussion.

12. Cf. *Ecce Homo*, "Genealogy of Morals."

13. Aquinas' quote is from *Summa Theologiae*, III, supplementum, Q. 94, Art. 1.

14. Cf. *Will to Power*, 184.

15. Letter to Peter Gast, Sils Maria, 18 July 1887, *L*, no. 154, p. 269.

16. *EH*, "Books," sec. 2 (note). Compare with Adolf Stöcker's remark in his anti-semitic speech, "Our Demands on Modern Jewry" (1879): "If the Christians continue to yield to the effects of the Jewish spirit that de-Germanizes and de-Christianizes them, this prophecy [that the glory of Germany will perish from the Jews] will certainly come true. . . . We would really have to be a nation without honor if we could not break these chains of an alien spirit and instead allowed ourselves to be totally Jewified." Stöcker's speech can be found in *Antisemitism in the Modern World: An Anthology of Texts*, ed. Richard S. Levy (Lexington: D. C. Heath and Company, 1991), 558-66. The anthology also includes selections by Wagner, *Modern* (1878); Heinrich von Treitschke's pamphlet, *A Word About Our Jews* (1879-80); and Theodor Fritsch, *The Desperate Act of A Desperate People* (1922).

17. John E. Groh, *Nineteenth Century German Protestantism* (Washington: University Press of America, 1982), 568.

18. Edward H. Flannery, *The Anguish of the Jews* (New York: Paulist Press, 1985), 164-66.

19. Groh, 568.

20. Léon Poliakov, *A History of Anti-Semitism*, v. 4 (New York: Vanguard Press, 1985), 16.

21. Paul Johnson, *A History of the Jews* (New York: Harper, 1987), 394. Ironically, Johnson, like Nietzsche, also mentions Dühring in the context of the social attacks from all sides on Jews: "It was Wagner's writings," Johnson says, "which provoked the furious outpourings of Eugen Dühring, who throughout the 1880s published a succession of widely read racial attacks on the Jews: the 'Jewish question', he declared, should be 'solved' by 'killing and extirpation'."

22. *Human*, 475.

23. See chapter 5 in Uriel Tal, *Christians and Jews in Germany: Religion, Politics, and Ideology in the Second Reich, 1870-1904* (Ithaca: Cornell University Press, 1975).

24. *Antichrist*, 25ff., 31, 40; *GM* I, 14ff.; *WP*, 197, 186: "The profound contempt with which the Christian was treated in the noble areas of classical antiquity is of a kind with the present instinctive aversion to Jews. . . . The New Testament is the gospel of a wholly ignoble species of man; their claim to possess more value, indeed to possess *all* value, actually has something revolting about it—even today."

25. Groh, 569. Stöcker was elected to the Prussian House of Deputies in 1879, where he served uninterruptedly until 1898. In 1881 Stöcker was also elected to the national Reichstag, where he held a seat until 1893, and was then reelected in 1898. For further discussion on Stöcker see Pulzer, ch. 10, "Stöcker and the Berlin Movement."

26. Stöcker, 66.

27. Tal, 257.

28. Stöcker, 59.

29. Stöcker, 66. See chapter 3 for the complete passage.

30. Quoted in Kaufmann's *Nietzsche*, 46.

31. Peter Bergmann, *Nietzsche: "The Last Antipolitical German"* (Bloomington: Indiana University Press, 1987), 144. Bergmann, whose fine historical work primarily focuses on biography and Nietzsche's letters—not his texts—writes that even though Nietzsche was not an antisemite, when his "Caesarism and anti-Christian atheism were inflamed, harsh invective would flow toward the Jews." As will become evident, however, the reverse is the case. Nietzsche's harsh invective toward ancient Judaism (especially in the *GM*) was principally directed toward Christian antisemitism. And alluding to Nietzsche's alleged "atheism" is irrelevant to the issue under discussion.

32. Bergmann, 172-73.

33. *Will to Power*, 89.

34. *Will to Power*, 203; Letter to Peter Gast, Sils-Maria, 20 June 1888, *SL*, p. 231. After announcing the age of Stöcker, Nietzsche adds: "—I draw conclusions and know already that my 'Will to Power' will be suppressed first in Germany." . . . The phrase from *WP* concerning "the sheep with horns" mentions the "court chaplains," which would allow readers to identify Stöcker as the object of Nietzsche's dig. The term "court chaplains" is found only in 1911, p. 502.

35. *Will to Power*, 347.

36. Ernest K. Bramsted, *Aristocracy and the Middle Classes in Germany: Social Types in German Literature 1830-1900* (1937; Chicago: University of Chicago Press, 1964), 132-33.

37. *Genealogy of Morals*, II, 11; III, 14; III, 26.

38. Peter Gay, *The Dilemma of Democratic Socialism* (New York, 1952), 97.

39. Georg Brandes, *Friedrich Nietzsche*, "An Essay on Aristocratic Radicalism," (1889; London, William Heinemann, 1914), 31. In *BGE* 253, Nietzsche regards the "mediocre Englishmen" as Darwin, John Stuart Mill, and Herbert Spencer. He is most likely referring to Mill's utilitarianism at the beginning of the *GM*.

40. Pulzer, 50-51.

41. George Mosse, *The Crisis of German Ideology* (New York: Schocken Books, 1981), 131-32. Gay, 95.

42. Jacob Katz, *From Prejudice to Destruction: Anti-Semitism, 1700-1933* (Cambridge, Mass.: Harvard University Press, 1980), 268ff. For a succinct discussion of Dühring as Nietzsche's intellectual nemesis, see Peter Bergmann's *Nietzsche*, 121-22 and 124-25.

43. Joseph Tennenbaum, *Race and Reich* (New York: Twaine, 1956), 12. Dühring's *The Jewish Question as a Problem of Race, Morals, and Culture* (1881), according to Tennenbaum, presented an almost complete Nazi program.

44. *EH*, "Wise," sec. 4; Bergmann, 124-25. For a discussion of Nietzsche and von Stein, see R. Stackelberg, "The Role of H. v. Stein in Nietzsche's Emergence as a Critic of Wagnerian Idealism and Cultural Nationalism," *Nietzsche-Studien* 5 (1976): 178-93. Wagner was skeptical of Dühring because he was not Christian; however, Dühring approved of von Stein's role in the Wagner household as Siegfried's tutor because Wagner and he shared a hatred of the Jews. Von Stein became 'Nietzsche's substitute' in the Wagner household after the break in 1878.

45. Gay, 95; Mosse, 131. Mosse regards Dühring's view of equal wills as "mythical." It can be described as mythical not in the sense that Dühring posits an initial beginning of the world, but rather an original 'essence' of human wills. Although Dühring was, according to Katz, a remarkable scholar who possessed a high degree of intelligence, he was nonetheless imbued with a "morbid mental constitution" (p. 265).

46. *Genealogy of Morals*, II, 11.

47. Ibid.

48. Ibid.; *Z* III "On Old and New Tablets," sec. 26: "The good are *unable* to create . . . they sacrifice the future to *themselves*—they crucify all man's future. The good have always been the beginning of the end." Compare the section in *GM* with *BGE* 259, which is most likely further commentary on Dühring's equal wills theory.

49. Cf. Keith Ansell-Pearson, *Nietzsche Contra Rousseau* (Cambridge: Cambridge University Press, 1991), 32ff. As stated, the undialectical reading of the goodness of humanity versus corrupt social institutions is an oversimplification of Rousseau's views; even so, it fundamentally represents Nietzsche and Dühring's reading of him; cf. especially Jean-Jacques Rousseau, "Discourse on the Origins and Foundations of Inequality Among Men" in *The First and Second Discourses*. Rousseau's general wills theory is a controversial and complex view that has been linked to the roots of totalitarianism. It is not my intention to confirm or deny the validity of those interpretations linking Rousseau with totalitarianism, but only to demonstrate Nietzsche and Dühring's respective sentiments toward a social order based on the primacy of will(s) in relation to the state, human nature, and morality. According to Pearson, Nietzsche exaggerates and distorts certain aspects of Rousseau's moral and political thought in an attempt to highlight his own challenge to the ethical foundations of both Christianity *and* Rousseau, whom Nietzsche regards as the modern philosopher of resentment *par excellence*; a secular successor to the Christian moral-tradition. See Pearson, 49ff.; *TW*, "Skirmishes," sec. 48; *WP* 94, 100, 1017.

50. *Will to Power*, 1027; *GS* 382; Z, prologue, sec. 4; *BGE* 257: "In the beginning, the noble caste was always the barbarian caste: their predominance did not lie mainly in physical strength but in strength of the soul—they were more *whole* human beings (which also means, at every level, 'more whole beasts')."

51. *Genealogy of Morals*, II, 11.

52. Dühring viewed individuals as "mere atoms" in a social and political body, but as the sovereign representatives of all society. For Dühring, socialization does not exclude individualization, but includes it (Gay, 99).

53. Bergmann, 136; *WP* 130. The Nazis, of course, later flipped these terms upside down. They regarded themselves as *Übermenschen*, and the Jews as *Üntermenschen*, subhuman beings.

54. Bergmann, 145.

55. *Antichrist*, 57-58.

56. *Twilight of the Idols*, "Skirmishes," sec. 34.

57. *Genealogy of Morals*, II, 11. The fundamental thesis of the *Genealogy* is, I believe, summarized by Nietzsche in the *Nachlass* under the heading of "My Five No's." Nietzsche states that his struggles are against (1) the feeling of guilt and the projection of punishment into the physical and metaphysical world, (2) the dangerousness of the Christian ideal and "latent Christianity" (e.g., as in music and socialism), (3) Rousseau's ideas including the view of human nature and the morality of guilt feelings of the Christian, "the morality of *ressentiment* [which is] a posture of the mob," (4) romanticism, in which "Christian ideals and the ideals of Rousseau unite," and (5) "the *predominance of the herd instincts*; against the inward hatred with which every kind of order of rank and distance are treated" (*WP* 1021).

58. *Will to Power*, 765. Compare with *GM* III, 15.

59. *Will to Power*, 353; *GM* III, 15.

60. Katz, 267. Although the term anti-Christian antisemitism signifies an opposition to Christianity, this does not mean that antisemites such as Dühring disdained Christianity to the degree that they abhorred Judaism and the Jews, or that antisemitism derived from an opposition to Christianity. Thus, Dühring and Stöcker could reach a common ground in their disdain for modern Jewry.

61. Cf. *GS* 345, 380; *BGE* 186, 202; and *Z* III, "On Old and New Tablets," sec. 2: "When I came to men I found them sitting on an old conceit; the conceit that they have long known what is good and evil for man. . . . I disturbed this sleepiness when I taught: what is good and evil *no one knows yet*, unless it be he who creates. . . . And I bade them overthrow their old academic chairs and wherever that old conceit had sat; I bade them laugh at their great masters of virtue and saints and poets and world-redeemers. I bade them laugh at their gloomy sages. . . . I sat down by their great tomb road among cadavers and vultures, and I laughed at their past and its rotting, decaying glory."

62. *Daybreak*, 205.

63. *Zarathustra*, II, "On the Virtuous."

64. *Zarathustra*, II, "On the Tarantulas"; *GS* 9, *Our eruptions.* —"Often the son already betrays his father—and the father understands himself better after he has a son. All of us harbor concealed gardens and plantings; and, to use another metaphor, we are, all of us, growing volcanoes that approach the hour of their eruption; but how near or distant that is, nobody knows—not even God."

65. *Genealogy of Morals*, III, 22.

66. *Genealogy of Morals*, I, 8.

67. *Genealogy of Morals*, I, 8.

68. *Genealogy of Morals*, III, 26.

69. *GM* I, 16. Edward Flannery in *The Anguish of the Jews*, interprets this passage the other way around: "Comparing them [the Jews] to the 'aristocratic' Germans and Chinese, he [Nietzsche] finds Jews 'fifth rate'" (p. 332). Flannery, a general reader of Nietzsche, fails to discern Nietzsche's clear disdain toward Germans and his admiration for modern Jews. Duffy and Mittelman are perplexed about the passage, and Kaufmann interprets the passage correctly, pointing out that Nietzsche is speaking against Germans and in praise of Jews, cf. the footnote to Kaufmann's translation (I 16). This illustration reveals how difficult it has been to demythologize the (popular) image of Nietzsche as an 'antisemite' after the Nazis claimed him as an ally.

70. An example of this occurs in *Daybreak* in which Nietzsche writes: "The command 'love your enemies!' had to be invented by the Jews, the best haters there have ever been" (377). Here Nietzsche is referring to Christians (perhaps Christian antisemites), as evidenced by the commandment 'love your enemies,' made famous through Jesus. Duffy and Mittelman misinterpret the passage, regarding it as a rare anti-Semitic comment after his break with Wagner. Attempting to discern 'which Jews' Nietzsche is referring to is not as confusing as it may appear, this passage is perhaps the most difficult to be found throughout his writings.

71. *Genealogy of Morals*, I, 14.

72. *Human, All-too-Human*, 475.

73. *Genealogy of Morals*, I, 11.

74. *Genealogy of Morals*, I, 5.

75. *Genealogy of Morals*, I, 8.

76. *Genealogy of Morals*, I, 11.

77. Ibid.

78. *Genealogy of Morals*, II, 17.

79. *Twilight*, "Improvers," sec. 2.

80. *Genealogy of Morals*, I, 11.

81. In *Ecce Homo* Nietzsche writes: "At this moment, for example, the German Kaiser calls it his 'Christian duty' to liberate the slaves in Africa: among us other Europeans this would then simply be called 'German'" (*EH* "The Case of Wagner," sec. 3). Nietzsche's views toward negroes [his term] do not dominate his thought; references are rare.

82. Quoted in Pulzer, 51.

83. *Twilight of the Idols*, "Improvers," sec. 4.

84. Quoted in Léon Poliakov, *The Aryan Myth*, trans. Edmund Howard (Chatto: Sussex University Press, 1975), 209. Cf. *Sämlitche Briefe*, 8: 324-25; *WP* 141-43, 145.

85. *Will to Power*, 145.

86. *Genealogy of Morals*, III, 26. Poliakov states that although Renan's Aryan myth was not biological in theory, it nonetheless stressed the Jews' inferiority and largely contributed to the racial theories of Arthur Gobineau (1816-82) and Wagner's stepson, Houston Stewart Chamberlain (1855-1927); see also Tal, 200, 280ff. As Poliakov notes, Renan assigns a common (linguistic) birthplace to the two great noble races, the Aryan and the Semitic, but sharply distinguishes between them as to the period of their influence. Renan writes: "The Semites have nothing further to do that is essential . . . let us remain Germans and Celts; let us keep our 'eternal gospel,' Christianity . . . only Christianity has a future." Renan employs the terms Semitic race or Jewish race on the one hand, or Indo-Germanic, Indo-European, or Aryan race on the other, although he prefers the latter term. It must be credited to Renan that after 1870-71 he issued warnings against seeking political advantage from the confusion between languages and races. See Poliakov, the *Aryan Myth*, 206-11, and Renan's *Histoire generale des langues Sémitiques* (Paris, 1878) for his primary views on Aryans and Semites.

Frank E. Manuel, *The Broken Staff: Judaism through Christian Eyes* (Cambridge, Mass.: Harvard University Press, 1992) correctly notes that Renan, in *The Life of Jesus*, speaks of the 'two great races' as equal spiritual poles, but does not address the *Histoire*, which was written years later, and presents his contention that the Jews, as Semites, comprised "a really inferior combination of the human race" (I, 16). Nor does Manuel mention Renan's antisemitism, which is blatant in *The Life of Jesus* alone. Manuel states that Renan was not referring to physiological heritage when speaking of Aryans and Semites (a point none of the above historians would dispute) and concludes that Renan "exerted an enormous influence on the appreciation of Judaism in the latter half of the nineteenth century" (p. 308). Nietzsche's estimation of Renan does not correspond with Manuel's. For additional discussions on Renan's racial views, see Katz, *Prejudice*, 133ff., and S. Almog, "The Racial Motif in Renan's Attitude toward Judaism and the Jews," *Zion* 32 (1967): 175-200.

87. Poliakov, *The Aryan Myth*, 300.

88. Golomb, 365ff.

89. *Daybreak*, 205. As Duffy and Mittelman note, this view, recorded in 1881, is distinct from the claim five years later in *Beyond Good and Evil* that the Jews *could*, but were not, heading toward mastery over Europe (309). They interpret this to mean that Nietzsche now believes that the Jews were not heading toward mastery, but only seeking assimilation. Considering the antisemitic climate Nietzsche was writing in, the aphorism in *Daybreak* would agitate those who were convinced that the Jews were involved in a secret conspiracy to rule the world economy. In *BGE*, Nietzsche tones it down somewhat.

90. *Beyond Good and Evil*, 225, 270.

91. *Genealogy of Morals*, I, 10.

92. Golomb, 365. If Golomb's thesis regarding Nietzsche's concept of power is accurate, which I agree that it is, it could be asserted that Nietzsche's idea of the will to power is in conflict with Dühring's notions of force and will. Whereas Dühring regards the interrelatedness between force (oppression) and will (freedom) as equally necessary for reshaping history and seeks to eliminate the Jews; Nietzsche elevates the positive power of will (freedom) over political force (oppression), and sees the Jews as a primary factor in creating and ushering in the new revaluation.

93. *Genealogy of Morals*, III, 26.

94. *Genealogy of Morals*, II, 2. Cf. *BGE* 212, 262, and also *EH*, "Wise," sec. 4, in which Nietzsche compares those (positive) decadents who struggle against wretched states and thus "turn out well," to (negative) decadents who choose disadvantageous means against those states. In regards to the former, Nietzsche writes: "He is always in his own company, whether he associates with books, human beings, or landscapes. . . . He believes neither in 'misfortune' nor in 'guilt'; he comes to terms with himself, with others; he knows how to *forget*—he is strong enough; hence everything *must* turn out for his best. Well then, I am the *opposite* of a decadent, for I have just described *myself*."

95. Cf. ch. 7 in Ofelia Schutte, *Beyond Nihilism* (Chicago: University of Chicago Press, 1984) for further discussion. Cf. *TW*, "Skirmishes," sec. 39.

96. *GM* I, 11.

97. *GM* I, 16; *BGE* 251.

98. *Genealogy of Morals*, preface, 7.

99. *Genealogy of Morals*, III, 14; III, 26.

100. Letter to Paul Deussen, Nice, 3 January 1888. *Sämtliche Briefe*, 8 vols. (Berlin: Walter de Gruyter, 1975-84), 8: no. 939, p. 220.

101. Letter to Franz Overbeck, Nice, 3 February 1888, *L*, no. 162, p. 282.

102. Letter to Elisabeth, Nice, end of December 1887. Quoted in Kaufmann's *Nietzsche*, 45.

103. Cf. suppressed part of letters of December 19th and 29th, 1887, reprinted in Curt Paul Janz, *Die Briefe Friedrich Nietzsche* (Zurich, 1972), 58-59; Bergmann, 173.

104. Theodor Lessing, *Untergang der Erde am Geist* (Hannover, 1924), 429; Bergmann, 150. Lessing (1872-1933) was a Zionist who wrote several general works on Nietzsche and applied many Nietzschean themes in analyzing, and providing solutions for, the contemporary Jewish condition. He was one of the first victims of Nazism. See Aschheim, *The Nietzsche Legacy in Germany*, 107-8.

105. *Zarathustra*, III, "The Wanderer."

106. Bergmann, 170. Taine strongly influenced Nietzsche's views on Rousseau and Napoleon; the historian believed that the Revolution led to a greater centralization of power, the destruction of authority, and social atomization. Taine regarded Napoleon as a synthesis of the beast and superbeast, as did Nietzsche. Ansell-Pearson, 33; Letter to Hippolyte Taine, Sils-Maria, 4 July 1887, *SL*, p. 294ff. Herzl referred to Nietzsche, only once, as a "madman"; cf. Aschheim, p. 104.

107. Letter to Paul Deussen, 3 January 1888, *Gesammelte Brief*, 5 vols. (Leipzig, 1907-9), 1:493; Bergmann, 173.

108. Letter to Carl Fuchs, Nice, 14 December 1887, *SP*, no. 127, p. 104.

109. *Genealogy of Morals*, I, 1ff.; *BGE*, 203.

110. For an opposing view of Nietzsche's critique of morality, see Phillipa Foot, "Nietzsche's Immoralism," *New York Review of Books* 11 (13 June 1991): 18-22. Foot, an analytic philosopher, essentially presents Nietzsche as an ethical relativist (there are no good or evil actions in themselves), on the basis of Nietzsche's insistence that 'there are no moral facts' (*TW*, "Improvers," sec. 1). Although she acknowledges that Nietzsche's morality is "perhaps" based on a principle of sublimation, she interprets remarks such as "everything evil . . . serves the enhancement of the species 'man' as much as its opposite does" (*BGE* 44), as providing a "license for injustice" (p. 20). The problem with Foot's approach to Nietzsche is commonplace. Namely, she tends to discuss Nietzsche's passages on 'good and evil' without any reference whatsoever to the concrete historical-political and religious-ethical issues prevalent during his time. She also tends to blame Nietzsche for Hitler's Germany (carrying the propagandic baggage that the Nazis "learned" from him—which unfortunately, is not the case, or they would have denounced antisemitism). The result is an oversimplification of Nietzsche's views which lead to, and become evident in, her unfolding assertions: "One must take account of Nietzsche's . . . vituperative attitude to Christianity" (p. 18). "Was he perhaps preaching in favor of a new morality rather than against morality as such? I think not" (p. 18). "Perhaps I am wrong in thinking of equality as necessary for the practice of justice"

(p. 20). She concludes: "His teaching has been sadly seductive in the past. Who can promise that it will never be seductive again?" (p. 22). In this underhanded fashion, Foot links an illusionary 'demise' of Christianity (assumed to be a moral pillar) to the rise of National Socialism, thus ignoring compatible elements between the two—not to mention the core of Nietzsche's ethical critique. Nietzsche's assertion that "there are no moral facts" does not denote that good and evil actions are illusions, but that no morality or institution should be exempt from criticism: the Christian state-church included.

6. *ANTICHRIST*

1. Letter to Franz Overbeck, Turin, 18 October 1888, *SP*, no. 148, p. 125: "Does anyone really doubt that I, as the old artillerist I am, could easily bring up my *heavy* guns against Wagner?— Everything decisive in this matter I held back—I have loved Wagner" (*CW* 1).

2. *Ecce Homo*, "Why I am a Destiny," sec. 1. Compare with *WP* 130: "Externally: age of tremendous wars, upheavals, explosions. . . . *Consequences*: (1) *barbarians* (at first, of course, below the form of culture so far [e.g. Dühring]." (2) *sovereign individuals* (where masses of barbarian force are crossed with a lack of all restraint regarding whatever has been). Age of the greatest stupidity, brutality, and the *masses*, and of the *highest individuals*." The term "E.g., Dühring" is found only in 1911 (p. 500).

3. *Genealogy of Morals*, III, 28.

4. *Antichrist*, 3.

5. *Genealogy of Morals*, I, 7.

6. *Genealogy of Morals*, I, 16.

7. Cf. 49 in *WP* (1888): "What a blessing a Jew is among Germans! How much dullness, how blond the head, how blue the eye the lack of *esprit* in face, word, posture; the lazy stretching-oneself, the German need for a good rest—not prompted by overwork but by the disgusting stimulation and overstimulation through alcoholica.—"

8. *Genealogy of Morals*, I, 16. That Nietzsche only refers to Judaism and Christianity as separate entities in these two instances after the slave revolt would only seem natural, particularly if it is assumed that Nietzsche's genealogy is linear and that his polemic is directed against the Christian tradition, which it indeed is. In these three passages he restates the three references in *BGE* which explicitly and solely concern Jews. After the revolt (*GM* I, 7; *BGE* 195) he first declares that Europe has inherited the best and the worst "poison" (*GM* I, 9; *BGE* 250). Then, at the end of the first essay in his final reference to the Jews (distinct from Jewish-Christians), he elevates them over the Germans (*GM* I, 16; *BGE* 251, "The Jews are the toughest, purest race living in Europe today"). The other three references to Jews in *BGE* concern the superiority of the Old Testament over the New as well as Greek literature (52); the Jews, Romans, Greeks, and

the French as creative geniuses in relation to the Germans (248); and the last one reads: "Jesus said to his Jews: 'The law was for servants—love God as I love him, as his son! What are morals to us sons of God!'" (164).

9. See also *AC* 26.

10. *Antichrist*, 58.

11. *Antichrist*, 39.

12. Ibid.

13. Ibid.

14. *Antichrist*, 35.

15. *Antichrist*, 40.

16. *Antichrist*, 36.

17. *Antichrist*, 51.

18. *Antichrist*, 39-40.

19. *Antichrist*, 41-48.

20. *Antichrist*, 47.

21. *Antichrist*, 42.

22. *Antichrist*, 33.

23. *Genealogy of Morals*, I, 8; I, 13ff.

24. *Antichrist*, 38.

25. *Antichrist*, 29-35, 40.

26. *Antichrist*, 27.

27. Ibid.

28. *Will to Power*, 1051. Nietzsche opposes the notion that the 'lesson' taught by Christ on the cross was "not to defend oneself" against the authorities and laws of this world (*WP* 170). "We pagans in faith . . . we believe in Olympus—and *not* in the 'Crucified'" (*WP* 1034).

29. *Antichrist*, 34.

30. *Antichrist*, 40. The "equality of *souls* before God" arises with the conception of Jesus as the Savior for Christians; thus, the hypocrisy inherent in such a notion. In the *GM*, the soul originates with the state, develops within Christianity, whose ascetic ideal becomes the goal to the beyond, which is nihilism. Nietzsche seeks to create a new possibility for the "Dionysian drama of the destiny of the Soul."

31. *Antichrist*, 44.

32. Ibid.

33. *Antichrist*, 25ff.

34. Whether Nietzsche's views are historically accurate is not the issue here. The point is to explicate Nietzsche's stance, which above all, seeks to discover where the conception of punishment and reward originated and how and why it was divinely sanctioned.

35. *Antichrist*, 27.

36. *Antichrist*, 25.

37. *Antichrist*, 43.

38. *Antichrist*, 16.

39. *Antichrist*, 19. Cf. sections 16-19 for the overall contrast between the Christian and Jewish God.

40. Nietzsche's predilection for Yahweh theologically supports his anthropology which—on the basis of the 'pathos of distance'—distinguished the ethics of the 'cultured' from that of the 'uncultured'—particularly antisemites. According to Nietzsche, the "former desire *to be just*, the others *to be judge*": "Thus, the philosopher has to say, as Christ did, judge not!" (*Mixed Opinions and Maxims*, 33).

41. *Antichrist*, 17.

42. *Antichrist*, 16.

43. *Antichrist*, 17.

44. Renan, *Jesus*, 123-24.

45. *Antichrist*, 29, 17; *TW*, "Skirmishes," sec. 2 and 6.

46. *Antichrist*, 10. Cf. Horton Harris, *The Tübingen School* (Oxford: Clarendon Press, 1975) for further discussion on that tradition.

47. Hayman, 325. Wellhausen, like Renan, attempted to date the process of deterioration in Judaism as early as possible, in order to confirm the modern theological conception that Christianity was the fulfillment of the true Israel; the rightful heir of Israel's prophetic religion. The historical explanation of the transference of election from unfaithful Israel to Christianity was of primary concern to both thinkers; cf. Tal, 280; Johnson, *Jews* 6, 10, 27.

48. Tal, 168.

49. The term *liberal Jews* is used to designate those who identified themselves as Jews, whether they regarded Judaism as a religion or as an ethnic group to which they

belonged. For further discussion see "Anti-semitism as a Reflection of Social, Economic and Political Tension in Germany" in *Jews and Germans from 1860-1933*, ed. David Bronsen (Carl Winter: Heidelberg, 1979).

50. Tal, 176. I am deeply indebted to Tal for the background of liberal Protestantism and its relationship to Judaism. See pp. 161-222 for a detailed discussion. The main points are summarized here. See also F. Lichtenberger, *History of German Theology in the Nineteenth Century*, trans. and ed. W. Hastie (Edinburgh: T & T Clark, 1889).

51. Tal, 160. Protestant theologian Albrecht Ritschl (1822-89) is to be distinguished from Nietzsche's teacher, the renowned classical philologist, Friedrich Ritschl (1806-76).

52. Tal, 169. The English translation of Ritschl's important "Festival Address on the Four Hundredth Anniversary of the Birth of Martin Luther" can be found in David W. Lotz, *Ritschl and Luther: A Fresh Perspective on Albrecht Ritschl's Theology in the Light of His Luther Study* (Nashville, 1974).

53. *Antichrist*, 47.

54. *Antichrist*, 52.

55. *Daybreak*, 84. "The manner in which a theologian, in Berlin as in Rome, interprets a 'verse of Scripture' . . . is always so audacious that a philologist can only tear his hair" (*AC* 52).

56. *Antichrist*, 46.

57. *Antichrist*, 37.

58. *Antichrist*, 44.

59. *Antichrist*, 37.

60. Renan, *Jesus*, 259ff. Renan never says that these visions of Jesus will come to pass in a literal or futuristic sense; the power of his argument, however, is that Jesus himself, "in his own mind," believed that they would.

61. Ibid., 186.

62. Ibid., 298-99.

63. Ibid.

64. *Antichrist*, 31. Renan, *Jesus*, 295.

65. Renan, *Jesus*, 224, 235, 391. The last passage echoes Renan's remark in his *Histoire generale des langues Sémitiques* (Paris, 1878): "Once this mission [monotheism] was accomplished, the Semitic race rapidly declined and left it to the Aryan race alone to lead the march of human destiny," quoted in Poliakov, *Aryan Myth*, 207.

66. Renan, *Jesus*, 358.

67. As the author's introduction to the English translation of the 1927 edition notes, Renan's *La vie de Jésus* sold like a Waverly novel among the academy and the populace alike, highly esteemed for its "beautiful style" which flourished throughout Renan's "brilliant" retelling of Jesus' story. Renan, the introduction continues, was a "supreme figure" among the scholars of his time, a simple, sincere, courageous saint, "even if judged by the teachings of the Galilean lake."

To Holocaust scholars and historians of antisemitism, however, Renan's storytelling is neither beautiful nor brilliant. Renan's *Vie de Jésus* together with Edouard Drumont's, *La France juive*, the latter of which paved the way for large-scale antisemitic propaganda in France, were the two antisemitic bestsellers in the latter half of the nineteenth century; cf. Poliakov, *Anti-Semitism*, IV: 39-40; *Myth*, 208.

Incredibly, that which outraged Nietzsche (and these historians) about Renan is overlooked—or disregarded—even today. In a 1968 English-speaking biography on Renan, Richard Chadbourne writes of Renan's "valiant" attempt to base an ethic largely on Christian principles without believing in its supernatural teachings: "A simple criterion guiding Renan is his testing of Christian works: 'How much they contain of Jesus.' He is far from the scandalous simplicity of Nietzsche's 'the last Christian died on the cross'" (Richard Chadbourne, *Ernest Renan* [New York: Twaine Publishers, Inc., 1968], 153).

68. *GM* III, 26; *WP* 128. Cf. Letter to Peter Gast, Nice, 24 November 1887, *SL*, p. 206. Others in this family include Kant, Saint-Beuve, Auguste Comte, Dühring, and Thomas Carlyle, whom Nietzsche compares to his beloved Emerson; cf. *TW* "Skirmishes," sec. 1ff.; *BGE* 44, 48.

69. *Twilight of the Idols*, "Skirmishes," sec. 1. Renan was, in fact, an ex-Catholic whom the Catholic Church denounced because of his non-divinization of Jesus. He was suspended from his professorship at Collège de France in 1862; declined a position as an Assistant Director of Department of Manuscripts in Imperial Library in 1864, in order to devote himself to his studies, but in 1871 was restored to his professorship. In 1879 he became a member of the Academy. From 1884 onward he was administrator of the Collège de France. Renan regarded himself as a liberal Protestant, but like Nietzsche, had no use for institutional religion or dogmatic Christianity. Unlike Nietzsche, Renan nonetheless viewed Christianity as an exemplary spiritual discipline (Katz, *Prejudice*, 133).

70. *Antichrist*, 31.

71. For a brief comparison of Renan and Dühring, see Katz, *Prejudice*, 265ff.

72. Renan, *Jesus*, 125, 160ff.

73. Ibid., 160 (ch. 7).

74. *Antichrist*, 32.

75. See the preface to vol. 7, *Marcus-Aurelius* in Renan's *Origins of Christianity*, for a summary of his position concerning Christianity's origins with Isaiah; his negativity regarding original Israel prevails throughout his writings. Nietzsche read Renan's *Origins* in the winter of 1887, "with much spite and—little profit," Letter to Overbeck, Nice, 23 February 1887, *L*, no. 149, p. 261.

76. *Antichrist*, 29. Cf. *Twilight*, "Errors," 7, in which Nietzsche writes that the priests at the head of ancient communities invented the doctrine of free will in order that they—or God—might punish and find others guilty: "Today, as . . . we immoralists are trying with all our strength to take the concept of guilt and the concept of punishment out of the world again, and to cleanse psychology, history, nature, and social institutions and sanctions of them, there is in our eyes no more radical opposition than that of the theologians, who continue with the concept of a 'moral world order' to infect the innocence of becoming by means of 'punishment' and 'guilt.' Christianity is a metaphysics of the hangman."

77. Renan, *Jesus*, 383-86.

78. Poliakov, *Antisemitism*, IV:9.

79. *Antichrist*, 31.

80. *Antichrist*, 46. Renan too esteems Pilate, but in order to stress that the Mosaic Law was responsible for Jesus' death. Romans, however, are also guilty, according to Renan.

81. *Antichrist*, 31, 45.

82. Quoted in Tal, 280.

83. *Ecce Homo*, "Destiny," sec. 7, trans. Hollingdale.

84. *Antichrist*, 55-54: "The pathological condition of his [the believer's] perspective turns the convinced into fanatics—Savonarola, Luther, Rousseau, Robespierre, Saint-Simon; the opposition-type of the strong spirit who has *become* free." See also the preface.

85. *Antichrist*, 59.

86. *AC* 58. Nietzsche continues to say that Paul utilized the symbol of "God on the cross" to unite all who lay at the bottom, the secretly rebellious, "the whole inheritance of anarchistic agitation in the Empire, into a tremendous power."

87. *Antichrist*, 38.

88. *Will to Power*, 1036.

89. *Ecce Homo*, "Why I am a Destiny," sec. 8.

90. *Antichrist*, 62.

CONCLUSION

1. Letter to Franz Overbeck, Turin, Christmas 1888, *L*, no. 194, p. 337. The game's name combines the pet names of Friedrich and Elisabeth; the letter was written during the week prior to Nietzsche's final breakdown.

2. *Genealogy of Morals*, preface, 8: "If this book is incomprehensible to anyone and jars on his ears, the fault, it seems to me, is not necessarily mine. It is clear enough, assuming, as I do assume, that one has first read my earlier writings and has not spared some trouble in doing so; for they are, indeed, not easy to penetrate."

3. Duffy and Mittelman, 303-4; Golomb, 380-81; Low, 382. "Most all commentators" is used here to denote a percentage of those few scholars who concentrate on Nietzsche's relationship to Jews and Judaism.

4. *Will to Power*, 864; Low, 387.

5. Low, 386.

6. Coutinho, 166. It is unclear as to what Coutinho means by Nietzsche's "supernational tendencies." If he is stating that Nietzsche was pro-nationalistic, he is clearly wrong.

7. Eisen, 11. Even so, continues Eisen, "Nietzsche could not but have felt ambivalent, knowing the dangers which would follow in the discovery that God was dead."

8. Eisen does not recognize that within the category of 'ancient Judaism,' Nietzsche distinguishes between original Israel and the priestly-prophetic strand.

9. Low, 383; Duffy and Mittelman, 302. At Leipzig (1866) Nietzsche placed an ad in the *Leipziger Tageblatt* for rooms in a "non-commercial area" because he wanted to get away from the Jews; cf. Hayman, 78.

10. Duffy and Mittelman, 30; cf. the letter to Rohde on Dec. 7 1882 (KGB 11/3, no. 227, p. 97) which is cited in *L*, p. 102, n. 96.

11. The *Birth of Tragedy* (1872) is silent about Jews.

12. "Every nation, every man has disagreeable, even dangerous characteristics; it is cruel to demand that the Jew should be an exception" (*H* 475). For Nietzsche's occasional comments on ancient Judaism, see *D* 38, 68, 72, 205; *GS* 135-39. As Duffy and Mittelman note, the threefold distinctions of Jews do not fully emerge—or become clear—until the later writings when he attributes the slave revolt as originating with the priestly-prophetic strand and regards them more negatively beginning with *BGE*. Duffy and Mittelman attribute this change to Nietzsche's failed relationship with Rée; however, it is rather a political ploy on Nietzsche's part.

13. Cf. *Z* I, "On the Thousand and One Goals." Here Nietzsche describes how the wills to power of the Greeks, Persians, Jews, and Germans, led them to formulate vari-

ous goals. In regards to the Jews, Nietzsche writes: "'To honor father and mother and to follow their will to the root of one's soul'—this was the tablet of overcoming that another people hung up over themselves and became powerful and eternal thereby." In Z IV, "Conversation with the Kings," Nietzsche uses the term Jew in reference to Christ. As noted however, although the *terms* Jews and Christians are sparse or non-existent, the text flourishes with Judeo-Christian imagery.

Werner Dannhauser, *Nietzsche's View of Socrates* (Ithaca, 1974) is to be credited with the observation that the term Christianity is not mentioned in *Zarathustra* (p. 241).

14. Quoted in Low, 383.

15. Prior to *BGE*, although Nietzsche consistently praises contemporary Jews, he was not totally uncritical of them (e.g. in *GS* 135 he states that the Jew did not have an appreciation for tragedy as did the Greeks, "in spite of all his poetic gifts and his sense for the sublime"). With *BGE*, he virtually has nothing but exaggerated praise for his Jewish contemporaries, often contrasting the Jews with decadent Germans, and the superior Old Testament with the New: To have glued the New Testament to the Old "is perhaps the greatest audacity and sin against the spirit that literary Europe has on its conscience" (*BGE* 52). Cf. 348 in book five of the *Gay Science* (which Nietzsche added and published in 1887); *BGE* 250; *GM* I, 16; III 22; *EH*, "Clever," sec. 7; *EH*, "Wagner," sec. 4, and appendices 3 and 4a; *WP* 49; etc. Nietzsche's elevation of the Jews during this time period is obviously not due to a conviction that Jews were perfect or racially pure; it simply served to rebut his political enemies who scorned his Jewish contemporaries. Cf. *EH*, "Books," sec. 2 (note 1).

16. Cf. Arthur Danto (New York: Columbia, 1965), "If he was not an anti-Semite, his language is misleading to a point of irresponsibility" (pp.166-67); Duffy and Mittelman, 313, 317; and Eisen, 7.

17. *Daybreak*, 84; Golomb, 379.

18. Duffy and Mittelman attribute Nietzsche's purely negative attack on prophetic Judaism in the *Genealogy* to his failed relationship with Rée, and to a "temporary diversion" to the early vestiges of his antisemitism (314), thus failing to recognize Nietzsche's political maneuver against Christian theology. They recognize, however, that his vehement attack against priestly Judaism (in the *GM*) is directly connected to the Christian culture of his time. The Rée hypothesis is untenable mainly because it remains unclear as to why Nietzsche would attack priestly-prophetic Judaism and not contemporary Jewry, to which Rée belonged.

The result of Nietzsche's stance against both forms of antisemitism is that anti-Christian antisemites could (eventually) use Nietzsche's anti-Christian anti-Judaic position (while ignoring his praise of ancient Hebrews and modern Jews); Christian antisemites could technically use nothing, but both groups could easily misquote him, which Elisabeth and the Nazis did. From a logical standpoint, Nietzsche's position was a no-win situation.

19. Letter to Franz Overbeck, Nice, 24 March 1887, *L*, no. 151, p. 264. Tal clearly sees Nietzsche's strategy: "Friedrich Nietzsche, wielding his mother tongue with unri-

valed vigor, sought to arouse his generation to the evils of the time, to the sterility of contemporary culture, ethics, and religion and to the ominous rise of political and spiritual despotism. He warned against attempts to find simple solutions for the existential problems of those days by stretching them on the procrustean bed of racial and political anti-Semitism as formulated by Paul deLagarde, Richard Wagner, and Professor Adolf Wahrmund" (47).

20. Copleston, 188; Duffy and Mittelman, 308-9; Eisen, 6; Low, 382. See especially *D* 38; *BGE* 195, 248.

21. *Zarathustra*, II, "On the Tarantulas."

22. *Will to Power*, 864.

23. *Will to Power*, 142, 145.

24. *Daybreak*, 205. According to Low, on the eve of the appearance of cultural and political Zionism in Europe, Nietzsche and Paneth discussed the question of the rebirth of Palestine (p. 388).

Nietzsche sent many of his early works, and works he had just completed, to Brandes in 1888; cf. *L*, pp. 283-84, no. 164. Brandes and Nietzsche, who never had a chance to meet in person, began exchanging letters, photographs, and ideas the previous year; the former coined the term 'aristocratic radicalism' to describe Nietzsche, which delighted him. Brandes was also an elitist who was disgusted with Germans. For the Brandes-Nietzsche correspondence see *SL*, p. 313ff., and also Georg Brandes, *Friedrich Nietzsche: An Essay On Aristocratic Radicalism* (1889), trans. A. G. Chater (London: William Heinemann, 1914).

25. Brinton, *Nietzsche*, 215. Kaufmann claims that there are many reasons why Nietzsche has been "one of the greatest scapegoats of all time." According to Kaufmann, during World War I British intellectuals found it convenient to attack a "German intellectual of stature . . . without losing a lot of time reading him." During World War II, this trend continued. And, says Kaufmann, Christian scholars "also needed outlets for their rancor." Overall, Kaufmann claims that sloppy scholars and writers could not vent their rancor against living colleagues, thus Nietzsche became their target (cf. the editor's introduction to Nietzsche's *Genealogy*, 9-10).

Kaufmann's assertions are accurate to a large degree, but do not adequately explain why Nietzsche was chosen as a target, for there are many other dead figures in history who are not scapegoats. Perhaps Christians have tended to portray Nietzsche—and his anti-Christianity—as compatible with National Socialism in order to divert attention away from the history of antisemitism firmly entrenched within Christianity itself (it must be noted, however, that some of the greatest Christian theologians of the twentieth century, such as Tillich, Bonhoeffer, and Jaspers, are exceptions to the general rule). In contrast, Jewish scholars, such as Stern, Tal, Heller, and Golomb, highlight Nietzsche's opposition to nineteenth-century Christianity and antisemitism, and do not look upon Nietzsche's anti-Christian stance with contempt. Initially, the scapegoating process needs to be traced from Wagner to Elisabeth and then to Hitler. The mixture of religion and politics becomes quite clear.

26. Heller, 63.

27. *The History of Germany Since 1789* (1958; New York: Frederick A. Praeger, 1968), 243.

28. *EH* "Destiny," sec. 4.

29. Historically, suspicion has not been directed toward the scruples of 'why' the Nazis used Nietzsche. Rather, Nietzsche's writings have been rendered suspect and are judged by the rare and partial standards of which elements, if any, are compatible or incompatible with National Socialism. This gives testimony to the Nazis as master propagandists, as will be discussed below. For further discussion of the Bayreuth Circle, see J. Lucien Radel, *Roots of Totalitarianism* (New York: Crane Russak, & Company, 1975), 112-17, and David Large, "Wagner's Bayreuth Disciples," in *Wagnerism in European Culture and Politics*, ed. David C. Large and William Weber (Ithaca: Cornell University Press, 1984).

30. Robert O. Butler, "Blonde Ambition," rev. of *Beyond the Fatherland: The Search for Elisabeth Nietzsche* by Ben MacIntyre, *Chicago Tribune Book Review*, 15 November 1992, sec. 14, p. 7.

31. *Human, All-too-Human*, 475.

32. *Daybreak*, 204. Compare with *GS* 9, and *Z* II, "On the Tarantulas."

33. *Genealogy of Morals*, II, 11; *BGE* 204, 259.

34. *Z* III, "On Old and New Tablets," sec. 26. See also *EH*, "Destiny," sec. 4, for an important commentary on sections 26 and 15 of "Tablets." See also *Z* II, "On Priests," "On the Virtuous," "On the Rabble," and "On the Tarantulas," the main sections in *Z* that address *ressentiment*.

35. *Antichrist*, 43.

36. *Zarathustra*, III, "On Passing By."

37. "I have been persecuted in recent times with letters and *Anti-Semitic Correspondence* sheets; my disgust with this party is as *outspoken* as possible, but the relation to Förster, as well as the after-effect of my former anti-Semitic publisher Schmeitzner, always brings the adherents of this disagreeable party back to the idea that I must after all belong to them. . . . Above all it arouses mistrust against my character, as if I publicly condemned something which I favored secretly. . . ." Quoted in Kaufmann, 45; Bergmann, 173.

38. Friedrich Nietzsche, *Gesammelte Werke*, Musarion-Ausgabe, 23 vols. (Munich, 1922-29), 3:52. *WP* 57. The translation is taken from Erich Heller's essay, "The Importance of Nietzsche," p. 5, which is more fluent than Kaufmann's.

39. *Beyond Good and Evil*, 251.

40. *Ecce Homo*, "Destiny," sec. 8.

41. MacIntyre, 162ff.

42. Cf. Förster-Nietzsche, 2:186-87, 249-52.

43. "In the present book I have also been forced to repel several attacks, yet I have not devoted much space to this feature; for those attacks of Nietzsche's last years are mainly derived from one book, Herr C. A. Bernoulli's *Overbeck-Nietzsche*, and this book has since been recognized as devoid of all significance" (Förster-Nietzsche, 2: preface, vii).

44. Leo Hirsch, "Friedrich Nietzsche und der Judische Geist," *Der Morgen* 10 (1934): 187; Aschheim, 96.

45. See *EH*, "Destiny," sec. 1: "I have a terrible fear that one day I will be pronounced *holy*: you will guess why I publish this book *before*; it shall prevent people from doing mischief with me."

46. According to de Lagarde, one ought "to despise those who—out of humanity!—defend these Jews or who are too cowardly to trample this usurious vermin to death. With trichinae and bacilli one does not negotiate, nor are trichinae and bacilli to be educated: they are exterminated as quickly and thoroughly as possible." Quoted in Bauer's *A History of the Holocaust*, 43.

47. Aschheim, 97; *Twilight of the Idols*, "Maxims," 8.

48. Adolf Hitler, *Mein Kampf*, trans. Ralph Manheim (1925; Cambridge: Riverside Press, 1943), 307.

49. Ruether, who was a pioneer in calling her tradition (in the 1970s) to recognize and renounce antisemitism in Christian theology—and reported that she suffered personal attacks from many fellow Christians for doing so—recognized that Christianity fertilized the ground for Nazism, but nonetheless regarded Nazism and Christianity as antithetical. She writes: "The Nazis, of course, were not Christians. They were indeed anti-Christian, despite their ability to co-opt the Church qua 'German Christianity'" (*Faith and Fratricide: The Theological Roots of Anti-Semitism* [Minneapolis: Seabury, 1974], 184). One can only imagine the increased severity of personal attacks that would have occurred had she called that chasm into question (which was essentially Nietzsche's plight and the plight of those who spoke up on behalf of Nietzsche's anti-Christianity during and after the Second World War).

SELECT BIBLIOGRAPHY

NIETZSCHE'S WRITINGS

The following is a chronological list. The date at the left indicates the year of first publication. The mark * after the original date indicates that the work was published after Nietzsche's insanity; the # indicates that parts of one book were written during different years. All works were originally written in German, although all titles are given here in English. The date of the English translation appears at the end of the entries. Walter Kaufmann's translations are used unless otherwise specified.

Nietzsche's collected works (and letters) are in German. See *Gesammelte Werke*.

The first note references of various works cited throughout the book do not necessarily appear in the bibliography.

1872 *The Birth of Tragedy*. Trans. Walter Kaufmann. New York: Vintage Books, 1967.

Untimely Meditations. Trans. R. J. Hollingdale. New York: Cambridge University Press, 1983. Consists of the following essays:
- 1873   1. David Strauss, the confessor and the writer
- 1874   2. On the uses and disadvantages of history for life
- 1874   3. Schopenhauer as educator
- 1876   4. Richard Wagner in Bayreuth.

1878 *Human, All-too-Human*. Trans. Marion Faber. Lincoln: University of Nebraska Press, 1984.

1878 *Human, All-too-Human*, vols. 1 and 2. Trans. R. J. Hollingdale. Cambridge: Cambridge University Press, 1986.

1879 1. *Mixed Opinions and Maxims*. The first sequel to *Human*.
1880 2. *The Wanderer and His Shadow*. The second sequel to *Human*.

1881 *Daybreak*. Trans. R. J. Hollingdale. Cambridge: Cambridge University Press, 1982.

1882 *The Gay Science*. Trans. Walter Kaufmann. New York: Random House, 1974.
   # Book five (pp. 279-348) added in 1887.

1883 *Thus Spoke Zarathustra*. Trans. Walter Kaufmann. New York: Viking Press, 1966.
   # Parts 1 and 2 were written in 1883; part 3, 1884; and part 4, 1885. The first public edition with part 4 appeared in 1892.

1886 *Beyond Good and Evil*. Trans. Walter Kaufmann. New York: Random House, 1966.

1887 *On the Genealogy of Morals*. Trans. Walter Kaufmann and R. J. Hollingdale. New York: Random House, 1967.

1888 *The Case of Wagner*. Trans. Walter Kaufmann. New York: Random House, 1967.

1889 *The Twilight of the Idols. The Portable Nietzsche*. Trans. Walter Kaufmann. New York: Viking Press, 1968.

1895* *The Antichrist. The Portable Nietzsche*. Trans. Walter Kaufmann. New York: Viking Press, 1968.
      * Written in 1888.

1895* *Nietzsche Contra Wagner. The Portable Nietzsche*. Trans. Walter Kaufmann. New York: Viking Press, 1968.
      * Written in 1888.

1908* *Ecce Homo*. Trans. Walter Kaufmann. New York: Random House, 1967.
      * Written in 1888.

Notebooks, Letters, and Miscellaneous

Philosophy in the Tragic Age of The Greeks. Trans. Marianne Cowan. New York: Gateway, 1962. This is an early essay (1862) that Nietzsche himself did not see fit to publish.

Philosophy and Truth: Selections from Nietzsche's Notebooks of the early 1870's. Trans. and ed. by Daniel Breazeale. New Jersey: Humanities Press, 1979.

Nietzsche: A Self-Portrait from his Letters. Trans. and ed. by Peter Fuss and Henry Shapiro. Cambridge, Mass.: Harvard University Press, 1971.

The Nietzsche-Wagner Correspondence. Ed. Elisabeth Förster-Nietzsche. Trans. Caroline V. Kerr. 1921. New York: Liveright, 1949. Letters between Wagner and Nietzsche from 1869-1876.

The Poetry of Friedrich Nietzsche. Ed. Philip Grundlehner. Oxford: Oxford University Press, 1986.

Selected Letters of Friedrich Nietzsche. Trans. and ed. by Christopher Middleton. Chicago: University of Chicago Press, 1969.

Selected Letters of Friedrich Nietzsche. Trans. A. N. Ludovici, ed. Oscar Levy. London: Soho Book Company, 1985.

The Will to Power. Trans. Walter Kaufmann and R. J. Hollingdale, ed. Walter Kaufmann. New York: Random House, 1967. Selections from Nietzsche's unpublished notebooks (1883-1888).

Select Secondary Sources

BIOGRAPHIES AND NIETZSCHE'S EARLY INFLUENCES

Binion, Rudolph. *Frau Lou: Nietzsche's Wayward Disciple*. Princeton: Princeton University Press, 1968.

Deussen, Paul. *Erinnerungen an Friedrich Nietzsche*. Leipzig: Brockhaus, 1901.

Förster-Nietzsche, Elisabeth (3 vols. Leipzig, 1895-1904). Volume 1 trans. by A. M. Ludovici as *The Young Nietzsche*; volume 2 trans. by P.V. Cohn as *The Lonely Nietzsche* (1912-1915).

Frenzel, Ivo. *Friedrich Nietzsche: An Illustrated Biography*. 1966. Trans. Joachim Neugroschel. New York: Pegasus, 1967.

Gutman, Robert. *Richard Wagner: The Man, His Mind, and His Music*. 1968. San Diego: Harvest, 1990.

Hayman, Ronald. *Nietzsche: A Critical Life*. 1980. New York: Penguin Books, 1984.

Hollingdale, R. J. *Nietzsche: The Man and His Philosophy*. 1965. London: Routledge and Kegan Paul, 1985.

Janz, Curt Paul, *Friedrich Nietzsche, Biographie*, 3 vols. Munich and Vienna, 1977-1978.

MacIntyre, Ben. *Forgotten Fatherland: The Search for Elisabeth Nietzsche*. New York: Harper Collins, 1992.

Newman, Ernest. *The Life of Richard Wagner*, vol. 4: 1866-83. New York: Knopf, 1946.

Peters, H. F. *Zarathustra's Sister: The Case of Elisabeth and Friedrich Nietzsche*. 1977. New York: Markus Wiener, 1985.

Pletsch, Carl. *Young Nietzsche: Becoming a Genius*. New York: Free Press, 1991.

Salomé, Lou. *Nietzsche*. 1894. Trans. and ed. Siegfried Mandel. Redding Ridge: Black Swan Books, 1988.

Schopenhauer, Arthur. *The World as Will and Representation*. 1814-1818. 2 vols. Trans. E. F. J. Payne. New York: Dover, 1969.

Strauss, David. *The Life of Jesus*. 1835. Trans. in London, 1865.

Strauss, David. *The Old Faith and the New*. 1873. Trans. Mathilde Blind. London: Asher & Co., 1874.

Wagner, Cosima. *Diaries*, vol. 1, 1869-77. Ed. Martin Gregor Dellin and Dietrich Mack, trans. Geoffrey Skelton. London and New York, 1978.

CRITICAL WORKS ON NIETZSCHE'S WRITINGS
AND PERSONALITY

Allison, David B., ed. *The New Nietzsche*. Cambridge, Mass.: MIT Press, 1977.

Ansell-Pearson, Keith. *Nietzsche Contra Rousseau*. Cambridge: Cambridge University Press, 1991.

Benz, Ernst. *Nietzsche's Ideen zur Geschichte des Christentums und der Kirche*. Leiden: E. J. Brill, 1956.

Bergmann, Peter. *Nietzsche: "The Last Antipolitical German"*. Bloomington: Indiana University Press, 1987.

Barth, Karl. "The Basic Form of Humanity." In *Church Dogmatics*, vol. 3, part two, ed. G. W. Bromiley and T. F. Torrance. Edinburg: T & T Clark, 1960.

Brandes, Georg. *Friedrich Nietzsche: An Essay on Aristocratic Radicalism*. 1889. London: William Heinemann, 1914.

Camus, Albert. "Nietzsche and Nihilism." In *The Rebel*, trans. by Anthony Brewer. New York: Vintage Books, 1956.

Copleston, Frederick. *Friedrich Nietzsche: Philosopher of Culture*. New York: Harper & Row, 1975.

Coutinho, A. C. "Nietzsche's Critique of Judaism." *Review of Religion* 3 (1939): 161-66

Duffy, Michael and Willard Mittelman. "Nietzsche's Attitudes Toward the Jews." *Journal of History of Ideas* 49 (1988): 301-17.

Eisen, Arnold M. "Nietzsche and the Jews Reconsidered." *Jewish Social Studies* 48.1 (1986): 1-14.

Foucault, Michel. "Nietzsche, Genealogy and History." In *The Foucault Reader*, ed. Paul Rabinow. New York: Pantheon, 1984.

Freud, Sigmund. "Discussion of Nietzsche: 'On the Ascetic Ideal' (Section 3 of *Genealogy of Morality*)." Scientific Meeting on 1 April 1908 in *Minutes of the Vienna Psychoanalytic Society* 1 (1906-1908), ed. Herbert Nunberg and Ernst Federn, trans. M. Nunberg. New York: International Universities Press, 1967, pp. 355-361. The discussants also include Alfred Adler and Otto Rank.

————. "Discussion of Nietzsche's *Ecce Homo*," Scientific meeting on 28 October 1908 in *Minutes of the Vienna Psychoanalytic Society* (1908-1910), ed. Herbert Nunberg and Ernst Federn, trans. M. Nunberg. New York: International Universities Press, 1967, pp. 25-33.

Geffré, Claude and Jean-Pierre Jossua, eds. "Nietzsche and Christianity." *Concilium* 145 (May 1981).

Golomb, Jacob. "Nietzsche's Judaism of Power." *Revue des Études juives*, 146-47 (July-December 1988): 353-85.

————. *Nietzsche's Enticing Psychology of Power*. Israel: Magnes Press, 1987.

————. "Jaspers, Mann and the Nazis on Nietzsche and Freud." *Israeli Journal of Psychiatry and Related Sciences* 18 (1981): 311-26.

Heidegger, Martin. "The Word of Nietzsche: God is Dead." In *The Question Concerning Technology*. New York: Harper and Row, 1977.

Heller, Erich. *The Importance of Nietzsche: Ten Essays*. Chicago: University of Chicago Press, 1988.

Hollinrake, Roger. *Nietzsche, Wagner, and the Philosophy of Pessimism*. London: George Allen & Unwin, 1982.

Jaspers, Karl. *Nietzsche and Christianity*. Trans. E. B. Ashton. Chicago: Gateway Editions, 1961.

Jung, Carl G. *Psychological Types*. New York: Pantheon, 1959. (Chapter III: "The Apollinian and the Dionysian"). Trans. H. Godwin Baynes.

————. *Two Essays on Analytical Psychology*. New York: Pantheon, 1953. (Chapter III: "The Other Point of View: The Will to Power"). Trans. R. F. C. Hull.

————. *Nietzsche's Zarathustra: Notes of the Seminar Given in 1934-1939 by C. G. Jung*. Ed. James L. Jarrett in 2 vols. Princeton: Princeton University Press, 1988.

Kaufmann, Walter. *Nietzsche: Philosopher, Psychologist, Antichrist*. 1950. 4th ed. Princeton: Princeton University Press, 1974.

Koelb, Clayton, ed. *Nietzsche as Postmodernist: Essays Pro and Contra*. Albany: SUNY Press, 1990.

Kuenzli, Rudolf E. "The Nazi Appropriation of Nietzsche." *Nietzsche-Studien* 12 (1983): 428-35

Küng, Hans. "Nietzsche: What Christians and Non-Christians can Learn." In *Does God Exist*, trans. Edward Quinn. New York: Vintage, 1981.

O'Flaherty, James C., Timothy F. Sellner, and Robert M. Helms, eds. *Studies in Nietzsche and the Judaeo-Christian Tradition*. Chapel Hill: University of North Carolina Press, 1985.

Richards, W. Wiley. *The Bible and Christian Traditions: Keys to Understanding the Allegorical Subplot of Nietzsche's Zarathustra*. New York: Peter Lang, 1991.

Schacht, Richard. *Nietzsche*. London: Routledge & Kegan Paul, 1983.

Schutte, Ofelia. *Beyond Nihilism*. Chicago: University of Chicago Press, 1984.

Silk, M. S., and J. P. Stern. 1981. *Nietzsche on Tragedy*. Cambridge: Cambridge University Press, 1984.

Stern, J. P. *A Study of Nietzsche*. Cambridge: Cambridge University Press, 1979.

——— . *Friedrich Nietzsche*. New York: Penguin, 1978.

Strauss, Leo. *Studies in Platonic Political Philosophy*. Chicago: University of Chicago Press, 1983.

Tillich, Paul. *The Courage to Be*. New Haven: Yale University Press, 1952. (Chapter I: "Courage and Life: Nietzsche").

——— . "The Escape from God." In *The Shaking of the Foundations*. New York: Charles Scribner's Sons, 1948.

——— . *A History of Christian Thought*. Ed. Carl E. Braaten. New York: Simon & Schuster, 1967. (Part 2, chapter IV, section F: "Nietzsche's Idea of Will-To-Power"; "Nietzsche's Doctrine of Resentment"; "The 'Death of God' and the New Ideal of Man").

Yovel, Yirmiyahu, ed. *Nietzsche as Affirmative Thinker*: Papers Presented at the Fifth Jerusalem Philosophical Encounter, April 1983. Martinus Nijhoff, 1986.

HISTORY, ANTISEMITISM,
AND JEWISH-CHRISTIAN RELATIONS

Aschheim, Steven. *The Nietzsche Legacy in Germany, 1890-1990*. Berkeley: University of California Press, 1992.

Almog, Shmuel. "The Racial Motif in Renan's Attitude toward Judaism and the Jews." *Zion* 32 (1967): 175-200.

——— . *Nationalism and Antisemitism in Modern Europe 1815-1945. Studies in Antisemitism*. Oxford: Pergamon Press, 1990.

Bauer, Yehuda. *A History of the Holocaust*. New York: Franklin Watts, 1982.

Borowitz, Eugene. *Contemporary Christologies: A Jewish Response*. New York: Paulist Press, 1980.

Bronson, David, ed. *Jews and Germans from 1860 to 1933: The Problematic Symbiosis*. Heidelberg: Carl Winter, 1979.

Eckhardt, Roy A. *Elder and Younger Brothers*. New York: Scribners, 1967.

Gay, Peter. *The Dilemma of Democratic Socialism*. New York, 1952.

Gutteridge, Richard. *Open Thy Mouth for the Dumb!: The German Evangelical Church and the Jews, 1879-1950*. Oxford: Basil Blackwell, 1976.

Hayes, Peter. *Lessons and Legacies: The Meaning of the Holocaust in a Changing World.* Evanston: Northwestern University Press, 1991.

Hilberg, Raul. *The Destruction of the European Jews.* New York: Holmes & Meier, 1985.

Katz, Jacob. *From Prejudice to Destruction: Anti-Semitism, 1700-1933.* Cambridge, Mass.: Harvard University Press, 1980.

———. *The Darker Side of Genius: Richard Wagner's Anti-Semitism.* Hanover: University Press of New England, 1986.

Kohn, Hans. *The Mind of Germany.* New York: Charles Scribner's Sons, 1960.

Levy, Richard S., ed. *Antisemitism in the Modern World: An Anthology of Texts.* Lexington: D. C. Heath and Company, 1991.

Low, Alfred D. *Jews in the Eyes of the Germans: From the Enlightenment to Imperial Germany.* Philadelphia: Institute for the Study of Human Issues, 1979.

Mann, Thomas. *Nietzsche's Philosophy in the Light of Contemporary Events.* Washington, D.C.: Library of Congress, 1948.

Mosse, George. *The Crisis of German Ideology.* New York: Schocken Books, 1981.

Poliakov, Léon. *The Aryan Myth.* Trans. Edmund Howard. Chatto: Sussex University Press, 1975.

———. *The History of Anti-Semitism.* 4 vols. New York: Vanguard Press, 1977-1985.

Pulzer, Peter. *The Rise of Political anti-Semitism in Germany and Austria.* Cambridge, Mass.: Harvard University Press, 1988.

Renan, Ernst. *The Life of Jesus.* Intro. John Haynes Holmes. New York: Random House, 1927.

Rosenberg, Stuart E. *The Christian Problem: A Jewish View.* New York: Hippocrene, 1986.

Rotenstreich, Nathan. *Jews and German Philosophy: The Polemics of Emancipation.* New York: Schocken, 1984.

Ruether, Rosemary Radford. *Faith and Fratricide.* Minneapolis: Seabury Press, 1974.

Schleunes, Karl A. "The Jewish Problem in the Second Reich." In *The Twisted Road to Auschwitz.* 1970. Chicago: University of Illinois Press, 1990.

Schweitzer, Albert. *The Quest of the Historical Jesus.* Intro. James M. Robinson. New York: Macmillan, 1968.

Stern, Fritz. *The Politics of Cultural Despair.* Berkeley, 1973.

Tal, Uriel. *Christians and Jews in Germany: Religion, Politics, and Ideology in the Second Reich, 1870-1914*. Ithaca: Cornell University Press, 1975.

Thomas, R. Hinton. *Nietzsche in German Politics and Society, 1890-1918*. 1983. La Salle: Open Court, 1986.

Viereck, Peter. *Metapolitics: The Roots of the Nazi Mind*. 1941. New York: Capricorn, 1961.

Weiss, David. *The Fascist Tradition*. New York, 1967.

INDEX

Adam 73, 163n. 78
"Always the rub-a-dub of justice" 54
anarchy, anarchism 60, 153
anarchist(s) 100–102, 132
    Jesus as "holy" 120, 130
anarchists and Christians 102–103, 113,
    117–118, 133
    See also antisemites
animals 53
    and humans 15, 77, 79, 81, 88
    Zarathustra's 89
    herd animals 36, 74, 128, 148
    herd formation 119
    herd morality 51, 100
    "no shepherd and one herd" 72
    See also beasts; priests; barbarians;
        tyrants; masses; swine; lambs;
        shepherd; sheep
annihilation 93, 120
antisemites 31, 34, 100, 102, 108, 142,
    147
    Christian antisemites 37, 42, 85–86,
        93, 99–100, 103–05, 117, 121,
        130–33, 139–141, 183n. 71
    antiChristian antisemites 72–73, 100,
        133, 141
    ignore N 91, 115, 153
    attack N 30, 37, 108, 111–112, 140,
        141, 146, 150, 204n. 37, 205n. 46
    See also antisemitism; Christians and
        anarchists; Stöcker; Dühring;
        Renan; Förster;
antisemites: N's quotes against 22, 36,
    37, 42, 92, 100, 102, 104, 108,
    131, 139, 142, 147
    "antisemitic goose" 35
    "antisemitic obstruction" 37

"antisemitic loudmouths" 56, 93
"antisemitic speculators" 56, 99
"antisemitic pamphlets . . ." 111
"absurd sheep with horns" 99
"damnable . . . antisemitism" 62
"moral masturbators" 111
"will to power of the weakest" 111
"having all antisemites shot" 39
    See also Jews, contemporary: N's
        quotes on
Antisemitische Correspondenz 111–12,
    141, 204n. 37
antisemitism
    history of 85–86, 96–99, 124–25
    Christian 45, 98–99, 103, 115–35
    anti-Christian 100, 103, 112,
    distinctions 98–99, 103, 141, 147,
        190
    political 65, 92–93, 98, 100, 203n. 19
    religious 124
    racial 134, 203n. 19
    See also Jews, persecution of
Apocalypse of John 118
Apollonian 13
Aquinas, St. Thomas 94
aristocracy, aristocratic, 60–61, 79, 94, 95,
    104–06, 110, 118, 128, 141, 142
Aristocratic radicalism 142, 188n. 39,
    203n. 24
"artists, saints and philosophers" 15, 16,
    159n. 31
Aryan(ism) 31, 41, 53, 100, 109
"Aryan influence, has corrupted" 142
Aryan Race 5, 40, 93, 113, 128, 149
    racial supremacy 105, 142
    race theories 100, 107–08, 192n. 86,
        198n. 65

215

466 2629

Printed in the United States
51536LVS00003B/79